INTRODUCTION TO SYRIAC

Key to Exercises
and
English-Syriac Vocabulary

by

Daniel M. Gurtner

IBEX Publishers
Bethesda, Maryland

Introduction to Syriac
Key to Exercises and English-Syriac Vocabulary
by
Daniel M. Gurtner

Manufactured in the United States of America

The paper used in this book meets the minimum requirements of the American National Standard for Information Services—Permanence of Paper for Printed Library Materials, ANSI Z39.48-1984

Ibex Publishers
Post Office Box 30087
Bethesda, Maryland 20824 U.S.A.
Telephone: 301-718-8188
Facsimile: 301-907-8707
www.ibexpublishers.com

Library of Congress Cataloging in Publication Data

Gurtner, Daniel M.
Key to exercises for Wheeler M. Thackston's introduction to Syriac and English-Syriac vocabulary / by Daniel M. Gurtner.
p. cm.
Answers to exercises in Syriac and romanized Syriac; readings in romanized Syriac with English translations.
Contents: Key to exercises — Key to readings — English-Syriac vocabulary — Corrigenda and addenda to the grammar.
ISBN 1588140458 (alk. paper)
1. Syriac language — Grammar — Problems, exercises, etc. I. Title

PJ5423 .T53 1999 Suppl.
492/.35—dc22
2006043690

Contents

Preface i

Key to Exercises

Lesson 1 1
Lesson 2 1
Lesson 3 3
Lesson 4 4
Lesson 5 5
Lesson 6 6
Lesson 7 7
Lesson 8 8
Lesson 9 10
Lesson 10 13
Lesson 11 14
Lesson 12 15
Lesson 13 17
Lesson 14 18
Lesson 15 21
Lesson 16 23
Lesson 17 24
Lesson 18 25
Lesson 19 27
Lesson 20 28

Key to Readings

From the *Pšiṭtā* 30
From Pseudo-Callisthenes' Legend of Alexander 32
The First Discovery of the True Cross 35
The Teaching of the Apostle Thaddeus 41
The Martyrdom of St. Barbara 49
From the Tale of Sinbad the Wise 53
From *The Cave of Treasures* 58
From *Kalilag and Demnag* 59
From a Metrical Sermon by Ephraem Syrus 60
From *The Syriac Book of Medicines* 62
A Flood in Edessa 64
From the *Chronicon Syriacum* of Barhebraeus,
The Taking of Babylon (Baghdad) by Hülägü Khan 67
From the Reign of Baidu Khan 69

English-Syriac Vocabulary 71

Corrigenda and Addenda to the Grammar 114

Preface

AS IS THE CASE WITH MOST STUDENTS OF SYRIAC, I learned this language almost entirely on my own. Though I am far from a Syriacist, I produced this key primarily for those also learning Syriac on their own or in small groups. I have also included an English-Syriac glossary to assist students with the English to Syriac translation exercises in Thackston's grammar. I have chosen to keep with Thackston's decision to use Estrangela font for its simplicity, and have retained that font even where Thackston's text uses Nestorian and Jacobite.

I would like to thank Farhad Shirzad at Ibex Publishers for immediately taking interest in the project and his patience in seeing it to fruition. I especially thank Prof. Wheeler M. Thackston for encouraging the production this project, and producing translations and transliterations of the extended readings from the end of the grammar. I also wish to thank Dr. Joseph Trafton and Mr. Jonathan A. Loopstra who kindly agreed to review drafts of this work for their accuracy. Thanks also goes to participants in a Syriac grammar class which I led at Tyndale House, Cambridge (UK), specifically Charles Echols, Peter Head, Caryn Reeder, and especially Tze-Ming Quek, Hilary Marlow, and Jane Heath. Each have helped ensure the accuracy of this key, though errors remain my responsibility alone. Corrections, suggestions, or comments can be sent direction to the author by email at syriackey@ibexpub.com.

For continuous encouragement in this project and others, I owe a debt of gratitude to Bill Barker, Jonathan Moo, Justin Hardin, and Charles Anderson.

This modest project is dedicated to Dr. Gary D. Pratico, who first instilled in me a rigorous ethic of studying Semitic languages and a deep appreciation for their beauty.

Daniel M. Gurtner
Bethel Seminary
St Paul, 2006

Daniel M. Gurtner (Ph.D., University of St Andrews) is Assistant Professor of New Testament at Bethel Seminary in St Paul, MN.

Lesson One

(a) 1. *slek men m\underline{d}ittā. He went up from the city.* 2. *^{c}erqa\underline{t} l-ṭurā She fled to the mountain.* 3. *^{c}raq men m\underline{d}ittā. They (m) fled from the city* 4. *sleqēn l-ṭurā. They (f) went up to the mountain.* 5. *n\underline{p}al ga\underline{b}rā. The man fell.* 6. *ke\underline{t}ba\underline{t} att\underline{t}ā. The woman wrote.* 7. *^{c}raq ^{c}ammā men hār\underline{k}ā. The people (m) fled from here.*[1] 8. *k\underline{t}a\underline{b} malkā l-^{c}ammā. The king wrote to the people.* 9. *^{c}raqun men tammān. They (m) fled from there.* 10. *šem^{c}a\underline{t} malk\underline{t}ā. The queen heard.* 11. *^{c}erqa\underline{t} att\underline{t}ā men m\underline{d}itta. The woman fled from the city.* 12. *^{c}raq ga\underline{b}rā men malkā. The man fled from the king.* 13. *selqa\underline{t} att\underline{t}ā men tammān. The woman went out from there.* 14. *n\underline{p}al ga\underline{b}rā men ṭurā. The man fell from the mountain.* 15. *lā ^{c}raq malkā men m\underline{d}ittā. The king did not flee from the city.* 16. *lā selqa\underline{t} att\underline{t}ā men hār\underline{k}ā. The woman did not go out from here.* 17. *lā šma^c ^{c}ammā. The people did not hear.* 18. *lā ke\underline{tb}a\underline{t} l-mal\underline{k}ā. She did not write to the king.* 19. *selka\underline{t} malk\underline{t}ā men ^{c}ammā. The queen went out from the people.* 20. *lā ^{c}raq ga\underline{b}rā l-\underline{t}ammān. The man did not flee to there.* 21. *selqa\underline{t} att\underline{t}ā l-m\underline{d}ittā. The woman went up to the city.*

(b) 1. ܥܪܩܬ ܐܢܬܬܐ ܡܢ ܓܒܪܐ *^{c}erqa\underline{t} att\underline{t}ā men ga\underline{b}rā*

2. ܢܦܠ ܠܛܘܪܐ *n\underline{p}al ṭurā*

3. ܠܐ ܟܬܒ ܓܒܪܐ ܠܡܠܟܐ *lā k\underline{t}a\underline{b} ga\underline{b}rā l-malkā*

4. ܠܐ ܫܡܥ ܥܡܐ *lā šma^c ^{c}ammā*

5. ܣܠܩ ܓܒܪܐ ܡܢ ܡܕܝܢܬܐ ܠܛܘܪܐ *sleq ga\underline{b}rā men m\underline{d}ittā l-ṭurā*

6. ܥܪܩ ܥܡܐ ܡܢ ܗܪܟܐ *^{c}raq ^{c}ammā men hār\underline{k}ā*

7. ܟܬܒ ܥܡܐ ܠܡܠܟܐ ܘܠܡܠܟܬܐ *k\underline{t}a\underline{b} ^{c}ammā l-malkā wa-l-malk\underline{t}ā*

8. ܣܠܩ ܡܢ ܬܡܢ *sleq men tammān*

9. ܟܬܒ̈ܝܢ ܠܓܒܪܐ *k\underline{t}a\underline{b}ēn l-ga\underline{b}rā*

10. ܢܦܠܬ ܡܕܝܢܬܐ ܠܡܠܟܐ *ne\underline{p}la\underline{t} m\underline{d}it\underline{t}ā l-malkā*

Lesson Two

(a) 1. *e\underline{b}a\underline{d} ga\underline{b}rā \underline{b}-ar^{c}ā. The/a man perished in/on the land.* 2. *l-mānā lā neṭra\underline{t} l-nāmōsā? Why did she/you (m) not keep the law?* 3. *sleqnan b-ṣa\underline{p}rā. We went out in the morning.* 4. *ne\underline{p}qe\underline{t} w-ezze\underline{t} l-nahrā. I went forth and went to the river.*

[1] Here I take "the people" as a collective, thus taking the singular verb. In order for "the people" to be the object ("He did not hear the people"), it would require the object marker which is introduced in Chapter 2. See also #17.

5. *ᶜḇar ᶜal nāmōsā. They (m) transgressed against the law.* 6. *kṯaḇ la-ḵṯāḇā malkā. The king wrote the book.* 7. *b-ramšā ᶜḇarn l-nahrā. In the evening we crossed over the river.* 8. *mānā emraṯ l-g̱aḇrā atttā? What did the woman say to the man?* 9. *ezzeṯ men mḏittā ḇ-ṣap̱rā. I went out from the city in the morning.* 10. *np̱aqton men mḏittā l-ṭurā. You went forth from the city to the mountain.* 11. *ᶜraq ᶜammā men qriṯā w-ezal la-mḏittā. The people fled from the village and went to the city.* 12. *gaḇrā qtal l-malkā. The man killed the king.* 13. *lā ᶜḇarnan ᶜal nāmōsā. We did not transgress the law.* 14. *mān eḥaḏ gaḇrā men qriṯā? What did the man take from the village?* 15. *sleq l-ṭurā w-ṯammān eḇaḏ. They went to the mountain and there they perished.* 16. *ma emraṯ l-ᶜammā?* OR *ma emart l-ᶜammā? What did she/you (m) say to the people?* 17. *eḇdaṯ ba-qriṯā atttā. The woman perished in the village.* 18. *l-mānā lā qeṭlaṯ l-malkā wa-l-malkṯā?* OR *l-mānā lā qtalt l-malkā wa-l-malkṯā? Why did she/you (m) not kill the king and the queen?* 19. *lā šemᶜeṯ l-g̱aḇrā. I did not hear/listen to the man.* 20. *eḥdeṯ kṯāḇā w-ezzeṯ l-nahrā. I seized the book and I went to the river.* 21. *Lā ᶜraqn men qriṯā ḇ-ramšā. We did not flee from the village in the evening.* 22. *lā qṭal l-atttā. They (m) did not kill the woman.* 23. *kṯaḇt l-malka ḵṯāḇā. She/you (m) wrote the book for the king.* 24. *ᶜerqeṯ men tammān w-ezzleṯ l-hārḵā. I fled from there and I came here.* 25. *emreṯ l-malkā ᶜal atttā. I spoke to the king about (concerning) the woman.* 26. *lā emarnan l-ᶜammā ᶜal malkā. We did not speak to the people about the king.* 27. *l-mānā la emarton l-malkā ᶜal nāmōsā? Why did you not speak to the king about the law?* 28. *l-malkā wa-l-malkṯā qtaln. We killed the king and the queen.*

(b) 1. *aykā eḇaḏ* ܐܝܟܐ ܐܒܕܘ

aykā ebadun ܐܝܟܐ ܐܒܕܘܢ

aykā eḇaḏ ܐܝܟܐ ܐܒܕ̈

aykā eḇaḏēn ܐܝܟܐ ܐܒܕ̈ܝܢ

2. *l-mānā lā nṭart l-nāmōsā* ܠܡܢܐ ܠܐ ܢܛܪܬ ܠܢܡܘܣܐ

3. *ᶜḇarnan l-nahrā ḇ-ramšā* ܥܒܪܢܢ ܠܢܗܪܐ ܒܪܡܫܐ

4. *emreṯ l-atttā ᶜal qrittā* ܐܡܪܬ ܠܐܢܬܬܐ ܥܠ ܩܪܝܬܐ

5. *l-mānā ezalton l-mḏittā* ܠܡܢܐ ܐܙܠܬܘܢ ܠܡܕܝܢܬܐ

6. *qtal l-malkā b-qrittā* ܩܛܠ ܠܡܠܟܐ ܒܩܪܝܬܐ

7. *Malkā ᶜḇar l-nahrā w-eḥaḏ l-mḏittā*

ܡܠܟܐ ܥܒܪ ܠܢܗܪܐ ܘܐܚܕ ܠܡܕܝܢܬܐ

8. *np̱aqnan w-sleqnan l-ṭurā b-ṣap̱rā*

ܢܦܩܢܢ ܘܣܠܩܢܢ ܠܛܘܪܐ ܒܨܦܪܐ

9. *mā emart l-g̱aḇrā* ܡܐ ܐܡܪ̇ܬ ܠܓܒܪܐ

10. *emreṯ l-ʿammā ʿal nāmōsā* ܐܡܪܬ ܠܥܡܐ ܥܠ ܢܡܘܣܐ

Lesson Three

(a) 1. *man ezal ʿammḵon. Who went with you (m. pl)?* 2. *nḥeṯ malkā la-mḏittā ʿam ʿammā. The king went down to the city with the people.* 3. *nesbeṯ l-ḵespā mennāḵ. I took money from you (m sg).* 4. *eḵal ʿamman. They (m) ate with us.* 5. *nḥeṯṯon ʿaḏ yammā. You (m. pl) went down as far as the sea.* 6. *ʿerqeṯ menneh. I fled from him.* 7. *šlaḥ lwāṯ malkā šliḥā. They (m.) sent a messenger to the king.* 8. *nsaḇ g̱aḇrā l-p̱uqdānā mennhon. The man received the commandment from them (m).* 9. *ezaln ʿaḏ qriṯā. We went as far as the village.* 10. *man ʿḇaḏ l-laḥmā? Who made the bread?* 11. *layt l-g̱aḇrā ḵespa. The man has no money.* 12. *sleq lwāṯ g̱aḇrā ḏa-ʿraq men mḏittā ḏ-layt bāh mayyā. They (m.) went out to the man who fled from the city which had no water in it.* 13. *layt b-arʿā nḇiyā. There is no prophet in the land.* 14. *layt lan laḥmā ḇ-ḇaytā. We have no food in the house.* 15. *lā ṇtarnan l-p̱uqdānā ḏa-nsaḇ nḇiyā men ṭurā. We did not keep the commandment which the prophet received from the mountain.* 16. *neḥteṯ men ṭurā w-ezzeṯ ʿaḏ yammā. I came down from the mountain and went as far as the sea.* 17. *man šlaḥ lāḵ lwāṯan? Who sent you to us?* 18. *atttā d-ʿeḇdaṯ laḥmā nep̱qaṯ w-selqaṯ ʿamm w-ʿammeh. The woman who made the bread went and went up with me and with him.* 19. *iṯ b-arʿā nahrā ḏ-iṯ beh mayyā. There is a river in the land in which there is water.* 20. *iṯ ba-mḏittā malkā w-malkṯā. There is in the city a king and a queen.* 21. *šlaḥ kespā la-mḏittā ʿam šliḥā. They (m.) sent money to the city with the messenger.* 22. *mānā emarton la-šliḥā ḏa-ʿraq men tammān? What did you (m. pl) say to the messenger who fled from there?* 23. *layt lāh baytā ḇa-qriṯā. She does not have a house in the village.* 24. *ezal nḇiyā lwāṯ ʿammā w-emar lhon l-mānā lā ṇtarton l-nāmōsā? The prophet went in the presence of the people and he said to them, "Why have you (m. pl.) not kept the law?"* 25. *ʿraq g̱aḇrā menn. The man fled from me.* 26. *eḵleṯ ʿammāḵ laḥmā. I ate the food with you (m.sg).* 27. *sleq men mayyā. He went up from the water.* 28. *np̱aq mennan. They (f. pl) went from us.* 29. *man emar lāḵ ʿal kespā ḏ-eḥaḏ malkā men ʿammā? Who told you about the money which the king took from the people?* 30. *neḥteṯ la-mḏittā w-nesbeṯ l-ḵespā men šliḥā. I went down to the city and I took the money from the messenger.*

(b) 1. *iṯ b-ḇaytā g̱aḇrā* ܐܝܬ ܒܒܝܬܐ ܓܒܪܐ

2. *man šlaḥ lwaṯhon la-šliḥā d-ezal la-mḏittā*

ܡܢ ܫܠܚ ܠܘܬܗܘܢ ܠܫܠܝܚܐ ܕܐܙܠ ܠܡܕܝܢܬܐ

3. *neḥteṯ l-nahrā ʿammāh b-ṣap̱rā* ܢܚܬܬ ܠܢܗܪܐ ܥܡܗ̇ ܒܨܦܪܐ

4. *layt lan kespā* ܠܝܬ ܠܢ ܟܣܦܐ

5. *nesbaṯ l-mayyā men gaḇrā* ܢܣܒܬ ܠܡܝ̈ܐ ܡܢ ܓܒܪܐ

6. *emarun li ʿal laḥmā ḏ-ʿeḵalun* ܐܡܪܘܢ ܠܝ ܥܠ ܠܚܡܐ ܕܐܟܠܘܢ

7. *qṭalun l-gaḇrā ḏ-ʿḇar l-nāmōsā* ܩܛܠܘܢ ܠܓܒܪܐ ܕܥܒܪ ܠܢܡܘܣܐ

8. *nsaḇ nḇiyā l-nāmōsā ʿal ṭurā* ܢܣܒ ܢܒܝܐ ܠܢܡܘܣܐ ܥܠ ܛܘܪܐ

9. *lā eḵlaṯ l-laḥmā ḏaʿḇaḏn* ܠܐ ܐܟܠܬ ܠܠܚܡܐ ܕܥܒܕܢ

10. *iṯ l-ḵon kespā ḇ-ḇaytā* ܐܝܬ ܠܟܘܢ ܟܣܦܐ ܒܒܝܬܐ

Lesson Four

(a) 1. *rḏap̱ malkā ḇāṯar bʿeldḇāḇeh. The king pursued his enemy.* 2. *šeḇqeṯ l-ʿaḇdā ḏ-hayklā. I forgave the servant of the temple.* 3. *eḥaḏ l-ḏahḇ b-ʿeldḇāḇ wa-ʿraq la-mḏittā. My enemy seized my gold and he fled to the city.* 4. *layt hārkā ḵespā ḏ-ḏilāḵ. There is no money here which belongs to you (m. sg.).* 5. *lā ʿḏar lan ʿaḇdan. Our servant did not help us.* 6. *rḏap̱ gaḇrā l-ʿaḇdeh. The man persecuted his servant.* 7. *rheṭ ʿaḇdā ḏ-hayklā ḇāṯar gaḇrā ḏ-eḥaḏ l-ḏahḇā ḏ-ḏileh. The servant of the temple ran after the man who seized the gold which belonged to him.* 8. *ezzeṯ la-qriṯā ḏa-nḇiyā. I went to the village of the prophet.* 9. *šḇaq l-ʿaḇdeh gaḇrā. The man forgave his servant.* 10. *lā ʿḏar li ḏahḇāḵ . Your gold did not help me.* 11. *šlaḥ malkā la-šliḥeh lwāṯāḵ. The king sent his messenger to you.* 12. *nsaḇ gaḇrā ḵespā mennhon. The man took the money from them.* 13. *ʿḇaḏ aykannā ḏa-p̱qaḏ lhon malkā ḏa-mḏittā. They did just as the king of the city commanded them.* 14. *emreṯ lāh aykannā ḏ-emart li. I spoke to her just as you spoke to me.* 15. *reḥṭeṯ bāṯarhon. I ran behind them (m.).* OR *I ran after them (m.).* 16. *rḏap̱ bāṯreh bʿeldḇāḇā ʿaḏ yammā w-ṯammān eḇaḏ. He pursued after the enemy as far as the sea, and there he perished.* 17. *qṭal la-ḇʿeldḇāḇeh d-malkā. They (m.) killed the king's enemy.* 18. *np̱aq nḇiyā men bayteh b-ṣap̱rā wa-sleq l-ṭurā. The prophet went forth from his house in the morning and he went up to the mountain.* 19. *reḏpeṯ la-ḇʿeldḇāḇ ba-mḏittā ḵollāh. I pursued my enemy throughout the city.* 20. *ʿḏar lan ʿammā ḵollhon. All of the people helped us.* 21. *emar li g̱aḇrā ḵollmeddem d-emraṯ leh attṯeh. The man told me everything which his wife said to him.* 22. *šḇaq kollmeddem d-eḥaḏ men hayklā wa-ʿraq. They left everything which they (m.) seized from the temple and they (m.) fled.* 23. *eḥdet kollmeddem d-ḏil w-ezzeṯ l-ḇayt. I seized everything which belonged to me and I went to my house.* 24. *rheṭnan bāṯar ʿaḇdā ḏ-gaḇrā aykannā ḏa-p̱qaḏ lan. We ran after the man's slave just as he commanded us.* 25. *eḵalt kolleh laḥma ḏ-ʿeḇdaṯ lāḵ attṯāḵ? Did you eat all the food that your wife made for you?* 26. *l-mānā lā ʿeḇdaṯ kollmeddem d-p̱aqdeṯ lāh? Why did she not* *do everything which I commanded her?* 27. *l-mānā šḇaq l-ḇaython d-ḇa-qriṯā w-ezal la-mḏittā? Why did they leave their house in the village and go to the city?*

(b) 1. *šḇaqn leh l-^{c}aḇdan ba-qriṯā* ܫܒܩܢ ܠܗ ܠܥܒܕܢ ܒܩܪܝܬܐ

2. *reḥteṯ men qriṯeh da-ḇ^{c}eldḇāḇ* ܪܗܛܬ ܡܢ ܩܪܝܬܗ ܕܒܥܠܕܒܒ

3. *rḏap̱ malkā ḇāṯar ḇ^{c}eldḇāḇā ḏ-^{c}ammeh b-ḵollah ar^{c}ā*

ܪܕܦ ܡܠܟܐ ܒܬܪ ܒܥܠܕܒܒܐ ܕܥܡܗ ܒܟܠܗ ܐܪܥܐ

4. *eḥaḏ ^{c}aḇdā l-ḏahḇeh d-malkeh wa-^{c}raq men ar^{c}ā*

ܐܚܕ ܥܒܕܐ ܠܕܗܒܗ ܕܡܠܟܗ ܘܥܪܩ ܡܢ ܐܪܥܐ

5. *eḥaḏt kollmeddem ddil* ܐܚܕܬ ܟܠܡܕܡ ܕܕܝܠ

6. *eḥaḏ gaḇrā kollmeddem da-bbayteh wa-nḥeṯ l-yammā*

ܐܚܕ ܓܒܪܐ ܟܠܡܕܡ ܕܒܒܝܬܗ ܘܢܚܬ ܠܝܡܐ

Lesson Five

(a) 1. *rḏap̱ malkē ḇāṯar b^{c}eldḇāḇē ^{c}aḏ mḏiṯthon. The kings pursued the enemies as far as their city.* 2. *lā šḇaqnan ^{c}aḇdē ḇ-hayklē. We did not leave the servants in the temples.* 3. *l-ḏahḇan eḥaḏ gaḇrē wa-^{c}raq la-mḏināṯā. The men seized our gold and they fled to the cities.* 4. *rḏap̱ l-^{c}aḇdē gaḇrē. The men pursued the servants.* OR *The men abused the slaves.* 5. *rheṭ ^{c}aḇdē ḇāṯar gaḇrē ḏ-eḥaḏ l-ḏahbhon dilhon. The servants ran after the men who seized their gold.* 6. *ezzeṯ l-quryā ḏa-nḇiyē. I went to the villages of the prophets.* 7. *lā šḇaq l-^{c}aḇdē. They did not forgive the servants.* 8. *lā ^{c}ḏar lāḵ dahbē. The gold did not help you.* 9. *šlaḥ malkē la-šliḥē lwāṯan. The kings sent the messengers into our presence.* 10. *nsaḇ gaḇrē l-ḵespē mennan. The men took the money from us.* 11. *^{c}ḇaḏ ^{c}aḇdē aykannā ḏa-p̱qaḏ lhon malkē. The servants did just as the kings commanded them.* 12. *emraṯ leh atttā aykannā ḏ-emrē lāh neššē. The woman told him just as the women told her.* 13. *rheṭ bāṯarhēn neššē. He ran after the women.* 14. *rḏap̱ bāṯar b^{c}eldḇāḇā ^{c}aḏ yammā w-ṯammān li qṭal. The enemy pursued me as far as the sea, and there he killed me.* 15. *kaḏ qṭal l-gaḇrā selqaṯ nap̱šeh la-šmayyā. When they killed the man his soul went up to heaven.* 16. *hā malaḵē ḏ-alāhā qreḇ leh la-nḇiyā. Behold, the angels of God drew near to the prophet.* 17. *šḇaq la-mḏittā wa-^{c}mar ba-qriṯā. He left the city and lived in the village.* 18. *qreḇ l-ḇaytāh d-emmhon. They approached the house of their mother.* 19. *man qṭal b^{c}eldḇāḇhon d-malkē? Who killed the enemy of the kings?* 20. *qerbaṯ malkuṯā ḏa-šmayyā. The kingdom of heaven drew near.* 21. *l-mānā rḏap̱ la-nḇiyē? Why did they persecute the prophets?* 22. *kaḏ nḥeṯ men ṭurē np̱aq w-ezal l-ḇayteh. When he went down from the mountains he went to his house.* 23. *qṭal l-nap̱šeh. He killed himself.* 24. *lā qṭal l-nap̱šhon. They (m.) did not kill their soul (OR themselves).* 25. *np̱aq nḇiyē men baytāh d-atttā. The prophets went forth from* *the woman's house.* 26. *rḏap̱ ^{c}ammā ḵollhon la-ḇ^{c}eldḇāḇeh d-malkā. All the people persecuted the enemy of the king.* 27. *^{c}mar neššē ḇ-quryā. The women lived in the villages.* 28. *kaḏ qreḇ b^{c}eldḇāḇā, ^{c}raq kollhon gaḇrē. When the enemy drew near, all of the men fled.* 29. *l-nāmōsā ḏ-alāhā ṇtar gaḇrā. The man kept the law of God.* 30. *nḥeṯ malaḵē men šmayyā. The angels descended from the heavens.* 31. *eḥdeṯ laḥmē ḵollhon men baytā w-selqeṯ l-ṭurē ^{c}am emm. I took all the food from the house and I went to the mountains with my mother.* 32. *hāḵannā emar nḇiyā ḵaḏ nsaḇ puqdānē ḏ-alāhā. Thus spoke the prophet when he took the commandments of God.*

(b) 1. *^{c}mar gaḇrē ḇ-quryā ḏ-malkuṯā* ܥܡܪܘ ܓܒܪ̈ܐ ܒܩܘܪ̈ܝܐ ܕܡܠܟܘܬܐ

2. *nḥeṯ malakē men šmayyā* ܢܚܬܘ ܡܠܐܟ̈ܐ ܡܢ ܫܡܝܐ

3. *Layt mayyā b-nahrē ḏ-ar^{c}ā* ܠܝܬ ܡܝ̈ܐ ܒܢܗܪ̈ܐ ܕܐܪܥܐ

4. *^{c}barēn neššē ^{c}al nāmōsē ḏ-malkē ḏ-malkuṯā*

ܥܒܪ̈ܢ ܢܫ̈ܐ ܥܠ ܢܡܘ̈ܣܐ ܕܡܠܟ̈ܐ ܕܡܠܟܘܬܐ

5. *rḏap̱nan l-^{c}aḇdē ḏa-b^{c}eldḇāḇē men kollhon hayklē ḏ-ar^{c}an*

ܪܕܦܢ ܠܥܒ̈ܕܐ ܕܒܥܠܕܒܒ̈ܐ ܡܢ ܟܠܗܘܢ ܗܝܟ̈ܠܐ ܕܐܪܥܢ

Lesson Six

(a) 1. *man-i hāḏē w-manu haw. Who is this (f) and who is that (m)?* 2. *meḥdā np̱aq men knušṯā w-ezal l-ḇaytāh d-emmhon. Immediately they departed from the synagogue and they went up to their mother's house.* 3. *emar leh ^{c}al attṯā ḏ-hi šeḥaṯ ennon. They spoke to him about the woman who sent them.* 4. *l-mānā la emart li att ^{c}al hāḏē kollāh. Why did you not speak to me about all of this?* 5. *atton-ennon melḥā ḏ-ar^{c}ā. You are the salt of the earth.* 6. *hāḏē hi mḏittā-y d-malkā ḏ-hāḏē ar^{c}ā. This is the city of the king of this land.* 7. *haw hu malkāh-u ḏ-mḏittā. That (man) is king of the city.* 8. *manu ḏ-ḏileh-i malkuṯā d-šmayyā. To whom does the kingdom of heaven belong?* 9. *aykannā ḏ-emar lan āp̱ enā emreṯ lhon. Just as they spoke to us, so also I spoke to them.* 10. *meḥdā ḵaḏ šem^{c}eṯ hāḏē nep̱qeṯ w-qerbeṯ l-nḇiyā. Immediately when I heard this I went forth and approached the prophet.* 11. *enā šliḥeh-nā ḏ-alāhā. I am God's messenger.* 12. *nḥeṯ men šmayyā malakā ḏ-hu šliḥeh d-alāhā wa-ḏbar l-nḇiyā l-maḏbrā. The angel that was God's messenger descended from heaven and led the prophet to the wilderness.* 13. *hādāy emmā d-^{c}eḇdaṯ lan laḥmā hānā. This is my mother, who made this food for us.* 14. *l-mānā eḥdaṯ emmāḵ kespā hānā mennāḵ. Why did your mother take this money from you?* 15. *ḏḇaron-ennon la-šmayyā malaḵē. The angels guided them to heaven.* 16. *b-ramšā sleqn w-ezaln la-knuštā. In the evening we left and went to the synagogue.* 17. *emar išo^{c} mšiḥā ḏ-naḥnan melḥā-nan ḏ-ar^{c}ā. Jesus Christ said, "we are the salt of the earth."* 18. *Manu gaḇrā ḏalkon ḏḇar lwāṯ. Who is the man who led you unto me?* 19. *l-mānā lā eḵal l-*

melḥā hay da-nsaḇn men mḏiṯtā. Why did they not eat that salt which we took from the city? 20. *hāḏē-i malktāh ḏ-arᶜā hāḏē. This is the queen of this land.* 21. *aykannā ḏa-šḇaqaṯ napšā l-pagrā selqaṯ ruḥā la-šmayyā. As the soul left the body, the spirit went to heaven.* 22. *reḏpeṯ la-ḇᶜaldḇāḇ l-meḏbrā w-ṯamman qeṭleṯ leh. I pursued my enemy to the wilderness and there I killed him.* 23. *kaḏ šmaᶜ la-nḇiyā meḥdā npaq w-ezal baṯreh. When they heard the prophet, immediately they went after him.* 24. *hāḏē atttā emmhoni ḏ-hālēn gaḇrē. This woman is the mother of these men.* 25. *hu ḏemar lāḵ kollāh hāḏē sliḥu ḏ-malkā ḏa-mḏiṯtā. He that told you all this is the messenger of the king of the city.* 26. *manu ḏa-ḏbar-ennon l-maḏbrā. Who is it that guided them to the wilderness?* 27. *manu ḏ-nesbaṯ hānon puqdānē menneh? Who is (the one) from whom you took those commandments?* 28. *aykannā eḇaḏ ḇ-maḏbrā hānon? How did they perish in the wilderness?*

(b) 1. *Hāḏē-y knuštā ḏ-kollhon ᶜammē ḏ-arᶜā*

ܗܕܐ ܗܝ ܟܢܘܫܬܐ ܕܟܠܗܘܢ ܥܡ̈ܡܐ ܕܐܪܥܐ

2. *Hānon gaḇrē-ennon ḇ-maḏbrā* ܗܢܘܢ ܓܒ̈ܪܐ ܐܢܘܢ ܒܡܕܒܪܐ

3. *It l-att l-gaḇrā ḏ-napšeh qeṭlaṯ l-hi*

ܐܝܬ ܠܐܢܬ ܠܓܒܪܐ ܕܢܦܫܗ ܩܛܠܬ ܠܗܝ

4. *Layt melḥā ḇ-ḇaytan* ܠܝܬ ܡܠܚܐ ܒܒܝܬܢ

5. *Malaḵē sleq l-šmayyā* ܡܠܐܟ̈ܐ ܣܠܩܘ ܠܫܡܝܐ

6. *Šliḥē hālēn ḏḇar ennon la-mḏinaṯā ḏ-malkē*

ܫܠܝܚ̈ܐ ܗܠܝܢ ܕܒܪܘ ܐܢܘܢ ܠܡܕܝܢܬܐ ܕܡܠܟ̈ܐ

7. *Manu-w ḏa-rḏap baṯreh la-ḇᶜeldḇāḇā ᶜaḏ nahrā*

ܡܢܘ ܗܘ ܕܪܕܦ ܒܬܪܗ ܠܒܥܠܕܒܒܐ ܥܕ ܢܗܪܐ

8. *Gaḇrā hānā šḇaq attṯeh ḇa-qriṯā*

ܓܒܪܐ ܗܢܐ ܫܒܩ ܐܢܬܬܗ ܒܩܪܝܬܐ

Lesson Seven

(a) 1. *ḥzayn l-ᶜêḏtā ḏa-ḇnaw b-haw aṯrā. We saw the church which they built in that place.* 2. *lā eṯêṯ lwaṯhon. I did not come to them.* 3. *bᶜā gaḇrā la-nḇiyā ḇ-ḵollāh mḏittā. The man searched for the prophet throughout the city.* 4. *l-mānā eṯayton l-harkā. Why did you (m.p.) come here?* 5. *manu ḏa-ḥzayt tamman. Who did you (m. s.) see there?* 6. *baṯār hāḏē sleq men ᶜêḏtā ḵollhon da-hwaw bāh. After this all who were in the church went from it.* 7. *emar išoᶜ da-ḇ-ḵoll-zḇan meskênē iṯ lḵon ᶜammḵon li ḏēn la ḇ-ḵoll-zḇan iṯ lkon. Jesus said, "You always have the poor with you, but you do not always have me with you."* 8. *daḇreh lwaṯan. He guided him to us.* 9. *manu ḏ-qaṭleh la-nḇiyā? Who is he who killed* *the prophet?* 10. *bnāṯā ḏ-haw gaḇrā lā eṯay. The daughters of that man did not come.* 11. *hāḵannā pqaḏtan malkṯā. In this way the queen commanded me.* 12. *kaḏ ḥzayn-ennon ḥḏiyn b-hon. When we saw them we rejoiced in them (m.p.).* 13. *hāna-w ᶜaḇdāḵ d-ᶜaḏran. This is your servant who helped me.* 14. *l-mānā lā šmaᶜkon. Why did he not listen to you (m.pl.)?* 15. *hu nṭreh l-puqdānā ellā hi lā nṭarteh. He kept the commandment but she did not keep it.* 16. *eḵal l-laḥmā ḵolleh. They ate all of the bread.* 17. *šḇaqn* (or *šaḇqan*) *ᶜam ḇᶜeldḇāḇā. We left with the enemy.* OR *He abandoned us with the enemy.* 18. *rḏapteh atttā l-ᶜaḇdāh men lwaṯāh. The woman drove her servant from her presence.* 19. *šalḥeh la-šliḥā l-hāḏē mḏittā malkā. The king sent the messenger to this city.* 20. *dahḇā ḏ-eḥdeh layt b-ḇayteh. The gold which he took is not in his house.* 21. *kaḏ ḥzaw ᶜêḏtā ḏa-ḇnā lhon malkā ḏa-mḏittā ḥḏi ḇāh. When they saw the church which the king of the city built for them they rejoiced in it.* 22. *hānā gaḇrā ḇreh-wā ḏ-alāhā. This man was the son of God.* 23. *kaḏ ramšā-wā ᶜḇarteh l-nahrā. When it was evening I crossed the river.* 24. *enā nsaḇteh l-ḵespā menneh. I took the money from him.* 25. *b-haw aṯrā ḇnaw ᶜêḏtā l-meskênē. In that place they built a church for the poor.* 26. *b-hānon yawmāṯā layt-wā lan laḥmā. In those days we had no bread.*

(b) 1. *emar da-ḇ-ḵoll-zban iṯ lan meskênē ᶜamman*

ܐܡܪ ܕܒܟܠܙܒܢ ܐܝܬ ܠܢ ܡܣܟܢ̈ܐ ܥܡܢ

2. *w-b-hanon yawmāṯā ḥḏi ḇ-ᶜêḏtā ḏa-ḇneh l-hon b-haw aṯrā*

ܘܒܗܢܘܢ ܝܘܡܬ̈ܐ ܚܕܝ ܒܥܕܬܐ ܕܒܢܗ ܠܗܘܢ ܒܗܘ ܐܬܪܐ

3. *Bnayyeh ḏ-hānā gaḇrā qṭal l-ḇᶜeldḇāḇā ḏa-mḏinaṯhon*

ܒܢ̈ܘܗܝ ܕܗܢܐ ܓܒܪܐ ܩܛܠ ܠܒܥܠܕܒܒܐ ܕܡܕܝܢܬܗܘܢ

4. *l-mānā šaḇqāḵ ba-qriṯā ḏ-layt bāh mayyā*

ܠܡܢܐ ܫܒܩܟ ܒܩܪܝܬܐ ܕܠܝܬ ܒܗ̇ ܡ̈ܝܐ

5. *dḇarteh menneh maḏbrā l-baytāh d-ḇarteh*

ܕܒܪܬܗ ܡܢܗ ܡܕܒܪܐ ܠܒܝܬܗ̇ ܕܒܪܬܗ

6. *Eḇaḏ ᶜal ṭurā ᶜammeh kespā ḏ-eḥḏeh mennhon meskênē*

ܐܒܕ ܥܠ ܛܘܪܐ ܥܡܗ ܟܣܦܐ ܕܐܚܕܗ ܡܢܗܘܢ ܡܣܟܢ̈ܐ

7. *hu w-bnaynāšā ḏa-qriṯeh nḥet ᶜal malkā d-qaṭleh l-ḇreh*

ܗܘ ܘܒܢ̈ܝܢܫܐ ܕܩܪܝܬܗ ܢܚܬܘ ܥܠ ܡܠܟܐ ܕܩܛܠܗ ܠܒܪܗ

Lesson Eight

(a) 1. *ḥāḏeyn-nan b-purqānnan b-yaḏ pārōqa. We are rejoicing in our salvation through the savior.* 2. *lā-wā ḇ-laḥmā ḇalḥōḏ ḥayē ḇarnāšā. Man was not living* *on bread alone.* 3. *enā lā saaleq-nā men baytā. I myself am not going from the house.* 4. *ḥāḏyā atttā ḇa-ḇrāh d-la ᶜāḇar l-nāmōsā. The woman is rejoicing in her son who is not transgressing the law.* 5. *eškḵhuh kaḏ ᶜāmrā ḇa-qritā hay. They found her (while) she was living in that village.* 6. *manu ḏ-ḇāᶜē att leh. For whom are you searching?* 7. *kaḏ hwā ramšā ᶜāḇrin l-nahrā. When it was evening, they crossed the river.* 8. *enā šaleḥ-nā leh l-hānā kṯāḇā lwāṯ-kon byaḏ hānā šliḥā. I am sending this book to you by means of this messenger.* 9. *ḥāzeyn atton l-hon. You are seeing them.* 10. *eškḥeṯ li aṯrā ḏ-ḇanē-nā ḇeh baytā. I found for myself a place in which I am building a house.* 11. *haw d-ḏaber laḵ bᶜeḏlḇāḇaḵ-u. That man who is guiding you is your enemy.* 12. *enā āmar-nā l-ḵon d-haw d-qṭlu pārōqan-u. I am telling you, "That one who they (m) killed is our savior."* 13. *ḥzaw lāḵ kaḏ nāpeq men baytāḵ. They saw you when you were going from your house.* 14. *b-ṣaprā ḏēn āzlin-waw l-ᶜêḏtā. But in the morning they went to church.* 15. *qṭlin-nan l-hon kollhon. We will kill them all.* 16. *alāhā pāres mraḥḥmānuṯeh ᶜal arᶜā ḵollāh. God is spreading his mercy over all the earth.* 17. *ᶜaḇdeh dēn d-qenṭrōnā ḥaḏ qriḇ-wā la-mmāṯ. w-šmaᶜ ᶜal išoᶜ. w-šaddar lwāṯeh qaššišē ḏa-yhuḏāyē. hennon dēn kaḏ eṯaw lwaṯ išoᶜ baᶜeyn-waw menneh w-āmrin. rhēm gēr l-ᶜamman. w-āp bēṯ-knuštā hu bnā lan. išoᶜ dēn āzel-wā ᶜammhon. kaḏ dēn la saggi raḥḥiq men baytā. šaḏdar lwāṯeh qenṭrōnā rāḥmaw. (But) the servant of a certain centurion was near death. And he heard about Jesus. And he sent to him the elders of the Jews. But when they came to Jesus, they sought from him and said, "Indeed, he loves our people. And so the house of the assembly (synagogue) he built for us. (But) Jesus went with them (m.). But when he was not very far from the house. The centurion sent to him his friends.*

(b) 1. *qenṭrōnā ḏ-ᶜaḇdeh qarriḇ la-mmāṯ šaddar lwaṯeh qaššišē ḏa-yhuḏāyē ḏa-šmaᶜin-waw ᶜal išoᶜ.*

ܩܢܛܪܘܢܐ ܕܥܒܕܗ ܩܪܝܒ ܠܡܡܬ ܫܕܪ ܠܘܬܗ ܩܫܝ̈ܫܐ
ܕܝܗܘܕ̈ܝܐ ܕܫܡܥܝܢ ܗܘܘ ܥܠ ܝܫܘܥ

2. *b-aṯrā hānā ḇnā šliḥā l-ᶜêḏtā l-ḡaḇrē wa-l-neššē ḏ-'aamriin bāh ba-mdittā*

ܒܐܬܪܐ ܗܢܐ ܒܢܐ ܫܠܝܚܐ ܠܥܕܬܐ ܠܓܒܪ̈ܐ ܘܠܢܫ̈ܐ
ܕܥܡܪ̈ܝܢ ܒܗ̇ ܒܡܕܝܢܬܐ

3. *Šāleḥ la-šliḥā lwaṯ malkā 'law ḏ-šmaᶜ*

ܫܠܚ ܠܫܠܝܚܐ ܠܘܬ ܡܠܟܐ ܕܫܡܥ

4. *Šaḇqan ᶜam bᶜeldḇāḇan* ܫܒܩܢ ܥܡ ܒܥܠܕܒܒܢ

5. *hākannā ḏ-malkā pqaḏ w-ap ᶜḇaḏ* ܗܟܢܐ ܕܡܠܟܐ ܦܩܕ ܘܐܦ ܥܒܕ

6. *bāṯreh kollhon npaq dēn mennāh mḏittā l-ṭurē*

ܒܬܪܗ ܟܠܗܘܢ ܢܦܩ ܕܝܢ ܡܢܗ̇ ܡܕܝܢܬܐ ܠܛܘܪ̈ܐ

7. *Ḥzaytonāh l-atttā ḏ-selqaṯ b-ṣaprā l-ḇaytāh d-rāḥemtāh?*

ܚܝܘܬܗ̇ ܠܐܝܬܘܬܐ ܕܫܠܡܘܬ݂ ܒܦܪܐ ܠܚܝܬܗ̇ ܕܢܣܒܬܗ̇

8. *Šem*[c]*et̲* [c]*al k̲ārōzut̲ā d̲a-nbiyā mennhon qaššišē*

ܫܡܥܬ ܥܠ ܟܪܘܙܘܬܐ ܕܢܒܝܐ ܡܢܗܘܢ ܩܫܝ̈ܫܐ

Lesson Nine

(a) 1. *gab̲rā ḥakkimā. The wise man.* 2. *Neššē ṭāb̲āt̲ā d̲-ṣêd̲ay. The good women who are beside me.* 3. *malkut̲ā ḥad̲t̲ā. The new kingdom.* 4. *bnāt̲eh saggiāt̲ā d̲-d̲ileh. His many daughters.* 5. [c]*êd̲t̲ā qadd̲išt̲ā. The holy church.* 6. *malkē rawrbē. The great kings.* 7. *yawmāt̲ā šappirē. The beautiful days.* 8. *bnaynāšā* [c]*attirē. The rich people.* 9. *melḥā bišt̲ā. The bad salt.* 10. *pag̲reh qaddišā. His holy body.* 11. *ruḥā qaddišā*[2]*. The holy spirit.* 12. *knušat̲ā saggi*[c]*āt̲ā. The many synagogues.* 13. [c]*êd̲at̲ā rawrbāt̲ā. The big churches.* 14. *mad̲brā rāb̲ā. The great desert.* 15. *emm ḥakkimt̲ā. My wise mother.* 16. *malak̲ē qaddišē. The holy angels.* 17. *b*[c]*eldb̲āb̲ē b̲išē. The wicked enemies.* 18. [c]*ab̲dē ṭāb̲ē ṣêd̲ēh. The good servants (are) beside her.* 19. *bāttē saggi*[c]*ē. The many houses.* 20. *puqdānhon rabbā. Their great commandment.* 21. *Rāḥmā ḥd̲attā d̲a-ḥlāp̲aw. The new friend which is for his sake.* OR *The new friend instead of him.* 22. *ar*[c]*āk̲ rabbt̲ā. Your great land.* 23. *qrit̲ā* [c]*attirt̲ā. The rich village.* 24. *qeryāt̲ā saggiāt̲ā. The many villages.* 25. *laḥmā saggi*[c]*ā ṣêd̲ayk. (There is) much bread beside you.* OR *There is much bread near you.* 26. *md̲itt̲ā qaddišt̲ā. The holy city.* 27. *rāḥmē* [c]*attirē. The rich friends.* 28. *qaššišā yud̲āyā. The Jewish elder.* 29. *md̲ināt̲ā raḥḥiqat̲ā. The distant cities.* 30. *baytā qarrib̲ā. The nearby house.*

(b) 1. ܚܟܝܡ ܗܘ ܓܒܪܐ *ḥakkim-u gab̲rā. The man is wise.*

2. ܛ̈ܒܢ ܐܢܝܢ ܢܫ̈ܐ ܕܨܐܕܝ *ṭāb̲ān-ennēn neššē d̲-ṣêd̲. The women beside me are good.*

3. ܚܕܬܐ ܗܝ ܡܠܟܘܬܐ *ḥad̲t̲ā-y malkut̲ā. The kingdom is new.*

4. ܣܓ̈ܝܐܢ ܐܢܝܢ ܒܢ̈ܬܗ ܕܕܝܠܗ *saggi*[c]*ān-ennēn bnāt̲eh d-d̲ileh. Many are the daughters who belong to him.* OR *He has many daughters.*

5. ܩܕܝܫܐ ܗܝ ܥܕܬܐ *qaddišā-y* [c]*êd̲t̲ā. The church is holy.*

6. ܪ̈ܘܪܒܝܢ ܗܘܘ ܡ̈ܠܟܐ *rawrbin-waw malkē. The kings were great.*

7. ܫܦܝ̈ܪܝܢ ܗܘܘ ܝܘ̈ܡܬܐ *šappirin-waw yawmāt̲ā. The days were beautiful.*

8. ܥܬܝ̈ܪܝܢ ܗܘܘ ܒܢܝ̈ܢܫܐ [c]*attirin-waw bnaynāšā. The people were*

[2] See Thackston's grammar, p. 30 n. 1.

rich.

9. ܒܝܫܐ ܗܝ ܡܠܚܐ *bišā-y melḥā. The salt is bad.*

10. ܩܕܝܫ ܗܘ ܦܓܪܗ *qaddiš-u pagreh. His body is holy.*

11. ܩܕܝܫܐ ܗܝ ܪܘܚܐ *qaddišā-y ruḥā. The spirit is holy.*

12. ܣܓܝܐܢ ܐܢܝܢ ܟܢܘܫܬܐ *saggiᶜān-ennēn knušāṯā. The synagogues are many.*

13. ܪܘܪܒܢ ܐܢܝܢ ܥܕܬܐ *rawrbān-ennēn ᶜêḏāṯā. The churches are big.*

14. ܪܒ ܗܘ ܡܕܒܪܐ *rāḇ-u maḏbrā. The desert is great.*

15. ܚܟܝܡܐ ܗܝ ܐܡܝ *Ḥakkimā-y emm. My mother is wise.*

16. ܩܕܝܫܝܢ ܗܘܘ ܡܠܐܟܐ *qaddišin-waw malaḵē. The angels were holy.*

17. ܒܝܫܝܢ ܗܘܘ ܒܥܠܕܒܒܐ *bišin-waw bᶜeldḇāḇē. The enemies were wicked.*

18. ܛܒܝܢ ܗܘܘ ܥܒܕܐ ܨܐܕܗ *ṭāḇin-waw ᶜaḇdē ṣêḏēh. The servants beside her were good.*

19. ܣܓܝܐܢ ܐܢܝܢ ܒܬܐ *saggiᶜan-ennēn bāttē. The houses are many.*

20. ܪܒ ܗܘ ܦܘܩܕܢܗܘܢ *rabb-u pukdānhon. Their commandment is great.*

21. ܚܕܬ ܗܘ ܪܚܡܐ ܕܠܚܠܦܘܗܝ *Ḥdeṯ-u rāḥmā ḏa-ḥlāpaw. The friend is new for his sake.*

22. ܪܒܐ ܗܝ ܐܪܥܟ *rabbā-y arᶜāḵ. Your land is great.*

23. ܥܬܝܪܐ ܗܝ ܩܪܝܬܐ *ᶜattirā-y qriṯā. The village is rich.*

24. ܣܓܝܐܢ ܐܢܝܢ ܩܪܝܬܐ *saggiᶜan-ennēn qeryāṯā. The villages are many.*

25. ܣܓܝ ܗܘ ܠܚܡܐ ܨܐܕܝܟ *saggi-u laḥmā ṣêḏayk. Much bread is beside you.*

26. ܩܕܝܫܐ ܗܝ ܡܕܝܢܬܐ *qaddišā-y mḏittā. The city is holy.*

27. ܥܬܝܪܝܢ ܗܘܘ ܪܚܡܐ *ᶜattirin-waw rāḥmē. The friends were rich.*

28. ܝܗܘܕܝ ܗܘ ܩܫܝܫܐ *yudāy-u qaššišā. The elder is Jewish.*

29. ܪ̈ܚܝܩܢ ܐܢܝܢ ܡܕܝ̈ܢܬܐ *raḥḥiqān-ennēn mḏinatā. The cities are distant.*

30. ܩܪܝܒܐ ܗܘ ܒܝܬܐ *qarriḇ-u baytā. The house is nearby.*

(c) 1. *bnaw l-hon ᶜêḏṯā ḥaḏtā ḇ-hu aṯrā. They built a new church for them in that place.* 2. *išoᶜ mšiḥā p̄ārōqa-w d-ᶜêḏṯā qaddišṯā. Jesus Christ is the savior of the holy church.* 3. *ᶜattirān-ennēn hālēn neššē. These women are rich.* 4. *ḥakkim-u haw d-la ᶜāḇer l-p̄uqdānē ḏ-alāhā. Wise is he who does not/will not transgress the commandments of God.* 5. *kaḏ ḥzā āḏām l-ḥawwā ḥḏi ḇāh saggi. When Adam saw Eve he rejoiced much in her.* 6. *biš-u ḏ-la nāṭer l-p̄uqdānē ḏ-alāhā ḏ-nāsbin bnaynāšā men mušē nḇiyā. Wicked is he who does not keep the commands of God which the people received from Moses the prophet.* 7. *lā ḥakkimin aytayhon bneyyeh d-atttā ᶜattirṯā. The sons of the rich woman are not wise.* 8. *ṭāḇān mellayhon d-naḇiyē. The words of the prophets are good.* 9. *raḇ-wā malkā ḏa-mdittē hānēn. The king of those cities was great.* 10. *mḏittē ḏ-malkā hānā rawrbān-ennēn. The cities of this king are great.* 11. *nāḥtin-waw malkē ᶜlayhon bᶜaldḇaḇēhon. The kings were descending upon their enemies.* 12. *ṭāḇ aytway-wā laḥmā ḏ-eḵlan b-ḇāttēhon. The bread which we ate in their houses was good.* 13. *b-koll-zban dēn eṯeyn šliḥēway d-alāhā lwaṯhon bnaynāšā. But the apostles of God always come to the people.* 14. *eṯā išoᶜ mšiḥā ḥlāp̄ayn. Jesus Christ came for our sake.* 15. *aytayhon bnaynāšā ḇa-mdittā raḇtā d-malkuṯā. The people in the city are the greatest of the kingdom.* 16. *bānē lan pārōqa malkutā ḥḏettā ḇ-šmayyē. The savior is building for us a new kingdom in heaven.* 17. *ᶜḇaḏ alāhā p̄ardisā l-kollhon bnaynāšā qaddišē. God made paradise for all the holy people.* 18. *kaḏ qreḇ l-qrittā lā ḥzaw leh l-g̱aḇrā haw. When they drew near the village they did not see that man.* 19. *l-mānā qtalhaw l-nabbi. Why did they kill the prophet?* 20. *dḇarun l-maḏbrā. They guided us to the wilderness.* 21. *ᶜḏar li ᶜaḇdēah. Her servants helped me.* 22. *ḥzaw lāḵ kaḏ qāṭel-att lāh l-attteh. They saw you when you were killing his wife.*

(d) 1. *Biš -aw bᶜaldḇaḇan* ܒܝܫ ܗܘܐ ܒܥܠܕܒܒܢ

2. *rawrbān hwaw ᶜêḏāṯā ḥḏittā ḏ-ḇnaw lhayn*

ܪܘܪ̈ܒܢ ܗܘܝ ܥ̈ܕܬܐ ܚܕ̈ܬܬܐ ܕܒܢܘ ܠܗܝܢ

3. *Saggiᶜin hwaw bnayyeh* ܣܓܝ̈ܐܢ ܗ̣ܘܘ ܒܢ̈ܝܗ

4. *Ḥdiṯin ennon batthon b-mdittā*

ܚܕ̈ܬܢ ܐܢܘܢ ܒ̈ܬܬܗܘܢ ܒܡܕܝܢܬܐ

5. *Yehbeṯ lāh la-ḵtābē d-yabt li* ܝܗܒܬ ܠܗ̇ ܠܟܬ̈ܒܐ ܕܝܗܒܬ ܠܝ

6. *Rabb b-malkuṯā hwaw bnayyi* ܪܒ ܒܡܠܟܘܬܐ ܗ̣ܘܘ ܒܢ̈ܝ

7. *Rba-ay hwa mdittā ḥadtā men haw dḥyayn bāh*

ܪܒܐ ܗ̱ܝ ܗܘܐ ܡܕܝܢܬܐ ܚܕܬܐ ܡܢ ܗܘ ܕܚܝܝܢ ܒܗ̇

Lesson Ten

(a) 1. *atton-ennon nuhrā d̲-ᶜālmā. You (mp) are the light of the world.* 2. *kad̲ nhār–wā ṣap̲rā d̲mek̲. They slept while the morning was bright.* 3. *ᶜraq ᶜab̲dā b̲iššā w-lā idaᶜ māreh d-aykā-u. The wicked servant fled and his lord did not know where he was.* 4. *hād̲ē-y mellt̲ā šarrirtā d̲a-nb̲iyē. This was the true word of the prophets.* 5. *bāt̲ar hād̲ē hp̲ak̲ kāhnā l-hayklā ᶜam talmid̲u. After this, the priest returned to the temple with his disciples.* 6. *eškaḥu kad̲ yāt̲eb̲ ᶜam rabbay-kāhnē. They found him as he was sitting with the chief priests.* 7. *kad̲ hap̲ket̲ l-baytā yat̲bet̲. When I returned to the house, I sat down.* 8. *šarrirāᶜit̲ lā id̲ᶜayn-nan. Truly we did not know.* 9. *dmek̲ ᶜab̲day malkā b̲-hayklā. The servants of the king went to sleep in the palace.* 10. *kad̲ hap̲ket̲ ḥzêt̲ nuhrā d̲-nāher b-ideh d-mārē b̲aytā. When I returned, I saw a light which was shining in the hand of the master of the house.* 11. *l-mānā rd̲ap̲tān men lwat̲āk̲. Why did you drive me from your presence?* 12. *saggi b̲āᶜeyn-wayn ellā la eškaḥnay l-māran. Many of us were searching but we did not find our master.* 13. *meskênā ḥad̲ ayt d-yat̲eb̲-wā lwat̲ tarᶜeh d-haw ᶜattirā. There is a poor man who was sitting before the gate of the rich (man)..* 14. *b-rāšit̲ ayt-aw hwā mellt̲ā. w-haw mellt̲ā ayt-aw-wā lwat̲ alāhā. w-alāhā it̲-aw-wā haw melltā. hānā it̲-aw-wā b̲-rāšit̲ lwat̲ alāhā. koll b-id̲eh-wa… In the beginning was the word. And the word was with God. And God was the word. This (one) was with God in the beginning. All (things) were (made) by his hand…*

(b) 1. *Ḥẓayt li nāḥet̲-nā la-qrit̲ā zᶜōrā qarrib̲-āh l-md̲ittā*

ܚܙܝܬ ܠܝ ܢܚܬ ܐ̱ܢܐ ܠܩܪܝܬܐ ܙܥܘܪܐ ܩܪܝܒܗ̇ ܠܡܕܝܢܬܐ

2. *It̲eb̲n ᶜam talmid̲an karrib̲eh at̲rā*

ܝܬܒܢ ܥܡ ܬܠܡܝ̈ܕܢ ܟܪܝܒܗ ܐܬܪܐ

3. *Rābb-wāt̲ malkut̲an b-yawmeh d-malkā*

ܪܒ ܗ̱ܘܬ ܡܠܟܘܬܢ ܒܝܘܡܗ ܕܡܠܟܐ

4. *Rd̲ap̲tiw menni*

ܪܕܦܬܝܘܗܝ ܡܢܝ

5. *yed̲ᶜet̲ d-ḥakkimin-waw bnaynāšā lā b-koll-zban*

ܝܕܥܬ ܕܚܟܝܡܝܢ ܗܘܘ ܒܢܝ̈ܢܫܐ ܠܐ ܒܟܠܙܒܢ

6. *Eškaḥneh leh b-hayklā*

ܐܫܟܚܢܗ ܠܗ ܒܗܝܟܠܐ

7. *Kad̲ rêš-ab̲āhāt̲ā yat̲eb̲-wa ᶜamhon talmideh w-rāḥmēh šarrireh iqed̲ ᶜêd̲tā*

ܟܕ ܪܫ ܐܒܗܬܐ ܠܝܬ ܗܘܐ ܥܡܗܘܢ ܬܠܡܝܕܘܗܝ ܘܪܚܡܘܗܝ
ܫܪܝܪܗ ܢܦܩ ܒܢܬܐ

Lesson Eleven

(a) 1. *enā-nā rāᶜyā ṭāḇā. rāᶜā ṭāḇā napšeh sāᶜam ḥlāp ᶜāneh. I am the good shepherd. The good shepherd puts down his soul for the sake of his sheep.* 2. *haw dēn išoᶜ qām qḏām hegmōnā wa-šleh hegmōnā w-emar leh. att-u malkā ḏa-yhuḏāyē. emar leh išoᶜ att emart. But then Jesus rose in front of the governor and the governor asked him and said to him, Are you the king of the Jews? Jesus said to him: "you said (so)."* 3. *qāymin-waw dēn rabbay-kāynē w-ᶜazzizazāᶜiṯ āḵlin-waw. But the chief priests were rising and they were strongly slandering him.* 4. *Qām men ṣlōṯeh w-eṯā lwāṯ talmiḏay w-eškaḥ-ennon kaḏ demkin. He rose from his prayer and he came unto his disciples and he found them as they were sleeping.* 5. *w-ᶜal išoᶜ l-ōrêšlem l-hayklā w-ḥzā kollmeḏem. And Jesus entered Jerusalem to the temple and he saw everything.* 6. *b-yawmē hêroḏes malkā eṯaw mgušē men maḏnḥā l-ōrêšlem w-āmrin. aykā malkā ḏa-yhudāyē... ḥzēn gēr kawkbeh b-maḏnḥā. In the days of Herod the king magi came from the east to Jerusalem and they said, "where is the king of the Jews," indeed we saw his star in the east...* 7. *Hānon dēn kaḏ šmaᶜ men malkā ezal w-hā qḏāmayhon ᶜdammā. d-eṯā qām lᶜel men aykā d-ayt-aw ṭalyā. But when they heard, they went out from the king and lo, it rose before them until it came above from where the child was.* 8. *Manu ḏ-sām l-kawkḇē ḇa-šmayyā. Who is he who put the stars in the heavens?* 9. *Kaḏ ḥzā hegmōnā ṭalyeh w-šāᶜel d-mān d-ᶜāḏer leh. When the governor saw his child, he rose and asked, "who is helping to him?"* 10. *Ḥzaw rāᶜawwāṯā ḏ-mitt ᶜānāhon kollhāh d-ḏilhon. The shepherds saw all their sheep which died which belonged to them.* 11. *Qām nḇiyā qḏām-aw w-āmar d-ᶜāᶜel-na l-baytāh d-aṯṯāḵ. The prophet rose before the king and said, "I am entering the house of your wife."* 12. *Kaḏ ḥzaw kāhnē nuhrā ḏa-ḇmaḏnḥā iḏa ᶜd-qāᶜem pārōqa ḏ-hu nuhrā ḏ-ᶜālmā. When the priests saw the light which is in the east they knew of the rising of the savior who is the light of the world.*

(b) 1. *Qāmeṯ qḏāmaw ᶜḏammā ḏ-iṯeḇ* ܩܡܬ ܩܕܡܘܗܝ ܥܕܡܐ ܕܝܬܒ

2. *ᶜaln bayteh d-gaḇrā ḇāᶜān-nan bᶜeldbāḇan*

ܥܠܢ ܒܝܬܗ ܕܓܒܪܐ ܒܥܝܢ ܚܢܢ ܒܥܠܕܒܒܝܢ

3. *Idaᶜ mellṯeh-waw da-nbiyā šarririn*

ܝܕܥܘ ܗܘܘ ܕܢܒܝܐ ܡܠܬܗ ܫܪܝܪܝܢ

4. *Eškaḥ yāṯaḇ b-maḏbrā ᶜammhon rāᶜawwāṯā*

ܐܫܟܚܘܢ ܝܬܒ ܒܡܕܒܪܐ ܥܡܗܘܢ ܪܥܘܬܐ

5. *Šarrirā^{c}iṯ lā yeḏ^{c}eṯ aykā hwā* ܫܪܝܪܐܝܬ ܠܐ ܝܕܥܬ ܐܝܟܐ ܗܘܐ

6. *Bāṯar haw hp̄aḵ hegmōnā l-^{c}êḏteh ^{c}ammhon talmiḏeh*

ܒܬܪ ܗܘ ܗܦܟ ܗܓܡܘܢܐ ܠܥܕܬܗ ܥܡܗܘܢ ܬܠܡܝܕܗ

7. *Eṯaw mgušē bā^{c}in l-ṭalyā kawkbeh ḥzaw b-šmayyā*

ܐܬܘ ܡܓܘܫܐ ܒܥܝܢ ܠܛܠܝܐ ܟܘܟܒܗ ܚܙܘ ܒܫܡܝܐ

8. *Yāṯbā-wayn ^{c}al l-ṭurā l^{c}el men l-mdittā*

ܝܬܒܐ ܗܘܝܢ ܥܠ ܠܛܘܪܐ ܠܥܠ ܡܢ ܠܡܕܝܢܬܐ

9. *Aykā mḏittā ḏ-malkā ḏ-ar^{c}ā hāḏē*

ܐܝܟܐ ܡܕܝܢܬܐ ܕܡܠܟܐ ܕܐܪܥܐ ܗܕܐ

10. *Raḏpeṯ bāṯar l-b^{c}eldḇāḇi lwāṯ maḏbrā, w-aykā qṭleṯ hennon*

ܪܕܦܬ ܒܬܪ ܠܒܥܠܕܒܒܝ ܠܘܬ ܡܕܒܪܐ ܘܐܝܟܐ ܩܛܠܬ ܗܢܘܢ

Lesson Twelve

(a) 1. *melltā ḏa-ktiḇā. The word which was written.* 2. *Puqdanē ḏa-pqiḏin l-aḇaw. The commandments which were commanded to his father.* 3. *Laḥmā ḏ-aḵil. The bread which was eaten.* 4. *malaḵā ḏ-šliḥ l-alāhā. The angel which was sent to God.* 5. *dahbā ḏ-aḥiḏ men hayklā. The gold which was seized from the temple.* 6. *Atttā ḏ-qtilā l-aḥi. The woman who killed my brother.* 7. *Mellē ḏ-šmi^{c}ān-way. The words which were heard.* 8. *ṭalyā ḏa-yliḏ. The child who was born.* 9. *kṯāḇē ḏ-simin lwāṯ aḇuḵ. The books which were put in the presence of your father.* 10. *Baytā ḏa-ḇnē-wā l-aḥo. The house which was built for his brothers.* 11. *kawkbē ḏa-ḥzin b-šmayyē. The stars which were seen in the heavens.* 12. *^{c}ānā ḏ-ba^{c}yā l-rā^{c}yā. The sheep which were sought by the shepherd.* 13. *mraḥḥmānuṯā ḏa-p̱risā ^{c}al bnaynāšā. The mercy which was spread over the people.* 14. *bnayyā ḏa-rḥimin l-aḇuhon. The sons who loved their fathers.*

(b) 1. *w-eḥaḏ ayti^{c}u l-bayteh d-raḇ kahnēh. w-šem^{c}ōn eṯa-wa baṯreh men ruḥqā. w-sām dēn nurā meṣa^{c}t dārtā. wa-ytaḇin-wu ḥḏārāh. wa-yaṯēḇ-wā ap̱ haw šem^{c}ōn baynāṯhon. w-ḥezāṯeh ^{c}laymtā ḥḏā ḏ-yaṯeḇ lwaṯ nurā. w-ḥeraṯ beh w-āmrā. Ap̱ hannā ^{c}ameh-wā. Hu dēn kp̱ar wemar. atttā lā yāḏe^c-nā leh. ap̱ att mennhon att. kêp̱ā ḏēn emar lā hwêṯ w-ḇāṯār ša^{c}ā ḥḏā ḥrênā emar šrirā^{c}iṯ ap̱ hānā ^{c}ameh-wā ap̱ glilāyā-u g̱ēr. āmar kêp̱a, gaḇrā lā yāḏē-nā mannā ḏ-emar att.*

And they seized him and brought him to the house of the high priests. And Simon was going behind him from a distance. Then they put a fire in the midst of the courtyard. And they were sitting around it. And Simon was also sitting among them. And a certain maiden saw him who was sitting beside the fire. And she paid heed to him (noticed him) and (she) said, This (man) was also with him. But he denied it and said. "Woman, I do not know him" You are also from them.

But Peter said. I am not. And after he said (that), another said, "Truly this (man) was also with him. for he also is a Galilean. Peter said, "Man I do not know what you are talking about."

2. *Emar leh pilāṭos. malkā att. amār leh išo*ᶜ. *att emart d-malkā enā. enā l-hāḏē iliḏ enā. wa-l-hāḏē eṯyeṯ l-*ᶜ*almā.*

Pilate said to him, "You are a king." (or, *"Are you a king?"*). *Jesus said to him, "You (yourself) said that I am a king. For this I was born. And for this I came into the world.*

3. *saggain –ennon awwānē ḇayt aḇi. Many are the lodgings (in) the house of my father.*

(c) 1. *Kaḏ qāmeṯ eškaḥeṯ dṯalmiḏi ḏmikin*

ܟܕ ܩܡܬ ܐܫܟܚܬ ܕܬܠܡܝܕܝ ܕܡܟܝܢ

2. *ezal l-aykā ḏa-yliḏ ṭalyā ḏ-kawkḇeh d-ḥza ḇ-maḏnḥā*

ܐܙܠ ܠܐܝܟܐ ܕܝܠܝܕ ܛܠܝܐ ܕܟܘܟܒܗ ܕܚܙܐ ܒܡܕܢܚܐ

3. *Ḥzāḵ aḥāḵ yāṯeḇin ba-mṣa*ᶜ*aṯ d-ḏārtā* ᶜ*ameh*

ܚܙܟ ܐܚܟ ܝܬܒܝܢ ܒܡܨܥܬ ܕܕܪܬܐ ܥܡܗ

4. *Kaḏ emar hegmōnā leh melkā ḏa-yhuḏāyē? Emar,* ᶜ*lā emreṯ d-malkā-nā. Emart att*

ܟܕ ܐܡܪ ܗܓܡܘܢܐ ܠܗ، ܡܠܟܐ ܕܝܗܘܕܝܐ؟ ܐܡܪ ܠܐ

ܐܡܪܬ ܕܡܠܟܐ ܐܢܐ ܐܡܪܬ ܐܢܬ

5. *Aykā ṯlāyē ḏa-yliḏin tammān* ܐܝܟܐ ܛܠܝܐ ܕܝܠܝܕܝܢ ܬܡܢ

6. ᶜ*laymā ḥār l-*ᶜ*laymtā ḏ-ra*ᶜ*yā l-*ᶜ*āneh d-aḇēh*

ܥܠܝܡܐ ܚܪ ܠܥܠܝܡܬܐ ܕܪܥܝܐ ܠܥܢܗ ܕܐܒܘܗ̇

7. *Emar Išo*ᶜ*, dmeskênē hwaw* ᶜ*ammayḵon b-koll-zban*

ܐܡܪ ܝܫܘܥ ܕܡܫܟܢܐ ܗܘܘ ܥܡܟܘܢ ܒܟܠܙܒܢ

8. *Kaḏ ḥzā l-*ᶜ*êḏtā ḥadtā ḏ-bnē malkā l-hon, ḥḏi raḇ*ᶜ*iṯ* ᶜ*am-aw*

ܟܕ ܚܙܐ ܠܥܕܬܐ ܚܕܬܐ ܕܒܢܐ ܡܠܟܐ ܠܗܘܢ، ܚܕܝ

ܪܒܥܝܬ ܥܡܗܘܢ

9. *Hākannā malkā ṗaqḏan* ܗܟܢܐ ܡܠܟܐ ܦܩܕܢ

10. *l-mānā lā eṯayton lwāṯ*ܠܘܬܢ ܠܡܢܐ ܠܐ ܐܬܝܬܘܢ ܠܘܬܢ

Lesson Thirteen

(a) 1. *l-mānā ṣāḇē att l-meḵtal ennon. Why do you want to kill them?* 2. *šlāmā šāḇeq enā lkon šlāmā ḏil yāheḇ enā. lā-wā aykannā ḏ-yāheḇ ᶜalmā enā yāheḇ enā l-kon. Peace I am leaving with you. My peace I am giving to you. Not as the world gives am I giving to you.* 3. *lā meškaḥ-nā l-meṯā lawtāḵ. I am not able to come with you.* 4. *ṣaḇin ennon l-meḵal leḥmāh. They are wanting to eat bread.* 5. *lā meškaḥ aytaw l-memar šrārā. He is not able to speak the truth.* 6. *eṯēn l-mešlāḵ ᶜal hāḏē. They are coming to ask you about this.* 7. *ṣḇā-nā la-meḥzākon. I want to see you.* 8. *w-laykā ḏ-ezal enā yaḏᶜin-ton. w-urḥā yaḏᶜin atton. emar leh tōmā. māran lā yaḏᶜin-nan l-aykā ezal att. w-aykannā meškaḥin-nan urḥā lmeddaᶜ. emar leh išoᶜ ennā-nā urḥā w-šrārā w-ḥayyē. lā naš eṯa lwaṯ aḇ ella ḇi. ellu yaḏᶜin-wayton aḇ l-aḇi yaḏᶜin-wayton. w-men hāšā yaḏᶜin atton leh. w-ḥziyton-ay. And you know to where I am going. And you know the way. Thomas said to him. Lord, we do not know where you are going. And how are we to find the way to know? Jesus said to him, "I am the way and the truth and the life. No one comes to my father except through me. If you knew me you would also know my father. And from now you (are) knowing him. And you saw him.* 9. *b-ḥaḏ-bšaḇbā ḏēn eṯaṯ maryam magdlāy b-ṣaprā l-bēṯ-qḇurā w-ḥzāṯ l-kêpā ḏ-šqilā men qaḇrā. w-reḥtaṯ eṯaṯ lwaṯ šemᶜōn kêpā. w-emarā l-hon d-šaḵlaw l-mārān men haw bēṯ-qḇurā. w-npaq šemᶜōn w-haw talmiḏā ḥrênā. w-eṯin-waw l-bēṯ-qḇurā w-rehtin-waw tartēhon akḥdā. haw dēn talmidā rheṯ qaḏmeh l-šemᶜōn w-eṯā qaḏmayā l-bēṯ qḇurā. But on Sunday Mary Magdelene went up in the morning to the sepulcher and she saw the stone which was lifted from the tomb. And she ran up to Simon Peter. And telling them that our lord was lifted from that sepulcher. And Simon went forth and that other disciple. And they were coming to the sepulcher and the two were running together. But that disciple ran before Simon and he came the first to the sepulcher.* 10. *kaḏ šlem yawmāṯā hpaḵ l-hon. išᶜō ḏēn talya pāš leh b-yerušalem w-yōsep w-emeh la iḏaᶜ. w-la eškaḥ-aw w-hpaḵ l-hon l-orêšlem. w-men bṯar tlāṯā yawmin eškaḥ-aw b-hayklā kaḏ yāṯeḇ mṣaᶜtā mallpānē w-šemaᶜ mennhon. When the days were over they returned (to them). But the child Jesus remained in Jerusalem but Joseph and his mother did not know. But they did not find him and they returned to Jerusalem. But after three days they found him in the temple sitting in the middle (of) teachers and listening to them.*

(b) 1. *bṯar tlātā yawmin, b-ḥaḏ-bšabbā, ezlaṯ l-ḇēṯ-qḇurā w-ešakḥat l-kêpā šqal-wa*

ܒܬܪ ܬܠܬܐ ܝܘܡ̈ܝܢ ܒܚܕܒܫܒܐ ܐܙܠܬ ܠܒܝܬ ܩܒܘܪܐ

ܘܐܫܟܚܬ ܠܟܐܦܐ ܫܩܠܗܘ

2. *Nāšin sām l-nurā ḇ-meṣᶜaṯ d-ḏārtā w-iṯeḇ ḥḏārah*

ܐܢܫܝܢ ܣܡܘ ܠܢܘܪܐ ܒܡܨܥܬ ܕܕܪܬܐ ܘܝܬܒܘ ܚܕܪ̈ܝܗ̇

3. *ᶜlaymtā ḥraṯ l-gaḇrā ḏ-ezal b-meṣᶜaṯ-hon w-yeḏᶜaṯ d-hwā ṯalmiḏā ḏ-išoᶜ*

ܚܙܬ ܠܡܠܟܐ ܕܐܙܠ ܒܡܨܥܬܗܘܢ ܘܢܒܥܬ ܕܗܘ̣ܐ ܐܬܠܟܣܢܕܪܐ
ܕܢܩܘܒܒܠܝܠܡܬܐ

4. *Layt lhon l-meskênē awwānā b̲-mad̲brā*
ܠܝܬ ܠܗܘܢ ܠܡܣܟ̈ܢܐ ܐܘܢܐ ܒܡܕܒܪܐ

5. *Bāṯar zᶜōr kad̲ ezal akḥdā mešqal l-kêp̲ā men aṯrāh*
ܒܬܪ ܙܥܘܪ ܟܕ ܐܙܠ ܐܟܚܕܐ ܡܫܩܠ ܠܟܐܦܐ ܡܢ ܐܬܪܗ̇

6. *En ḥzeṯ lāḵ iṯbeṯ lāḵ.* ܐܢ ܚܙܬ ܠܟ ܐܬܒܬ ܠܟ

Lesson Fourteen

(a) 1. impf 3 m. pl ("they will go up") *nêzlon* ܢܐܙܠܘܢ

2. impf 3 f. sg/2 m. sg ("you will go forth") *teppoq* ܬܦܘܩ

3. impv m. sg *eḥod̲* (ܐܚܕ "seize") ܐܚܘܕ

4. impf 3 f. pl *neḥdyān* (ܚܕܝ "they will rejoice") ܢܚܕ̈ܝܢ

5. impf 3 m. sg *ned̲mak̲* (ܕܡܟ "he will return") ܢܕܡܟ

6. impf 2 f. pl *teᶜbdān* (ܥܒܕ "you will make") ܬܥܒ̈ܕܢ

7. impf 1 com pl *neḥḥon* (ܢܚܬ "we will go down") ܢܚܘܢ

8. Impf 2 f. sg *tepleyn* (ܦܠܐ "you will turn") ܬܦܠܝܢ

9. impf 2 m. sg/3 f. pl *teḥḥoṯ* (ܢܚܬ "you will go down") ܬܚܘܬ

10. impf 3 m. pl *nerḥṭun* (ܪܗܛ "they will run") ܢܪܗܛܘܢ

11. impf 3 f. pl *neb̲dān* (ܐܒܕ "they will serve") ܢܐܒ̈ܕܢ

12. impf 2 f. pl *tešlḥān* (ܫܠܚ "you will send") ܬܫܠ̈ܚܢ

13. impf 1 com pl *neṯē* (ܐܬܐ "we will go up") ܢܐܬܐ

14. impf 1 com sg *eṭar* (ܢܛܪ "I will keep") ܐܛܪ

15. impf 2 m. pl *teṯbun* (ܬܒ "you will seek") ܬܬܒܘܢ

16. impf 3 f. sg/2 m. sg *taqad̲* (ܝܩܕ "she will burn") ܬܐܩܕ

17. impf 1 com sg *eḥa* (ܚܙܐ "I will see") ܐܚܙܐ

18. impf 2 f. sg *tek̲tbin* ("you will write") ܬܟܬܒܝܢ

19. impf 1 com pl *nehpok̲* ("we will turn") ܢܗܦܘܟ

20. impf 2 m. pl *tep̲ros* (ܦܪܣ "you will spread") ܬܦܪܘܣ

21. impf 3 f. pl *ned̲ᶜān* (ܝܕܥ "they will know") ܢܕܥܢ

22. impf 2 m. pl *tet̲un* (ܐܬܐ "you will come up") ܬܐܬܘܢ

23. impf 2 m./3 f. sg *teb̲nē* (ܒܢܐ "you will build") ܬܒܢܐ

24. impf 1 com pl *nehwā* (ܗܘܐ "we will be") ܢܗܘܐ

25. impf 3 f. pl *nenhrān* (ܢܗܪ "they will shine") ܢܢܗܪܢ

26. impf 2 m. pl *teᶜdrun* (ܥܕܪ "you will help") ܬܥܕܪܘܢ

27. impf 2 m./3 f. sg *tešboq* (ܫܒܩ "you will leave") ܬܫܒܘܩ

28. impf 2 f. pl *tekṭlān* (ܩܛܠ "you will kill") ܬܩܛܠܢ

29. impf 2 m./3 f. sg *têmar* (ܐܡܪ "you will say") ܬܐܡܪ

30. impf 2 f. sg *ted̲ᶜin* (ܝܕܥ "you will know") ܬܕܥܝܢ

31. impf 1 com sg *et̲ab̲* (ܝܬܒ "I will seek") ܐܬܒ

32. impf 3 m. sg *neᶜroq* (ܥܪܩ "he will flee") ܢܥܪܘܩ

33. impf 2 m. pl *teᶜlun* (ܥܠܠ "you will go in, enter") ܬܥܠܘܢ

34. impf 2 m./3 f. sg *tqum* (ܩܘܡ "you will rise") ܬܩܘܡ

35. impf 3 m. sg *nemmot̲* (ܡܘܬ "he will die") ܢܡܘܬ

36. impf 2 f. pl *tesimān* (ܣܝܡ "you will put") ܬܣܝܡܢ

37. impf 2 m. or f. sg *teḥor* (ܚܪ "he will gaze") ܬܚܘܪ

38. impf 3 m. pl *neb̲ᶜōn* (ܒܥܐ "they will seek") ܢܒܥܘܢ

39. impf 2 f. sg *tešalin* (ܫܐܠ "you will ask") ܬܫܐܠܝܢ

40. impf 3 m. sg *tesaq* (ܣܩܐ "he will sack") ܬܣܩ

41. impf 3 m. sg *neḥzē* (ܚܙܐ "he will see") ܢܚܙܐ

42. impf 3 m. sg *nerdop̱* (ܪ̇ܕܦ "he will persue") ܢܪ̇ܕܘܦ

43. impv m. sg *aḵol* (ܐܟܠ "eat!") ܐܟܘܠ

44. impf 3 m. sg *nerḥam* (ܪ̇ܚܡ "he will love") ܢܪ̇ܚܡ

45. impf 2 f. pl *tešmcān* (ܫܡܥ "you will hear") ܬܫܡ̈ܥܢ

46. impf 3 m. pl *neškḥun* (ܫܟܚ "he will find") ܢܫܟܚܘܢ

47. impf 2 f. sg *teḏbrin* (ܕܒܪ̇ "you will say") ܬܕܒܪ̇ܝܢ

48. impf 3 f. pl *neḵprān* (ܟܦܪ̇ "they will deny") ܢܟܦܪ̈ܢ

49. impf 2 m. pl *teqrbun* (ܩܪ̇ܒ "you will draw near") ܬܩܪ̇ܒܘܢ

50. impf 1 com sg *ecol* (ܥܠܐ "I will raise up")ܐܥܘܠ

51. impv m. pl *taw* (ܐܬܐ "go up") ܬܘ

52. impf 1 com sg *ettel* (ܢܬܠ "I will give")ܐܬܠ

53. impf 3 m. pl *nep̱wšun* (ܦܫ "they will stay, remain") ܢܦܘܫܘܢ

54. impf 2 m./3 f. sg *tmuṯ* (ܡܝܬ "you will die") ܬܡܘܬ

55. impf 1 com sg *eḥzē* (ܚܙܐ "I will see") ܐܚܙܐ

56. impf 3 m. pl *neḏcun* (ܝܕܥ "they will know") ܢܕܥܘܢ

57. impf 1 com sg *eḥdel* (ܕܚܠ "I will fear") ܐܕܚܠ

(b) 1. Three months *tlāṯā yarḥē* ܬܠܬܐ ܝܪ̈ܚܐ

2. Ten years *cesrā šnayyā* ܥܣܪܐ ܫܢ̈ܝܐ

3. eight days *tmānyā yawmē* ܬܡܢܝܐ ܝܘ̈ܡܐ

4. three hours *tlāṯā šāce* ܬܠܬܐ ܫܥ̈ܐ

5. seven men *tmānyā gaḇrē* ܬܡܢܝܐ ܓܒ̈ܪܐ

6. nine women *tšac neššē* ܬܫܥ ܢܫ̈ܐ

7. the second month *trayyānā yarḥā* ܬܪܝܢܐ ܝܪܚܐ

8. the fourth house *rḇicāyā baytā* ܪܒܝܥܝܐ ܒܝܬܐ

9. the fifth teacher *ḥmišāyā mallpānā* ܚܡܝܫܝܐ ܡܠܦܢܐ

10. the first good word *qadmāyā melltā ṭabā* ܩܕܡܝܐ ܡܠܬܐ ܛܒܐ

(c) 1. *ṣābē-wā l-mesak. He wanted to go up.* 2. *la meškaḥ ena l-mpāš. He was not able to stay.* 3. *Ṣābin-aw l-mḥar bāh. They wanted to delay in in her.* 4. *meškaḥ-wêt l- meḥzyeh. He is able to see him.* 5. *ṣābē baytā l-mabnā. Wanting to build a house.* 6. *la meškaḥ-wa l-mdittā l-mezal. He was not able to go to the city.* 7. *la ṣābē l-mebad. Not wanting to perish.* 8. *ṣbi att namōsā l-meṭar. You (are) desiring to observe the law.* 9. *la ṣbā li l-metleh. Not wanting me to give him.* 10. *la ṣbā enā le-mlektlek. I am not wanting to kill you.*

(d) 1. *ettol* ܐܬܘܠ. 2. *nedhlun* ܢܕܚܠܘܢ. 3. *tedmok* ܬܕܡܘܟ. 4. *tebnē* ܬܒܢܐ. 5. *neppol* ܢܦܘܠ. *nezlān* ܢܐܙܠܢ̈ *neytān* ܢܐܬܝܢ̈. 7. *têdᶜeyn* ܬܐܕܥܝܢ. 8. *neḥḥot* ܢܚܘܬ. 9. *attēn* ܐܬܝܢ. 10. *tesloq* ܬܣܠܘܩ. 11. *tqum* ܬܩܘܡ. 12. *nsumun* ܢܣܘܡܘܢ. 13. *êtē* ܐܬܐ. 14. *teḥdeyn* ܬܚܕܝܢ. 15. *eḥzē* ܐܚܙܐ. 16. *eti* ܐܬܝ. 17. *lā nmitun* ܠܐ ܢܡܝܬܘܢ. 18. *tpāšin* ܬܦܫܝܢ. 19. *tšelām* ܬܫܐܠܢ̈. 20. *tbᶜē* ܬܒܥܐ. 21. *nehwon* ܢܗܘܘܢ. 22. *tḥor* ܬܚܘܪ. 23. *tekol* ܬܐܟܘܠ.

Lesson Fifteen

(a) 1. *nebᶜēw. they will build him.* 2. *teḥodēh. you will seize her.* 3. *epqodkon. I will visit you.* 4. *neprasēh. they will spread her.* 5. *tešbakonān. you will leave me.* 6. *tešlḥek. you will send you.* 7. *eṭrᶜēw. I will keep him.* 8. *nemrēh. they will tell her.* 9. *neldēw. they will beget him.* 10. *edᶜek. I will know you.* 11. *teklonēw. you will eat it.* 12. *nedbran. they led me.* 13. *tebraynyēw. you crossed it.* 14. *nerḥmekon. they love you.* 15. *nesimnēw. she will put him.* 16. *ebᶜwē. I will seek him.* 17. *neḥzunan. he will see me.* 18. *tebnēh. she will build it.* 19. *eḥzēk. I will see you.* 20. *neprsunāy. he will spread it.* 21. *tešboqin. you will leave us.* 22. *nebᶜinek. they will seek you.* 23. *nerdpunāy. they will pursue him.* 24. *tektbēh. she will write her.* 25. *tekolēw. you will eat it.* 26. *ektlāk. I will kill you.* 27. *tešbqnēy. you will stop him.* 28. *neqtlan. they will kill us.* 29. *tešmᶜēw. she will hear him.* 30. *eᶜbdeh. I will serve him.*

(b) 1. *w-emar l-hon matlā hānā. manu mennkon gabrā leh mā ᶜerbin. w-en nêbad ḥad mennhon. lā sbeq tešᶜin w-tšᶜā b-dabrā. w-azal bāᶜē l-haw d-ebad ᶜedmā d-neškaḥwē. w-mā d-eškḥeh ḥādē. w-šākel leh ᶜal katpāteh. w-ātē l-*

bayteh. w-qārē l-rhēmāw w-lšāb̲ēw. w-āmar l-hon. ḥad̲ ᶜam d-eškaḥet̲ ᶜerab̲ d-ab̲id̲. amar enna l-kon. d-hākannā t̲-ehwē ḥad̲ut̲ā b̲-šmayyā ᶜal ḥad̲ ḥaṭṭāyā d̲-tāᶜeb̲ aw ᶜal tešᶜin. w-tešᶜā zaddiqin d-lā met̲baᶜyā l-hon tyāb̲ut̲ā.

And he told them this parable. There is a certain man among you who had many sheep. And if one from among them perished, will he not leave behind 99 in the wilderness And he will go seeking that which perished until he found him? And he who found him will rejoice. And he put him upon his shoulders. And went up to his house. And he called his friends and his neighbors. And he said to them. Rejoice with me because I found my sheep with was lost. I am saying to them. Of thus there will be more gladness in heaven upon one sinner who repents than upon the ninety and nine righteous for whom repentance is not necessary.

2. *b-haw dēn zab̲nā. et̲o nešin emar leh ᶜal glilāyā hānon d-pilgos ḥlet̲ d-mhon ᶜam deb̲hon. w-ᶜenā išoᶜ w-emar l-hon. sab̲rin atton d-hennon glilāyē ḥaṭṭayn-waw yattir men kollhon glilāyē. d-hākannā hwā-ennon lā. amar-nā l-kon dēn. dāp̲ kollkon en lā ttubun. hākannā tebbdun. aw hānon tmāntaᶜsar d-npal ᶜalhon magdlā b-šilōḥā w-qtal ennon. sbarin atton d-ḥaṭṭin-wā yattir men kollhon bnaynāšā d-emrin b-orêšlem. lā. Amar-nā d̲-an la ttubun kollkon akwāthon tab̲dun.*

But in that time. The people went up (and) they spoke to him concerning those Galileans whose blood Pilate mingled with their sacrifices. And Jesus replied and said to them, "You (were) thinking that these Galileans were sinner more than all of the Galileans. Because this happened to them? However, I am saying to you. That also all of you if you are not good. Thus you will perish. Or those eighteen on whom the tower in Siloam fell and killed them. You were thinking that they were sinners more than all the people which are living in Jerusalem. No. I say to you, that if you do not repent, all of you like them will perish.

(c) 1. *Hānā yarḥā nešlom bāt̲ar yawmē ḥammšē*

ܗܢܐ ܝܪܚܐ ܢܫܠܘܡ ܒܬܪ ܝܘ̈ܡܐ ܚܡ̈ܫܐ

2. *Hpokayn l-ōrêšlem w-bᶜoyn l-ṭalyā d̲-pāš tamman*

ܗܦܘܟܝܢ ܠܐܘܪܫܠܡ ܘܒܥܘܝܢ ܠܛܠܝܐ ܕܦܫ ܬܡܢ

3. *Lā yed̲ᶜat̲ aykā msām l-ᶜerbā d̲-šeqlat ᶜal katpāt̲ā*

ܠܐ ܝܕܥܬ ܐܝܟܐ ܡܣܡ ܠܥܪܒܐ ܕܫܩܠܬ ܥܠ ܟܬܦܬܗ̇

4. *Lā met̲baᶜyā li d-eᶜnē* ܡܬܒܥܝܐ ܠܝ ܐܥܢܐ

5. *Aykannā id̲eᶜn l-urḥā b̲-d-t̲ezol*

ܐܝܟܢܐ ܝܕܥܢ ܠܐܘܪܚܐ ܒܕܬܐܙܠ

6. *Ep̲uš hārkā l-eštā yarḥē* ܐܦܘܫ ܗܪܟܐ ܠܐܫܬܐ ܝܪ̈ܚܐ

7. *Ellu t̲eb̲ᶜōnān teškoḥi b̲-b̲ayteh d-ab̲i*

ܐܠܘ ܬܒܥܘܢܝ ܬܫܟܚܘܢܝ ܒܒܝܬܗ ܕܐܒܝ

8. *Ellu b̲ᶜayt teškaḥi b-b̲ayteh aḥi*

ܐܠܘ ܒܥܝܬܝ ܬܫܟܚܝ ܒܒܝܬܗ ܐܚܝ

9. *Lā yahbet̲ l-āk̲ kollmeddem d-ṣāb̲ē*

ܠܐ ܝܗܒܬ ܠܟ ܟܠܡܕܡ ܕܨ̈ܒܐ

(d) 1. *kteb̲teh* ܟܬܒܬܗ. *ektob̲eh* ܐܟܬܘܒܗ. 2. *pqad̲ti* ܦܩܕܬܝ. *tepqod̲i* ܬܦܩܘܕܝ. 3. *prasnhon* ܦܪܣܢܗܘܢ. *neproshon* ܢܦܪܘܣܗܘܢ. 4. *qeṭlat̲eh* ܩܛܠܬܗ. *teqtoleh* ܬܩܛܘܠܗ. 5. *rdap̲āh* ܪܕܦܗ̇. *ned̲rop̲āh* ܢܪܕܘܦܗ̇. 6. *šbaqtnā* ܫܒܩܬܢܐ. *tešbaqnā* ܬܫܒܩܢܐ. 7. *nsab̲nek* ܢܣܒܢܟܝ. *nensbunek̲* ܢܣܒܘܢܟܝ. 8. *eškaḥnāk̲* ܐܫܟܚܢܟ. *neškaḥnāk̲* ܢܫܟܚܢܟ. 9. *šeltoni* ܫܐܠܬܘܢܝ. *tšeluni* ܬܫܐܠܘܢܝ. 10. *nṭarnanāk̲* ܢܛܪܢܢܟ. *nenṭṭorāk̲* ܢܛܪܘܟ. 11. *ekaltāh* ܐܟܠܬܗ̇. *tekolāh* ܬܐܟܘܠܗ̇. 12. *bnêt̲eh* ܒܢܝܬܗ. *eb̲neh* ܐܒܢܝܗ. 13. *bᶜaytan* ܒܥܝܬܢ. *teb̲ᶜēn* ܬܒܥܐܢ. 14. *ḥzāk̲* ܚܙܟ. *teḥzāk̲* ܬܚܙܟ. 15. *sāmtonāh* ܣܡܬܘܢܗ̇. *tsumunāh* ܬܣܘܡܘܢܗ̇. 16. *ḥzayti* ܚܙܝܬܝ. *teḥzeyni* ܬܚܙܝܢܝ.

Lesson Sixteen

(a) 1. *kanneš ennon. He gathered them. 2. šarrit̲ l-mallāp̲u. I began to teach.* 3. *eṣallā. I pray.* 4. *mallep̲-wā. He was teaching.* 5. *nmallun. "they will speak".* 6. *mšarriyēn. "beginning".* 7. *mṣalleyn.* "praying" 8. *mkannāšu. "to assemble".* 9. *Ṣallit̲ ᶜalaw. I prayed for them.* 10. *šarri l-mqaṣṣāyeh l-laḥmā. He began to break the bread.* 11. *šarryat̲ lmešḥak̲. It began to get dark.* 12. *nagged̲*eh. *"he beat him".* 13. *neb̲arrek̲ lšameh. They blessed his name.* 14. *nallpluni. "they teach me".* 15. *šarri mnaggdin l-hon. They began beating them.* 16. *šarrit̲ lammallālu. I began to speak.* 17. *lā b̲arrek̲t att. She did not bless you.* 18. *lā t̲naggdin. Do not beat.*

(b) 1. *att dēn emat̲ d-mṣallē att. ᶜol ltawwānek̲. w-eḥod̲ tarᶜek̲. w-ṣallā l-ab̲ok̲ d-b̲-kesyā. W-ab̲ok̲ d-ḥāzē b̲-kesyā nparrek b-gelyā.*

You, however, when you pray, go into your inner room and shut your door. And pray to your father privately. and your father, who sees in secret, will reward you openly.

2. *w-hwā d̲-kad̲ hu mṣallē b̲-dukktā ḥdi. Kad̲ šlem. Emar leh. Ḥad̲ men talmidēw: marran allep̲ayn l-mṣallāyu aykanna d̲-ap̲. Yōḥannān allep l-talmidēw. āmar l-hon išo^c. Emart. d-mṣallin atton hākannā hwayton amrin abon db-šmayyā. Net̲qaddaš[3] šmak̲. Tattā malkut̲ak nhawwā ṣebyānak aykannā. d-b-šmayyē ap̲ b-ar^{c}ā.*

And while he was praying in a place he rejoiced. When he finished, he said to him. One from his disciples (said), "Master, teach us to pray just as also. John taught his disciples. Jesus says to them, "You say. When you are praying, you are in this way saying, "Our father which (is) in heaven. May your name be blessed. May your kingdom come, you will be done just as. In heaven also in earth.

3. *Šqal išo^c laḥmā. W-barrek̲ w-qṣā. W-yab̲ l-talmiddēw. w-emar sob̲ ek̲ol hāno p̲agrā*

And Jesus took the bread. And he blessed and he broke (it) for his disciples. And he said: Take, eat. This is my body.

4. *meṭṭul hānā hā enā mšaddar enā lwat̲kon nbiyē w-ḥakkimē w-sāp̲rē. mennhon kaṭṭlin atton wzqappin atton wmennhon mnaggdin atton. b-kannuštkon. W-terdpun ennon men mdinā la-md̲inā*

For this, behold, I sent unto you prophets and wise men and scribes. from them killing you and crucifying you and from them beating you. in their synagogues. And you pursued them from city to city.

5. *tub̲ dēn šarri-wā mallep̲ ^{c}āl yad̲ yammā. Et̲kannaš lwāt̲eh kenšē. saggiā. Ak̲ d-nass nt̲ub̲ leh b-sp̲ittā b-yammā w-kolleh kenšā qā^{c}em. -wā ^{c}al ar^{c}ā ^{c}al yad̲ yammā*

Again, however, he was beginning teaching beside the sea. And many multitudes were gathered to him. So much so that they pressed him (to) retreat into a boat on the sea. And all his assembly rose on the earth beside the sea.

Lesson Seventeen

(a) 1. *ašlini meddem. You lent me something.* 2. *ad̲rek̲āh ḥeššok̲ā. He overtook darkness.* 3. *Aḥḥeb̲ayk. he loved you.* 4. *taḥḥebni. you loved us.* 5. *taḥḥebinni. you loved us.* 6. *ad̲rek̲aw. he overtook him.* 7. *Šarri l-mahhru. He began to bother me.* 8. *eḥbet̲eh. I loved her.* 9. *neḥḥtaw. he will send me down.* 10. *neḥḥik̲on. he will give them life.*

(b) 1. *w-emar l-hon manu mennkon d-ayt raḥmā w-nazzel lwat̲eh. b-p̲elgut-lêlyā w-nammer leh raḥmā ašelin tlāt̲. Griṣēn. Meṭṭul d-raḥmā etā lwat men urḥā w-*

[3] *Netqaddaš* "may be blessed". the pattern of this verb and of *etkannaš* below will be introduced in §19.1.

layt. meddem d-asim leh w-haw raḥmeh men l-gaww n^{c}annā w-nemar. Le. Lā ṯahharni d-hā ṯar^{c}ā aḥid-w w-benni ^{c}ammi. b-^{c}aršā. Lā enā d-equm w-ettel lāk

And he said to them. Who from among them which there is to him a friend he went up to him. in the middle of the night. And he will say to him. My friend my lending three. loaves of bread. Because of a friend he came to me from a road, and I do not have. anything which I can give him and that his friend to the inside will answer and he will say. To him. Do not bother me. (For) lo, there he was seizing and my sons with me. in bed. I am not able to rise and give (it) to him.

2. *hākannā g̱ēr alāhā l-^{c}ālmā aykannā ḏ-l-ḇreh iḥiḏāyā nettel. D-kollman d-m-haymen beh lā nêbad ellā nehwon leh ḥayyē d-l-^{c}ālmā. Lā uēr šaddar alāhā l-ḇareh l^{c}almā. d-neḏoniaw l-^{c}almā. Ellā ḇ-iḏeh.*

For God so loved the world. As he gave his only son. That the one believing in him will not perish but there will be to him eternal life. But God did not send his son to the world. to judge the world. But he did not give life to the world through him.

3. *emar l-hon išo^{c}. Qallil aḥrin zaḇnā nuhrā ^{c}emkon. hlkw ^{c}ed iṯ l-kon nuhrā-wā. D-lā ḥeššokā neḏrakkon. W-men d-mahleḵ b-ḥeššoḵā. Lā yālē l-aykā kad iṯ l-kon nuhrā. Haymen b-nuhrā d-bēnaw d-nuhrā tahwun. halēn mallel išo^{c} w-ezal mennhon.*

Jesus said to them, "after a while the light was with you. Walk as though (you have) light. That your vow (is) darkness. And from which you are walking in darkness. Not knowing to where he is going until there is no light to them. They believe in the light. You who are my sons will be light. These (things) Jesus spoke and he went up from them.

4. *man d-šema^{c} malli w-lo naṭar l-hon. enā lā dān enā leh. Lā gēr. ayt d-edon l-^{c}almā. Ellā d-eḥḥā l-^{c}almā.*

And whoever shall hear my words, and not observe them, I do not judge him. For I did not come to judge the world, but to bring life to the world. (John 12:47)

Lesson Eighteen

(a) 1. *Atttā ḏ-meṯaqryā maryam. The woman who is called Miriam.* 2. *meddem d-meṯqrē mešḥā. Whatever is called oil.* 3. *Haw d-eṯemer li. That which was spoken to me.* 4. *malkuṯā ḏ-šmayyā ḏ-meṯdmyā l-^{c}sar btulēn. The kingdom of the heaven which is like ten virgins.* 5. *meṯb^{c}aw ḏ-lā neṯemar hānā. It was necessary that he not say this.* 6. *mānē d-mezdbenēn. Vessels which were bought.* 7. *mlē metamran. Words which are being said.* 8. *gabrē ḏ-meṯqarin kênēn. Men who were called just.* 9. *T^{c}urā ḏ-lā metpteḥ. A door which was not opened.* 10. *gabrā d-ezdqep̱. a man who was crucified.*

(b) 1. *āp̱ enā āmar enā l-kon. šel w-neṯiheḇ l-kon. b^{c}aw w-teškḥun. q w-neṯpteḥ l-kon. koll gēr d-šā^{c}el nāseḇ. w-ḏ-b^{c}ā meškaḥ. w-dḇākeš meṯpleḥ.*

So also I am saying to you: They asked and to you. They sought and you found. Knock and it will be opened to you. For all those asking (are) receiving. And the one seeking is able. And the one knocking it will be opened to him.

2. *tub̲ šmaᶜton d-et̲emer d-rḥem l-krib̲ek̲. w-šni l-b̲ᶜaldbāb̲ak̲. enā d̲ēn āmar enā l-kon. aḥheb̲ l-bᶜaldbāb̲kon. w-b̲arrek̲ l-menn d-lāṭ l-k̲on. w-ᶜeb̲ad̲ d-šappir d-sanā l-kon. w-ṣall ᶜal aynin d-dabbarin l-kon b-qtirā w-rad̲pin l-kon. aykannā d-tehwon b-noē d̲-ab̲ok̲on d-blšmayyē haw d-mednaḥ šemšeh ᶜal tab̲ē w-ᶜal bišē. w-mḥāt̲ meṭreh ᶜal kênē w-ᶜal ᶜawwālē.*

And again you heard that it was said, "Love your neighbor. And hate your enemy." But I am saying to you, Love your enemies. and bless those from the ones who are cursing you. And do what is good (unto) those which hate you. And pray for any which are leading you by force and persecuting you. That you may be children of your father who is in heaven, who causes his sun to rise upon the good and upon the wicked. and sends his rain upon the just people and upon the unjust. (Matthew 5:43-45)

3. *haydēn et̲dmē malkutā d-šmayyē l-ᶜsar bt̲ulēn. hennēn d-nsab̲ lampêdēyn l-npaq l-urᶜā ḥatnā w-kalltā. ḥammeš dēn menhayn ḥakkimēn-way. w-ḥammeš saklēn. w-hennēn sakkaltā nsāb̲ lampêdēyn. w-lā nsāb̲ ᶜamheyn mešḥā. hennēn dēn ḥakkimtā nsāb̲ b-mānē ᶜam lampêdēyn. kad̲ awḥar dēn ḥat̲nā nām kollheyn w-dmek̲ w-pelgeh d-lêlyā dhwāt̲ qᶜāt̲ā. hā ḥat̲nā at̲ā. puqaw l-urᶜeh. haydēn qām kolhēn btultē hālēn. w-taqqen lampêdēyn. emarn dēn hānēn sakkaltā l-ḥakkimtā. habeyn lan men mešḥakin deh ad̲ᶜek̲ lhon lampêd̲eyn. ennēy hānnēn ḥakkimtā w-emarn. l-mā lā nespeq nespaq lan w-lak̲ēn. ellā zallēn lwat aylēn d-mezblan w-zeb̲nēn lakēn. w-kad̲ ezal l-mezban. Et̲ā ḥat̲nā. w-aylēn d-meṭayyēbn-ay ᶜal ᶜameh l-bayt ḥlōlā. etṯhed̲ turᶜā. b-ḥartā d̲ēn ayti ap̲ hānnēn bt̲ultā ḥranyātā w-emrēn mrān mrān. pt̲eḥ lan. hu dēn ᶜnā w-amar l-hēn. āmên amar ennā l-kēn. d-lā yadᶜnē lkēn.*

Then the kingdom of heaven is like ten virgins. They who took their lamps and went out to meet the bridegroom and the bride. But five from among them were wise. And five foolish. And the foolish ones took their lamps. And they did not take oil with them. But the wise ones took (some) in vessels with their lamps. But when the bridegroom delayed. All of them slumbered and they slept and in the middle of the night there was an outcry. Lo, the bridegroom comes. go out to meet him. Then all of these virgins stood up. And they got their lamps ready. But those foolish ones were saying to the wise ones. Sell to us from your oil, for behold, our lamps went out. those wise ones answered and were saying. Lest there is not sufficient for us and for you. But go unto those who sell, and buy for yourselves And when he went up to buy, the bridegroom came. And those who were ready went with him into the house of marriage. And he closed the door. In the end, however, also those other virgins came saying, "Lord, lord!" Open for us! But he answered and said to them. Truly I am saying to you. That I don't know you. (Matthew 25:1-2)

Lesson Nineteen

(a) 1. *Kenšē saggē ḏ-meṯkannšin. The great crowds which were being gathered together.* 2. *Lampeḏayhēn d-btulāṯā skaltā mettaqqanin-waw. Their lamps which the foolish virgins were not being constituted.* 3. *Kollmeddem meṯtayyeḇ-wā. Everything was ready.* 4. *Eṯpallag mayyā l-mušē. The waters were divided for Moses.* 5. *Lā ezṣahhreṯ. I was not aware.* 6. *eṯtašši ḇnaynāšā ḇattēhon. The men hid themselves in their houses.* 7. *Meṯb^{c}i-i halēn d-neštallmun. Having sought these which were completed.* 8. *Gaḇrā ḏ-lā mezdahhar. The man which was not being aware.* 9. *Lā meškaḥ d-neṯmallā hānā. He did not find this which we filled.* 10. *Neššē ḏ-meṭṭaššin b-gaww baṯihēn. Women which were hiding inside their houses.*

(b) 1. *Isō^c dēn ḥzāh lemmeh w-l-talmidā haw d-rḥem-wa ḏ-qam. w-emar l-emmeh atttā. hā breḵ. w-emar l-ṯalmiḏā haw. hā emmāḵ. w-men hay šā^{c}tā dbarāh talmiḏā haw lwaṯeh. bāṯar hālēn iḏa^c išō^c d-koll meḏem eštallam. w-dneṯmallā kṯāḇā. emar ṣhē ennā.*

But Jesus saw his mother and the disciple whom he loved, standing by. And he said to his mother, "Woman." Behold your son. And he said to that disciple. Behold your mother. And from that hour that disciple led her unto him. After these Jesus knew that everything was completed. And that the scripture was fulfilled. He said, "I am thirsty". (John 19:26-28)

2. *w-kaḏ eṯkannaš rebbōtā ḏ-kenšē saggai aykannā ḏ-ndayyšun ḥaḏ l-ḥaḏ šarri l-memar l-ṯalmiḏēy. luqdam ezdahhar b-npeškon ḥmirā ḏ-prišē. d-aytaw nsaḇ b-appē. layt dēn meddem d-ḵmā d-lā neggli. w-lā d-meṭṭšeḥ d-lā netidda^c. Koll gēr d-b-ḥeššōḵā emarton b-nahhirā n. w-meddem d-b-tawwānē b-ednē laḥḥešton. ^{c}al eggārē netkrez. āmar ennā lkon dēn lreḥmeḥ. lā ṯeḏḥlun men aylēn d-qattlin pagrā. w-men bāṯarken layt l-hon meddem yattir l-me^{c}beḏ.*

And when the great many multitude was gathered together as they trampled one to another, Jesus began to speak to his disciples. First of all beware for yourselves of the leaven of the Pharisees, which is hypocrisy. For there is nothing which hidden, as will not be revealed. And there is nothing hidden that will not be made known. For all which they say in darkness in light and whatever you whisper in the closets in the ears it will be broadcast upon rooftops. And to you, my friends, I say Do not fear from those who kill the body. And afterwards there is nothing more for them to do. (Luke 12:1-4)

3. *w-kaḏ mepu šêḏā. d-eṯaw ḥaršā. hwā ḏ-kaḏ haw šêḏā. Mallel haw ḥaršā. w-eṯdammar kenšē. nāšā ḏēn menhon emar. b-ḇ^{c}elzboḇ rêšā ḏ-daywā mepu hānā ḏaywā. eḥrênā ḏēn mensin kaḏ mensin leh āṯā men šmayyā šā^{c}el-waw. išō^c dēn d-yaḏē^c-wa maḥšbāthon. emar l-hon. koll malku ḏ-tetpallag nepšāh teḥrak. w-baytā d-^{c}al w-nāmeh metpalleg. npal. W-en sāṭānā ^{c}al nepšeh eṯpallag. aykannā makluṯeh.*

And when he was casting out a demon that was mute, it happened that when the demon had gone, the mute (person) spoke. And the crowds were astonished. But people from among them said, "By Beelzebub, the head of demons, this (man) drives out evil spirits. And others, to tempt him, asked him for a sign from heaven. But Jesus knew their thoughts. He said to them. Every kingdom which is divided upon itself will be destroyed. And a house which upon itself is divided will fall. And if Satan is divided against himself, how will his kingdom stand?

Lesson Twenty

1. *w-šeleh ḥaḏ men rêšānē wemar leh. mallpānā ṭābā. mānā e^{c}abbeḏ ḥayyē ḏal^{c}ālam. āmar leh išo^c. mānā qāra att li ṭāḇā. layt ṭābā ellā en ḥaḏ alāhā. puqdānē yāḏe^c att. lā teḵtol. w-lā tgur. w-lā tegnoḇ w-lā ṯasheḏ sāhduṯā d-šurqā. yaqqar l-aḇoḵ w-lemmaḵ. āmar leh. hālēn kollhēn neṯreṯ ennēn men ṭalyuṯi. kaḏ šma^c dēn išo^c. emar leh. ḥassirā lāḵ. zabben kollmeḏem d-ayt lāḵ. l-meskênē. w-ṯehwā lāḵ simtā ḇ-šmayyē. w-ṯā battari. hu dēn kaḏ šma^c hālēn. krayt leh. ^{c}attir-wā g̱ēr ṭāḇ. w-kaḏ ḥzā išo^c d-keryeṯ leh. Emar. aykannā ^{c}aṯlā l-aylēn d-ayt l-hon neksē. d-ne^{cc}lon l-malkuteh d-alāhā. dlilā-y l-g̱amlā ḏ-b-ḥr d-b-ḥrōrā ḏ-mḥaṭṭā ne^{c}ol. aw ^{c}attirā l-malkuteh d-alāhā. āmrin leh aylēn d-šmaw. w- meškaḥ l-mḥā. išo^c dēn emar. aylēn d-lwaṯ bnaynāšā lā meškaḥn. lwaṯ alāhā meškaḥn l-mehaw.*

And one from the noblemen asked him he said to him. Good teacher. What must I do to inherit eternal life? Jesus said to him, "Why are you calling me good? No one is good except one, God. You know the commandments. You shall not kill. And you shall not commit adultery. You shall not steal and you shall not bear false witness. Honor your father and your mother. He said to him. All of these I have kept from my childhood. But when Jesus heard these (words), He said to him. You are still lacking one thing. Sell everything which there is to you. And give to the poor. And you will have treasure in heaven. And follow after me. But when he heard these, He was sad. For he was very rich. And when Jesus saw his sadness, He said. How difficult is it for those who have riches to enter the kingdom of God! It is easier for a camel to enter the eye of a needle than a rich person the kingdom of God. Those who heard (him) said to him, "Who (then) finds life?" Jesus said, "Those (things) which by people cannot be, with God can be." (Luke 18:18-27)

2. *Beh b-haw yawmā qrabaw nāšā men prišē. w-emrēn leh. puq zal lāk mekkā. meṭṭul d-hêrōdes ṣābē l-meqtlāk. āmar l-hon išo^c.zlaw emr-aw l-ta^{c}lā hannē. d-hā mpaq enā šêdē āswātā^{c}bad enā yawmānā w-mḥār. w-l-yawmā meštamlā enā. bram w-lā li d-yawmānā w-mḥār es^{c}or w-l-yawmā ḥrênā ezal. meṭṭul d-lā meškaḥā d-nbiyā nêbad l-bar men orêšlem. qetlat nbēy w-regmat l-aylē d-šlihēn lwat-āh. kmā zabnin ṣbit l-mekinaš bnayk ak tarnāgultā d-kānešā parrugāh tḥēt geppēāh. w-lā ṣbiton. hā meštbeq l-kon baytkon ḥarbā. āmar enā l-kon gēr. d-lā teḥzon-ni ^{c}dammā d-tamrun. brayk-u d-etā b-šmeh d-māryā.*

In that day the people came some of Pharisees and said to him. Go from here, because of Herod wants to kill you. Jesus said to them. "Go say to that fox. "Behold, I cast out demons and perform healings, today and tomorrow, and on the third day I shall be consummated. However, I must labor today and tomorrow, and on the following day I will depart, for it cannot be that a prophet should perish away from Jerusalem. She killed the prophets and she stoned those who were sent to her. How many times I would have gathered her children like a hen which gathers her chicks below her wings, but you were not willing? Behold your house is left to you desolate. For I say to you. That you will not see me until you will say. Blessed is he who comes in the name of the Lord. (Luke 13:31-35)

3. (26:36) *Haydēn etā ᶜamhon išoᶜ l-dukktā gedsmen. w-emar l-talmidēw. tab harkā. ᶜad ezal eṣlā.* (26:37) *w-dkar l-kêpā w-letrayhon bnay zebday, w-šrē l-metkmaru w-l-mettᶜawu.* (26:38) *w-emar l-hon. kriā-i lāh l-nepši ᶜdammā l-mawtā. Waw li harkā w-šahraw ᶜami.* (26:39). *W-pdaw w-lil. w-npal ᶜal appaw. w-msaḷlē-wā w-amar. Abi. en meškḥā, nᶜabrneḥ ksā hānā. bram lā lāk d-enā ṣābē enā lā ak att.* (26:40). *w-etē lwat talmidēw. w-eškaḥ ennon kad demmakin w-emar l-kēpā. hākanna lā eškaḥton ḥdā šāᶜ d-tešrom ᶜami* (26:41) *ettᶜir w-ṣall. d-lā taᶜlon l-nesyonā. ruḥā mettibā, pegrā dēn krih.* (26:42) *tub ezal d-tartēn zabnēn. ṣal w-emar. Abi. en lā meškaḥ hānā ksal d-naᶜbar lā en eštēteh. ᶜinayhon gēr yawrēn-way.* (26:44) *w-šbaw ennon w-ezal tub ṣli d-alt zabnēn. w-lāh l-melltā emar.* (26:45) *haydēn etā lwat talmēd-aw. w-emar l-hon. dmek mekkêl ettniḥ. hā metet šāᶜtā. w-breh d-enšā meštlem b-yadhon d-ḥattēyā.* (26:46) *w-wmaw nêzal. hā metā haw d-mešlam li.*

(26:36) *At that time Jesus went up with them to the place of Gethsemane. And he said to his disciples. Sit here, while I go and pray.* (26:37) *And he took Cephas and the two sons of Zebedee, and began to be dejected and sorrowful* (26:38). *And he said to them. There is anguish in my soul, even unto death. Wait for me here, and watch with me.* (26:39). *And retiring a little, he fell on his face, and he prayed and said. My father. If it can be so, let this cup pass from me. Yet not as I choose, but as you.* (26:40). *And he came to his disciples, and found them asleep. And he said to Cephas. So, could you not watch with me one hour?* (26:41) *Wake up and pray. Lest you fall into temptation. The spirit is willing, but the body is weak.* (26:42). *Again he went away a second time. And he said. My father, if it cannot be that this cup pass, except that I drink it, your will be done.* (26:44) *And he left them, and went again and prayed a third time, and used the same words.* (26:45) *At that time he came to his disciples. And he said to them. Sleep henceforth and rest. Behold the hour has come. And the son of man will be handed over into the hands of sinners.* (26:46) *Arise, let us go. Behold, he that betrays me has come.* (Matthew 26:36-42, 44-46)

From the *Pšiṭṭā: Kārōzuṯā ḏ-maṯṯay*
The Gospel of Matthew 11:28-30

Taw lwaṯ kollkon layyā w-šqili mawblā. w-ena eniḥkon. šḵolaw niri ʻaliḵon. w-yalpaw meni. ḏ-niḥ ena w-maḵḵiḵ b-laḇi. w-meškaḥin atton nyāḥā l-nep̱šēṯkon. niri g̱ēr bassim-aw. w-mawbli qlilā-y.

Come to me all of you (who are) weary, and my burden load. And I will calm you. Take my yoke upon you. And learn from me. Because I am calm and I am humble in my heart. And you (will) find rest for your soul. But my yoke is pleasant. And my burden is light.

From the *Pšiṭṭā: Kārōzuṯā ḏ-maṯṯay*
The Gospel of Matthew 7:24-27

Koll hāḵêl d-šmē’ mlē hālēn w-ʻeḇaḏ l-hayn. neṯdammā l-gaḇrā ḥaḵimā haw da-ḇnā ḇnā ḇayteh ʻal šōʻā. w-nḥeṯ meṭrā. W-eṯaw nahrawwāṯā. wa-nsaḇ ruḥē w-eṯtarraw beh b-ḇaytā haw. w-lā np̱al. šaṯesēw gēr ʻal šōʻā simān—way. w-koll men da-šmʻē mlē hallēn w-lā ʻaḇeḏ lhayn. neṯdammā l-g̱aḇrā saklā ḏ-ḇnā ḇayteh ʻal ḥālā. w-nḥeṯ meṭrā w-eṯaw nahrawwāṯā. w-nsaḇ ruḥē. w-eṯtarraw b-ḇaytā haw. wa-np̱al. W-hwāṯ map̱pulteh raḇḇā.

Thus everyone fully hearing these and does them. He is like a wise man who builds his house upon the rock. The rain came down and the rivers rose. And the winds came up and beat against that house. And it did not fall. For his foundation was upon a rock. And everyone who has fully heard these (things) and is not doing them. He is like a foolish man who builds his house upon sand. And the rain came down and the rivers rose. And the winds came up. And they beat against that house. And it fell. And there was a great collapse.

From the *Pšiṭṭā: Kārōzuṯā ḏ-maṯṯay k:a-yw*
Gospel of Matthew 20:1-16

Damyā gēr malkuṯā ḏ-šmayyā l-gaḇrā mārā ḇaytā ḏa-np̱aq b-ṣap̱rā. ḏ-nag̱or pāʻlē l-karmeh. qaṣ dēn ʻam b-yawmā p̱aʻlē men dênārā. w-šaḏdar ennon l-ḵarmeh. w-np̱aq ba-ṯlāt šayyēm. w-ḥzā ḥrānē ḏ-qimeyn bšuqā wa-ḇtileyn. w-emar l-hon. zlaw ap̱ eṯton l-ḵarmā. w-meḏdem d-wālē yahēḇ enā l-ḵon. hennon dēn ezlaw. w-np̱aq tuḇ b-šeṯ wa-ḇtšaʻ šāʻēn. wa-ʻbaḏ hāḵwāṯ. w-lap̱pay ḥḏaʻsrē šāʻēn. np̱aq w-eškaḥ ḥrānē ḏ-qimeyn wa-ḇtileyn. w-emar l-hon. manā qimeyn aṯton yawmā ḵolleh w-baṭṭlin. amrēn leh. d-lā nāš eg̱arn. amar l-hon. zlaw ap̱ aṯton l-ḵarmā. w-meḏdem d-wālē nesbeyn atton. kaḏ hwā ḏēn ramšā. emar marrā ḵarmā l-raḇ bayteh. qri paʻlē yaḇ l-hon ag̱rahon. w-šrā men ḥrênā w-ʻḏammā l-qaḏmēy. w-eṯaw hānon d-ḥḏaʻsrē šaʼin. nsaḇ dinar dinar. w-kaḏ šqal. ʻal marrā ḇaytā wemrin. hālēn ḥrāyā ḥḏā šāʻā. w-ešawiṯ ennon ʻamman d-šaqln yuqreh d-yawhmā w-ḥummeh. hu ḏēn ʻenā w-emar l-ḥaḏ menhon. ḥaḇri lā meʻwal bāḵ. lā-wa ḇ-dinar qṣeṯ ʻami. saḇ dilaḵ wzal. ṣāḇā enā ḏēn d-l-hānā ḥriā eṯtel aḵ d-lāḵ. aw lā šliṭ li meḏdem d-ṣāḇā enā aʻbeḏ b-ḏili. aw ʻaynāḵ bišā ḏ-enā ṯāḇ enā. hāḵannā nehwon ḥrēyā qaḏmēyā. w-qaḏmēyā ḥrēyā. sgiayn ennon gēr qrēyā w-z 'orēn gaḇēyā.

(1) *But the kingdom of heaven is like a master (man) who went forth in the morning. To hire laborers to his vineyard.* (2) *And he contracted with the laborers for dinar per day. And he sent them to his vineyard.* (3) *And he went forth in three hours. And he saw others standing in the market and being idle. And he said to them. You also go to the vineyard. And what is necessary I will give you. And they went. And again he went forth in sixth and in the ninth hour. And he did likewise. And around about the eleventh hour. He went forth and found others standing around and doing nothing. And he said to them. Why are you standing around all day and doing nothing?* (7) *(They) say to him. (because) nobody has hired us. (He) says to them. You also go to the vineyard. And whatever is necessary will be given you.* (8) *And when it was evening. The master of the vineyard said to his steward. Call the laborers, give them their wages. And commence from the last unto the first.* (9) *And those of the eleventh hour came. They took each a dinar.*(11) *And when they received (it). They complained to the master of the house,* (12) *and said. These last worked one hour. And you have made them equal with us, who have borne the burden of the day and its heat. He then answered and said to one from among them. My friend, I do not do ill to you. Was it not for a dinar that you contracted with me?* (14) *Take your property and go. For I am wanting to give to this last as to you.* (15) *Or do I not have the authority (to do) whatever I want with my property? Or (is) your eye wicked, because I (am) good?*(16) *Thus the last will be first. And the first last. For many of them have been called, but few of them have been chosen.*

From the *Pšiṭtā: men kārōzuṯā ḏ-luqā b:a-k*
From the gospel of Luke 2:1-20

Hwā dēn b-yawmtā hānon w-npaq puqdannā men agusṭus qesar d-netktob kolleh 'ammā d-uḥdānā. (b) hādē maktbānutā qadmitā hwat b-hegmōnutā d-qewrinos b-suryā. (g) w-ezal-wa kollnāš d-netktab b-mditteh. (d) sleq-wa dēn ap yosep men nāṣrat mdittā d-glilāyā l-ihud. l-mditteh d-dawid d-metqriyā baytlḥem. meṭṭul d-awtwi-wa men bayteh –men šarbeteh d-dawid. (h) 'am maryam mkirteh kad baṭnā d-tammān netkteb. (w) w-hwā d-kad tammān ennon. Etmlyaw yawmtah d-taled. (z) w-yaldet brah bukrā. W- b-'azrurē b-oryā. meṭṭul d-layt-wa l-hon dukktā aykā d-šrayn –waw. (ḥ) rā'awwātā dēn ayt-wā l-hon dukktā aykā d-šarin-wā tammān. w-neṭṭrin maṭṭartā d-lêlyā 'al mar'yāthon. (ṭ) w-hā mlākā d-ettā lwathon. w-tešboḥteh d-māryā anhret elihon. w-dḥel deḥltā rabtā. (y) w-emar l-hon malakā. lā tadḥlon. Hā gēr mesbar enā l-kon ḥdōtā rabtā dethwā l-kolleh 'almā. (yā) ettled l-kon gēr yawmnā parukā.d-it-aw māryā mšiḥā. b-mditteh d-dawid.(yb) w-hādē l-kon ātā.b-škaḥin atton 'wellā d-karrēk 'ōlā b-'azrurē w-sim b-oryā. (yg) w-men šel etḥzaw. 'am mlākā saggiyā ḥaylawwātā d-šmayyā kad mešbḥin l-alāhā w-emrin. (yd) tešboḥtā l-alahā b-mrōmā. w-'al ar'ā šalmā. w-sabrā ṭba l-bnaynāšā. (yh). W-hwā d-kad ezal men lwathon mlakē. mlal r'ōtā ḥad 'am ḥad w-emrēn. nerdē 'dammā l-baytlḥem. w-naḥzā l-melltā hadē d-hwat. ayk d-māryā awda' lan. (yw) w-etaw msarhbā'it w-eškaḥ l-maryim w-l-

yosep. w-l-'awwālā d-sim b-ōryā. (yz) w-kad ḥzāw. l-melltā d-etmallet 'amhon 'alaw ṭalyā. (yḥ) w-kollhon d-šma'. etdammar 'al aylēn d-etmlal r'ōtē. (yṭ) Miryim dēn neṭrā-wat kollhēn mlē hallēn. wmepḥmā belbah.(k) w-hpak r'ōtē hānon kad mešbaḥin w-mahllin. l-allahā 'al koll d-ḥaz w-šma' aykannā d-etmlal 'amhon.

(1) For it was in those days a decree went forth from Caesar Augustus that every person register in his jurisdiction. (2) This was the first census in the governorship of Quirinious in Syria. (3) And everyone went to enroll in his town. (4) Indeed Joseph also went up from Nazareth, (a) city of Galilee to Judea. To the city of David which is called Bethlehem. Because he was from the house and from the lineage of David. (5) With Mary his betrothed, then pregnant, to be enrolled. (6) And it happened when they were there, that her days to give birth were completed. (7) And she gave birth to her first-born son. And she wrapped in swaddling clothes. And she placed him in a manger. For there was no place where they could lodge. (8) Then there were shepherds in the place where they were stopping. (who) kept watch at night over their flocks. (9) and behold, an angel of the Lord came to them. And the glory of the Lord shone upon them. And they feared a great fear. (10) And the angel said to them. Do not be afraid. For behold, I bring to you great gladness which will be for all people. (11) For a savior has been born to you today. who is the Lord Messiah. In the city of David. (12) And this is a sign to you. You will find a baby wrapped in swaddling clothes and being set in a manger. (13) And at once they saw. With the angel a great host of heaven, as (they were) glorifying God and saying. (14) Glory to God in the highest. and on earth peace. And good tidings to men. (15) and it was that when the angels went from among them to heaven. They spoke tending flocks one with another and saying. Let us go down to Bethlehem. And let us see this event which has happened. As the Lord made known to us. (16) And they went hastily. And they found Mary and to Joseph. And the baby setting in a manger. (17) And when they saw. They made known the thing which was spoken unto them concerning the child. (18) And all that they heard. They were astonished concerning what they were told them by those keeping flocks. (19) Then Mary kept laid up all these things, and stored them in her heart. (20) And the shepherds returned as (they were) glorifying God and saying. To God concerning all that they saw and heard, as it was told them.

From Pseudo-Callisthenes' Legend of Alexander
men Taš'īṯā ḏ-Aleksandros bar P̱īlīpos
From the Story of Alexander son of Philip

Haydēn Aleksandros men tamman ašqel wa-l-Maqedonyā ezal. w-eṯā la-ṯhūmā d-P̱āres. wa-šrā 'al nahrā Deqlaṯ. w-Aleksandros b-izgaddūṯā lwāṯ Daryuš ezal. 'ḏammā ḏ-'al l-Ḇāḇel. w-eṯaw Pārsāyē w-awda'(w) l-Ḏaryuš malkā. w-ḵaḏ emar(w): w-Ḏaryuš kaḏ l-Aleksandros ḥzā. eṯrḵen w-l-Aleksandros sgeḏ. meṭṭul d-sāḇar (h)wā da-mhīr alāhā iṯaw d-eṯtaḥti. wa-l-'uḏrānā d-P̱ārsāyē eṯā. meṭṭul d-eskêmeh l-eskêmā d-alāhē msabbah (h)wā. meṭṭul da-ḵlilā da-ḇ-rêšeh asīr (h)wā l-zallīqē msabbah. wa-lḇūšā da-lḇīš hwā b-ḏahḇā snīnā zqīr (h)wā. w-ḇarzanqē d-ḇa-ḏrā‘aw b-sêmā .ṭāḇā ‘ḇīḏīn (h)waw. w-msānaw d-ḏahḇā. wa-qmāreh men margānyāṯā wa-zmargḏē ‘ḇīḏ (h)wā. w-Ḏaryuš qā’em (h)wā w-ḇ-eskêmeh meṯbaqqē (h)wā. w-‘esrā alpīn parrāšē nāṭray-haṣṣeh lwāṯeh qāymīn (h)waw. d-nāṭōrē dileh ‘ḇīḏīn (h)waw. haydēn l-Aleksandros šā’el (h)wā. d-att man att. Aleksandros emar. izgaddā-nā ḏ-Aleksandros. d-men Aleksandros šlīḥūṯā aytêṯ lāḵ. w-hāḵannā emar: d-eštawḥart li qrāḇā l-me‘baḏ. w-Maqeḏonāyē āmrīn: d-meṭṭul d-lebbeh d-Ḏaryuš špel ba-qrāḇā. ‘al hāḏē mḥīr la-qrāḇā l-mêṯā. hāšā hāḵêl att lā tqawwē. ellā šloḥ li d-emaṯ šāḇē att **[p. 155]** *l-taḵtōšā l-mêṯā. haydēn Daryuš emar leh. da-lmā att qnomāḵ Aleksandros att w-lā hwayt izgaddā. meṭṭul d-mellē saggi lḇībā’iṯ mmallel (h)wā Aleksandros. w-lā mmallel (h)wā nīḥā’iṯ ak gaḇrā izgaddā. āmar leh Daryuš: enā men mellayk lā meṯrahhaḇ-nā. att hāšā ak ‘yāḏā ḏ-izgaddē šarūṯā qḏām(y) l‘as. meṭṭul d-āp̱ Aleksandros b-izgaddē dil(y) hāḵan ‘ḇaḏ. haydēn Dāryuš b-‘arseh agges (h)wā. w-ḥêraw w-rawrḇānaw qḏāmaw estmeḵ(w). wa-l-quḇleh d-Ḏāryuš Aleksandros d-hāwē izgaddā. wa-bnaynāšā kollhon tammihīn (h)waw beh. da-ḇ-p̱agreh z‘or (h)wā. w-mellaw ḥarrip̱ān (h)way. w-ḵaḏ l‘as(w). ḥamrā b‘aw. w-Aleksandros koll mānā ḏ-ḏahḇā d-awšeṭ(w) leh. ḥamrā ‘al ar‘ā ešaḏ (h)wā. w-mānē b-ḥanneh sā’em (h)wā. haydēn kaḏ ḥzaw d-mānā ‘āḇeḏ. l-Ḏaryuš awda‘ (h)waw. w-Ḏaryuš kaḏ šma‘. men ‘arseh qām. wa-lwāṯ Aleksandros eṯā w-emar leh. d-ō ‘āḇeḏ neṣḥānē. meṭṭul mānā d-ak hālēn ‘āḇeḏ att. d-ḵollhon mānē ḏ-maštyā b-ḥannāḵ sāmt. Aleksandros emar. meṭṭul d-kaḏ mār(y) Aleksandros emaṯ d-šarūṯā l-ḥêraw ‘āḇeḏ (h)wā. kollhon mānay maštyā ḏ-ḏahḇā l-hon yāheḇ (h)wā. āp̱ enā sabbret d-āp̱ beh ba-znā ‘āḇeḏ att. ellā hāšā en layt lāḵ d-ak hānā ‘yāḏā. hā mānay maštyā qḏāmayk. pqoḏ w-ḏahḇāḵ m‘aṭṭep̱-nā lāḵ. haydēn Daryuš emar. āp̱ enā peqdeṯ d-ḏahḇāḵ lwāṯāḵ narmōnāy. w-P̱ārsāyē kolhon b-Aleksandros ḥāyrīn (h)waw. w-ḵaḏ tammihīn (h)waw meṭṭul d-mellaw ḥayltānyān (h)way w-malyān ida‘ṯā. kaḏ haḵêl men mārawwāṯā ḥaḏ. d-iṯaw (h)wā Pusāq šmeh: d-men qḏēm b-izgaddūṯā men Daryuš l-Maqedonyā eštaddar (h)wā lwāṯ P̱ilipos aḇū d-Aleksandros: w-ḵaḏ b-Aleksandros* **[p. 156]** *ḥattīṯā’iṯ eṯbaqqi yaḏ‘eh (h)wā. wa-ḇ-leššānā pārsāyā l-Ḏaryuš emar (h)wā. ō ‘āḇeḏ .ṭāḇāṯā Daryuš malkā. pqoḏ da-l-hānā izgaddā b-nāṭōrāṯā zhirā’iṯ nnaṭṭrūn. meṭṭul d-huyu qnomeh d-Aleksandros. w-men ḥzāṯeh yāḏa‘-nā leh w-mestakkal-nā. haydēn kaḏ Daryuš w-ḥêraw w-rawrḇānaw šma‘(w). šarri(w) ḥaḏ ‘am ḥaḏ la-mmallālū w-ḇ-Aleksandros meṯbaqqeyn (h)waw. haydēn Aleksandros iḏa‘. w-men bēṯ meštūṯā qām. wa-l-ṯar‘ā ḏ-malkā šwar. ‘am hānon kollhon mānay dahḇā da-ḇ-ḥanneh aḥīḏ (h)wā. w-‘al tar‘ā ḏ-ḇēṯ malkā gaḇrā ḥaḏ nāṭōrā eškaḥ. kaḏ b-iḏeh qaysā d-arzā ḥaḏ kaḏ dleq aḥīḏ (h)wā. w-qaṭleh w-nasbeh menneh. w-‘al sūsāyeh rḵeḇ. wa-ḇ-‘eqbeh ba‘ṭeh. w-haw qaysā kaḏ nūrā meṯnaḇršā (h)wāṯ qḏām ‘aynaw d-sūsāyā lḇīḵ (h)wā w-sūsāyā beh b-zahrā ḏ-nūrā b-urḥā msarhḇā’iṯ rheṭ (h)wā. w-la-sp̱ar nahrā ḥaḏ eṯā. haydēn izgaddē bāṯreh np̱aq(w) qallilā’iṯ. w-meṭṭul ḥāšōḵā d-lêlyā sugāhon b-gaww gumāṣē wa-ḇ-neq‘ē np̱al(w). Aleksandros dēn b-ḥaylā d-alāhē l-nahrā haw ‘ḇar. w-ḵaḏ l-haw gabbā ḏ-nahrā ‘ḇar. w-reglaw qaḏmāyāṯā ḏ-sūsāyā l-yaḇšā smeḵ. mayyā hānon da-maglḏīn (h)waw meḥdā pšar (h)waw. w-reglaw ḥrāyāṯā ḏ-sūsāyā b-gaww nahrā nḥeṭ (h)way. w-Aleksandros men sūsāyā l-yaḇš_ā šwar. w-sūsāyā b-nahrā .ṭḇa‘. haydēn kaḏ izgaddē la-sp̱ar nahrā eṯaw. wa-ḥzaw d-Aleksandros l-nahrā haw ‘ḇar. w-*

hennon d-ne'brūn bāṯreh lā eškaḥ(w). haydēn tmah(w) w-ḥaḏ l-ḥaḏ āmrīn (h)waw. d-rabbu gaddeh d-Aleksandros da-l-nahrā ḏ-hāḵan rabb ma'barṯā yaḇ leh. w-eškaḥ l-me'breh. w-ḵaḏ pnaw. lwāṯ Daryuš eṯaw. w-awda'(w) l-Ḏaryuš 'al pulạ̄teh w-ma'barṯeh d-Aleksandros da-l-nahrā. Daryuš b-'āqṯā rabbṯā (h)wā. w-men šelyā āṯā eṯhazyaṯ leh. ṣalmeh gēr d-Ḵusraw malkā. haw **[p. 157]** *d-Ḏaryuš rāḥem (h)wā leh. b-ḇēṯ maštyā 'al estā ṣīr (h)wā. w-men šel(y) eṯqp̱el (h)wā men estā. wa-l-'aynaw d-Ḏaryuš 'al ar'ā np̱al. Aleksandros dēn men da-l-nahrā 'ḇar. men raḥteh w-men 'amleh ettnīḥ. w-qām b-reglaw mhalleḵ (h)wā. wa-ḇ-g̱aww haw ḥeškā d-lêlyā l-Amoros rêš guddā balḥoḏaw ḥzā. w-ḵaḏ b-'āqṯā rabb_ṯā meṭṭul Aleksandros qā'em (h)wā w-ḇāḵē. haydēn Aleksandros kollhēn mellē ḏa-'ḇar 'law l-Amoros emar (h)wā.*

Then Alexander set forth from there and went to Macedonia, and he came to the border of Persia and camped by the river Tigris, and Alexander set out on an embassy to Darius until he entered Babylon. The Persians came and informed Darius the king, and when they told him and when Darius saw Alexander he bowed down and prostrated himself before Alexander because he thought that he was a skilled god who had been sent down and was come to the aid of the Persians because his appearance was made to resemble the appearance of the gods, for the crown that was fastened to his head was made to resemble rays, the clothing he was wearing was formed of pure gold, the armor on his arms was made of beautiful silver, his sandals were of gold, and his belt was made of pearls and emeralds. And Darius was standing, scrutinizing his appearance, and ten thousand horsemen of his bodyguard, were standing in his presence, for they had been made his guards. Then he asked Alexander, "Who are you?" Alexander said, "I am Alexander's envoy who have brought you a message from Alexander, and thus he said: 'You have hesitated to do battle with me, and the Macedonians say that Darius' heart is cowardly in battle. For this reason he delays to come to battle. Now do not wait thus, but send me [a message, saying] when you desire to come **[p. 155]** *to the battlefield.' " Then Darius said to him, "Are you not yourself Alexander? You are no envoy." For Alexander was speaking very bold words and not speaking calmly like an envoy. Darius said to him, "I am not frightened by your words. Now, according to the custom of ambassadors, partake of a banquet in my presence, because so also did Alexander do for my ambassadors." Then Darius reclined on his couch, and his noblemen and grandees reclined before him, and opposite Darius was Alexander, who was [pretending to be] an ambassador. All the people were astonished by him, for in body he was small, but his words were severe. When they had partaken [of the food], they called for wine. Every vessel of gold they set before him, Alexander poured the wine on the ground and placed the vessel in his lap. When they saw what he was doing, they informed Darius, and when Darius heard, he arose from his couch and went to Alexander and said to him, "O doer of adventures, why are you doing this, putting all the vessels of the banquet in your lap?" Alexander said, "Because when my lord Alexander made a banquet for his nobles, he gave them all the banquet vessels of gold. I thought that so also in a like manner you would do too, but now, if you have no such custom, here are the banquet vessels before you. Command, and I will return* *your gold to you." Then Darius said, "I too order that they lay down the gold before you." All the Persians were looking at Alexander, and they were astonished because his words were powerful and filled with knowledge. Then one of the lords, whose name was Pusaq, who had previously been sent by Darius to Macedonia to Philip, Alexander's father, when he scrutinized Alexander accurately,* **[p. 156]** *he recognized him, and in the Persian language he said to Darius, "O doer of good deeds, King Darius, command that they keep this ambassador under watch securely, because he is himself Alexander, and from the sight of him I recognize him and understand." Then, when Darius and his nobles and grandees heard, they began to speak with each other, scrutinizing Alexander. Then Alexander realized, and he arose from the banquet hall and leapt to the king's gate along with all the golden vessels he was holding in his lap. At the gate of the king's palace he found a guard holding a branch of cedar in his hand as a torch. He killed him, took it (the torch) from him, mounted his horse, and spurred it with his heel. He held the branch with the fire burning before the horse's eyes, and the horse ran speedily down the road by the light of the fire. He came to the bank of a river. Then envoys set out after him swiftly, but because of the darkness of the night many of them fell into pits and holes. Then Alexander, with the power of the gods, crossed the river, and when he crossed to the other side of the river and the front legs of the horse rested against the dry land, the water, which was frozen, suddenly melted, and the hind legs of the horse sank into the river. Alexander jumped from the horse onto the dry land, and the horse sank into the river. Then, when the envoys came to the river bank and saw that Alexander had crossed the river, they were unable to crossed after him, so they were perplexed and said to each other, "Alexander's fortune is great that found a crossing of such a large river and was able to cross." When they returned and came to Darius and informed Darius of Alexander's escape and crossing of the river, Darius was in great sadness. Suddenly a vision was seen by him, as the image of King Chosroës,* **[p. 157]** *whom Darius loved, which was depicted on the wall in the banquet hall, suddenly became detached from the wall and fell to the ground before Darius' eyes. Alexander then rested from having crossed the river, from his running and his labor, and he rose and walked on foot. In the midst of the darkness of the night he saw Amoros, the head of his band, standing alone and weeping in great grief over Alexander. Then Alexander told Amoros all the things that had happened to him.*

The First Discovery of the True Cross

Taš'īṯā ḏa-Škaḥṯeh d-Mār(y) Ṣlīḇā Qaddīšā: d-aykan eštkaḥ qaḏmā'īṯ b-yaḏ Prọṭōnīqē attṯeh da-Qlawdiyōs Qesar. Māran, 'ḏarayn(y) b-raḥmayḵ, āmên.

The Story of the Discovery of My Lord the Holy Cross: How It Was First Found by Protonice, the Wife of Claudius Caesar. My Lord, help me with your mercies. Amen.

Men bāṯar messaqṯeh d-Māran Išō' d-la-šmayyā: beh b-zabnā haw kaḏ ezal (h)wā Šem'ōn Kêp̱ā l-R(h)ōmē: w-aḵrez tamman mellṯā ḏ-alāhā: šem'aṯ (h)wāṯ Prọṭōnīqē attṯeh da-Qlawdiyōs Qesar: haw d-'aḇḏeh Ṭīberyōs trayyānā b-

malkūṯeh: kaḏ āzel (h)wā d-naqreḇ ʻam bnay Espānyā da-mraḏ (h)waw ʻlaw: hī dēn hāḏē atttā: kaḏ īṯaw (h)wā Šemʻōn b-R(h)ōmē: ḥāzyā (h)wāṯ_teḏmrāṯā w-ḥaylē tammīhē d-sāʻar (h)wā ba-šmeh d-Māran Mšīḥā. w-kep̱raṯ b-ḥanpūṯā ḏ-aḇāhēh d-qāymā (h)wāṯ bāh: wa-ḇ-ṣalmē d-ḥanpūṯā d-sāg̱ḏā (h)wāṯ l-hon. w-ḇa-Mšīḥā Māran mhaymnā (h)wāṯ w-sāg̱ḏā (h)wāṯ leh: ʻam kollhon aylēn da-nqīp̱īn (h)waw leh l-Šemʻōn: w-āḥḏā (h)wāṯ leh b-īqārā rabbā. **[p. 158]**

w-men bāṯar hāḵannā ṣḇāṯ (h)wāṯ d-āp̱ l-Ōrêšlem teḥzē: w-ḏūkkyāṯā_aylēn da-ḇ-hēn estʻar(w) ḥaylē tammīhē w-ṯahhīrē d-Māran Īšōʻ Mšīḥā. w-qāmaṯ (h)wāṯ ḥp̱īṯāʼīṯ: w-neḥtaṯ lāh men R(h)ōmē_l-Ōrêšlem: hī wa-ṯrayn bnēh ʻammāh wa-ḥḏā barṯāh bṯūltā. w-ḵaḏ mṭāṯ (h)wāṯ da-ṯeʻʻōl l-Ōrêšlem: šemʻaṯ w-nep̱qaṯ kollāh mḏīttā l-ūrʻāh: w-qabblūh (h)waw b-īqārā rabbā: ak da-l-malkṯā mārṯeh d-aṯrā ḏ-ḇēṯ-R(h)ōmāyē. b-zaḇnā dēn haw: Yaʻqōḇ ʻḇīḏ (h)wā mḏabbrānā w-p̱āqōḏā ḏa-mḏīttā: b-ʻêḏtā ḏ-ḇanyā (h)wāt lan tamman b-Ōrêšlem.

w-ḵaḏ šmaʻ d-meṭṭulmānā eṯāṯ (h)wāṯ l-ṯamman: qām (h)wā meḥdā w-ezal ṣēḏēh. w-ʻal lwāṯāh aykā d-šāryā (h)wāṯ: b-āpadnā rabbā ḏ-malkē d-ḇēṯ-Herōdes. w-ḵaḏ ḥzāṯeh (h)wāṯ: qabblāṯeh (h)wāṯ b-ḥaḏūṯā rabbṯā: āp̱ leh ak da-l-Šemʻōn Kêp̱ā. w-ḥawwyāh ḥaylē d-asyūṯā: āp̱ hū ak Šemʻōn. w-emraṯ leh: ḥawwā lī Gāg̱ūlṯā: hay d-ezdqep̱ bāh Māran Mšīḥā: wa-qaysā ḏa-ṣlīḇūṯeh d-eṯṯlī (h)wā beh men y(h)ūḏāyē: wa-qaḇrā haw d-ḇeh ettsīm. haydēn āmar lāh hū Yaʻqōḇ: hālēn tlāṯayhon d-ṣāḇyā malkūṯeḵ d-teḥzē: ṭḥēṯ īḏā ennon da-y(h)ūdāyē: w-hānōn āḥḏīn l-hon. w-lā šāḇqīn lan d-nêzal wa-nṣallē tamman qḏām Gāg̱ūlṯā w-qaḇrā: w-āp̱-lā qaysā ḏa-ṣlīḇeh ṣāḇeyn d-nettlūnāy lan. w-lā (h)wā hāḏē balḥōḏ: ellā āp̱ merdap̱ rāḏp̱īn lan: d-lā naḵrez w-nsabbar ba-šmeh da-Mšīḥā: w-zaḇnāṯā ṭūḇ saggīʼāṯā āp̱ bēṯ-asīrē ḥāḇšīn lan.

w-ḵaḏ šemʻaṯ hālēn hī Prōṭōnīqē malkṯā: bāh b-šāʻṯā peqdaṯ w-aytī(w) la-qḏāmēh l-Ḥunyā bar Ḥannān kāhnā: w-la-G̱ḏalyā bar Qaypā: wa-l-Y(h)ūḏā bar Šālōm: rêšā ḏa-y(h)ūḏāyē. w-emraṯ l-hon malkṯā: ašlem(w) Gāg̱ūlṯā w-qaḇrā w-qaysā ḏa-ṣlīḇā l-Yaʻqōḇ w-l-aylēn d-šālmīn leh: lā nāš neḵlē ennon men da-nšammšūn tamman ak ʻyāḏā ḏ-ṯešmšaṯhon. w-ḵaḏ **[p. 159]** hāḵannā peqdaṯ (h)wāṯ l-ḵāhnē: qāmaṯ (h)wāṯ d-ṯêzal w-ṯeḥzē ennēn l-ḏūkkyāṯā hālēn: w-āp̱ d-ṯašlem aṯrā haw l-Yaʻqōḇ w-l-aylēn d-ʻammeh. w-ḇāṯarken ʻallaṯ l-qaḇreh d-Māran: w-eškḥaṯ (h)wāṯ b-g̱awweh d-qaḇrā tlāṯā zqīp̱ē: ḥaḏ d-Māran: w-ṯrēn d-hānon gayyāsē da-zqīp̱īn (h)waw ʻammeh: ḥaḏ men yammīneh w-ḥaḏ men semmāleh. w-ḇeh b-ʻeddānā d-ʻellaṯ (h)wāṯ l-qaḇrā hī malkṯā w-ḇnēh ʻammāh: bāh b-šāʻṯā nep̱laṯ (h)wāṯ barṯāh bṯūlṯā w-mīṯaṯ d-lā kêḇā wa-ḏ-lā kurhānā wa-ḏ-lā ʻellṯā meddem. w-ḵaḏ ḥzāṯ (h)wāṯ Protonīqē d-miṯaṯ lāh barṯāh men šelyā: berkaṯ (h)wāṯ ba-ṣloṯā ba-ḇḵāṯā: wa-mṣallyā (h)wāṯ b-g̱awweh d-qaḇrā w-āmrā (h)wāṯ hāḵannā: Mšiḥā d-y(h)aḇ napšeh l-mawtā ḥlāp̱ kollhon bnaynāšā: w-ezdqep̱ b-aṯrā hānā: w-ettsim b-qaḇrā hānā: ak alāhā maḥḥē-ḵoll qām: w-aqim ʻammeh l-saggiʼē: lā nešmʻun y(h)udāyē zāqōp̱ē w-ḥanpē_taʻyē: hānon d-ḵep̱reṯ b-ṣalmayhon w-ḇa-g̱lip̱ayhon wa-ḇ-ḏeḥlathon d-ḥanpūṯā: w-neḥdōn li kaḏ mahhlīn bi w-nêmrūn: d-ḵollāh da-hwāṯ lāh hāḏē: ʻal d-ḵep̱raṯ b-allāhē d-sāg̱ḏā (h)wāṯ l-hon: w-awdyaṯ ba-Mšiḥā d-lā yāḏʻā (h)wāṯ leh: w-ezlaṯ (ezzaṯ) da-ṯyaqqar dukkṯā ḏ-qaḇreh wa-ṣlibuṯeh. w-en enā lā šāwyā-nā d-eštmaʻ: ʻal d-seg̱ḏeṯ l-beryāṯā ḥlāp̱ayk: ḥūs att meṭṭul šmāḵ sgiḏā: d-lā tuḇ netgaddap̱ b-aṯrā hānā: ak da-g̱addep̱(w) ʻlayk ba-ṣliḇūṯāḵ.

w-ḵaḏ hālēn ba-ṣlōṯāh āmrā (h)wāṯ: qḏām aylēn d-iṯ (h)waw tamman: qreb lwāṯāh brāh qaššišā w-āmar lāh: šma‘(y) meddem d-āmar-nā qḏām malkuṯeḵ. enā hāḵannā sāḇar-nā b-re‘yān(y) wa-ḇ-meḥšḇaṯ(y): d-hānā mawtā ḏ-hāḏē ḥāṯ(y) d-menšel(y): lā (h)wā sriqā’īṯ hwā: ellā su‘rānā (h)u hānā tammihā: d-alāhā meštabbaḥ beh: w-lā (h)wā rešmeh neṯgaddap̱ beh: ak da-sḇar(w) aylēn da-šma‘(w) hāḏē: hā ‘āllin l-qaḇrā hānā ḏa-Mšiḥā w-eškaḥnan tlāṯā zqip̱ē: w-lā yāḏ‘inan aynā (h)u mennhon zqip̱ā hu d-eṯtli beh Mšiḥā. hāšā dēn b-mawtāh d-hāḏē ḥāṯ(y) **[p. 160]** *meškḥīnan d-neḥzē w-nêlap̱: d-aynu zqip̱eh da-Mšiḥā: lā gēr mahmē men aylēn da-mhaymnin beh. malkṯā dēn Prọtoniqē: kaḏ ṭāḇ marrirā (h)wāṯ nap̱šāh b-‘eddānā haw: ḥḏaṯ (h)wāṯ b-re‘yānāh ak ḥeḵmṯāh: d-ḵênā’iṯ wa-ṯriṣā’iṯ emar brāh hālēn. w-qerbaṯ meḥdā w-šeqlaṯ (h)wāṯ hi b-iḏēh ḥaḏ men hālēn zqip̱ē: w-sāmṯeh ‘al šladdāh d-ḇarṯāh d-ramyā (h)wāṯ qḏāmēh: w-emraṯ (h)wāṯ ba-ṣlōṯāh: Mšiḥā d-ḥawwi ḥaylē tammihē b-aṯrā hānā: ak d-šma‘nan w-haymennan. en dilāḵ (h)u Mār(y) hānā zqip̱ā: wa-ḇ-haw eṯtalyaṯ nāšūṯāḵ men marrāḥē: ḥawwā ḥaylā ‘azzizā wa-ṯqip̱ā ḏ-allāhūṯāḵ d-‘am nāšūṯāḵ ḥḏā (h)wāṯ. w-ṯaḥḥē hāḏē barṯ(y) wa-ṯqum: w-neštabbaḥ bāh šmāḵ: kaḏ panyā nap̱šeh l-g̱aww pag̱rāh: w-neḇhṯun zāqōp̱ayk: w-neḥḏōn sāg̱ōḏayk. w-qawwyaṯ (h)wāṯ ‘eddānā saggi’ā: men bāṯar d-emraṯ hālēn. w-bāṯarken šqalṯeh (h)wāṯ la-zqip̱ā haw men šladdāh d-ḇarṯāh: w-sāmaṯ (h)wāṯ haw ḥrênā. w-emraṯ tuḇ ba-ṣlōṯāh: alāhā haw da-ḇ-ramzeh qāymin ‘ālmē w-ḇeryāṯā: w-ṣāḇē b-ḥayyē d-ḵollhon bnaynāšā d-meṯp̱nēn lwāṯeh: w-lā mahmē men bā‘ūṯā ḏ-aylēn d-ḇā‘ēn leh. en dilāḵ (h)u Mār(y) hānā zqip̱ā: ḥawwā ḥaylā ḏ-neṣḥānayk ak da-m‘āḏatt: w-ṯaḥḥē hāḏē bart(y) wa-ṯqum. w-neḇhṯun ḥanpē sāg̱ḏay l-beryāṯā ḥlāp̱ayk: w-nawdōn mhaymnē šarrirē: d-meṯp̱ṯaḥ pumhon l-ṯešbḥāṯāḵ qḏām aylēn d-ḵāp̱rin bāḵ. w-aggraṯ (h)wāṯ tuḇ ṭawrā saggi’ā: w-haydēn šqalṯeh (h)wāṯ la-zqip̱ā haw da-ṯrēn men barṯāh: w-sāmaṯ haw da-ṯlāṯā ‘al barṯāh. w-ḵaḏ bā‘yā (h)wāṯ da-ṯrīm ‘aynēh la-šmayyā: w-ṯep̱taḥ pumāh ba-ṣlōṯā: bāh b-šā‘ṯā w-ḇeh b-‘eddānā: ak meṭrap̱ temrā ḏ-‘aynā: da-qreḇ (h)wā zqip̱ā haw la-šladdā ḏ-ḇarṯāh: ḥyāṯ (h)wāṯ barṯāh men šelyā w-qāmaṯ. wa-mšabbḥā (h)wāṯ la-Mšiḥā: d-aḥḥyāh ba-zqip̱eh.*

malkṯā dēn Prọtoniqē: kaḏ ḥzāṯ (h)wāṯ d-aykannā ḥyāṯ barṯāh: ettzi‘aṯ w-eṯrahhḇaṯ ṭāḇ: w-mšabbḥā (h)wāṯ la-Mšiḥā d-haymnaṯ beh: **[p. 161]** *d-ḇreh (h)u d-alāhā ḥayyē. āmar lāh brāh: ḥzayt mārt(y): d-ellu hāḏē lā hwāṯ yawmānā: gaḏšā d-šāḇqin (h)wayn zqip̱ā hānā ḏa-Mšiḥā da-ḥyāṯ beh ḥāṯ(y): w-āḥḏin (h)wayn wa-myaqqrin (h)wayn d-ḥaḏ men hānon gayyāsē qāṭōlē. ella hāšā hā ḥāzēn w-ḥāḏeynan b-hāḏē. w-alāhā d-sa‘rāh l-hāḏē: yattirā’iṯ eštabbaḥ bāh. w-šqalṯeh malkṯā Prọtoniqē la-zqip̱eh da-Mšiḥā: w-y(h)aḇṯeh (h)wāṯ l-Ya‘qōḇ: ak d-neṯṭar b-iqārā rabbā. w-p̱eqdaṯ (h)wāṯ d-neṯbnē benyānā rabbā wa-šḇiḥā ‘al Gāg̱ulṯā w-‘al qaḇrā: ak d-neṯyaqqrān dukkyāṯā hālēn da-zqip̱ā wa-ḏ-qaḇrā: w-nehwē tamman bēṯ-wa‘dā la-ḵnušṯā ḏ-ṯešmešṯā. malkā dēn kaḏ ḥzāṯ (h)wāṯ: d-ḵenšaṯ nāšūṯā kollhon da-mḏittā l-ḥzāṯā ḏ-su‘rānā hānā: peqdaṯ da-ḏ-lā taḥpiṯā ḏ-iqārā ḏ-malkāṯā têzal (h)wāṯ barṯāh ‘ammāh galyā’iṯ l-āpadnā ḏ-malkā haw d-šāryā (h)wāṯ beh: ak d-neḥzē kollnāš wa-nšabbaḥ l-alāhā. ‘ammā dēn da-y(h)udāyē wa-ḏ-ḥanpē: hennon da-ḥḏi(w) (h)waw b-šurāyāh d-hāḏē: eṯkmar (h)waw b-šulāmāh d-hāḏē. ṭāḇ gēr mnāḥin (h)waw ellu lā hwāṯ hāḏē: d-ḥāzēn (h)waw d-saggi’ē mennhon haymen (h)waw beh ba-Mšiḥā. yattirā’iṯ dēn d-ḥāzeyn (h)waw d-saggi’ān (h)way āṯwāṯā w-ṯeḏmrāṯā ḏ-hāwyān (h)way men* *bāṯar sulāqeh: yattir men hānēn d-hāwyān (h)way men qḏām sulāqeh. w-āp̱ l-aṯrawwāṯā raḥḥiqē ezal (h)wā .tebbeh d-su'rānā hānā: w-āp̱ la-šliḥē kollhon aylēn da-msabbrin (h)waw la-Mšiḥā. w-hwā (h)wā šelyā b-'êḏtā ḏ-Ōrêšlem: w-ḇa-mḏināṯā da-ḥḏārēh. w-aylēn d-lā ḥzaw āṯā hāḏē: 'am aylēn da-ḥzaw: āp̱ hennon mšabbḥin (h)waw l-alāhā.*

w-ḵaḏ selqaṯ malkṯā Proṭoniqē men Ōrêšlem l-R(h)ōmē mḏittāh: koll mḏittā aydā d-'āllā (h)wāṯ lāh: la-ḥzāṯā ḏ-ḇarṯāh ḥāḇsin (h)waw nāšā d-neḥzōn. w-ḵaḏ 'allaṯ l-R(h)ōmē: ešta''yaṯ qḏām Qlawdiyos Qesar **[p. 162]** *kollhēn hālēn d-est'ar (h)way ṣêḏēh: d-aykan miṯaṯ barṯāh w-ḇāṯarken ḥyāṯ. w-ḵaḏ šma' (h)wā Qesar hālēn: pqaḏ (h)wā d-neppqūn kollhon y(h)udāyē men R(h)ōmē w-men aṯrā ḏ-Iṭalyā. kaḏ b-ḵolleh aṯr_ā haw su'rānā hānā meṯmallal (h)wā men saggi'ē: wa-qḏām Šem'ōn Kêp̱ā ešta''yaṯ (h)wāṯ hi Proṭoniqē teḏmurṯā hāḏē: w-ḵoll meddem d-s'ar (h)waw šliḥē ḥaḇraw. w-qḏām kollnāš maḵrzin (h)waw: d-nešm'ūn āp̱ aylēn d-lā šma'(w) w-iḏa'(w): w-nedd'un aylēn da-ḇ-iḏan s'ar w-sā'ar Māran galyā'iṯ: d-neštabbaḥ šmeh d-Māran men kollnāš l-'ālam 'ālmīn: āmēn.*

hālēn hāḵēl da-ṯnayt ennon qḏāmayḵon: d-ṯedd'un w-ṯeṯbayynun da-ḵmā rabbā haymnuṯeh da-Mšiḥā: l-aylēn da-nqip̱in leh šarrirā'iṯ. āp̱ Ya'qōḇ dēn mḏabbrānā ḏ-'êḏtā ḏ-Ōrêšlem: haw d-hu b-'aynaw ḥzā l-su'rānā hānā: hu āp̱ kaṯbeh w-šaddreh la-šliḥē ḥaḇraw: la-mḏittā d-iṯ (h)way b-aṯrawwāṯhon. w-āp̱ hennon šliḥē kṯaḇ(w) w-awda'(w) l-Ya'qōḇ kollmeddem da-'ḇaḏ Mšiḥā b-iḏayhon: w-meṯqreyn (h)waw qḏām kolleh kenšā ḏ-'êḏtā wa-qḏām kolleh 'ammā. šlāmā.

After the ascension of Our Lord Jesus into heaven, at the time when Simon Peter went to Rome and preached there the word of God, he was heard by Protonice, the wife of Claudius Caesar, the one whom Tiberius made second in his kingdom when he went to fight with the Spaniards who had revolted against him. This woman, then, while Simon was in Rome, saw the miracles of amazing powers that he did in the name of Our Lord Christ. She renounced the paganism of her fathers which she practiced and the idols of paganism which she worshiped, and she believed in Christ Our Lord and worshiped him along with all those who followed Simon, and she held him in great honor. **[p. 158]**

After this she wanted to see Jerusalem and those places in which the amazing and marvelous powers of Our Lord Jesus Christ had been done. She arose earnestly and went down from Rome to Jerusalem, she and two sons with her and one virgin daughter. When she was about to enter Jerusalem, all the city heard [of her approach] and went out to greet her, and they received her with great honor, as for the queen, the lady of the land belonging to the Empire of the Romans. At that time Jacob had been made the leader and commander of the city in the church that had been built for us there in Jerusalem.

When he heard why she had come there, he arose at once and went to her. He came to her where she was staying, in the great palace of the kings of the House of Herod. When she saw him, she received him with great gladness, as she had [received] Simon Peter. He too, like Simon, showed her powers of healing. She said to him, "Show me Golgotha, where Our Lord Christ was crucified, and the wood of the cross on which he was raised by the Jews, and the tomb in which he was placed." Then Jacob said to her, "These three which Your Majesty wants to see are under the control of the Jews, and they have seized them. They do not let us go and pray there before Golgotha and the tomb. Neither do they want to give us the wood of the cross. Not only this, but also they persecute us so that we not preach or spread the word in the name of Christ, and very many times they imprison us in prison.

When Protonice heard these things, she immediately gave a command, and they brought before her Huniah son of Hannan the priest, Gedaliah son of Caiaphas, and Judah son of Shalom, the chief of the Jews. To them she said, "Hand over Golgotha, the tomb, and the wood of the cross to Jacob and to those who follow him. Let no one prevent them from serving there in accordance with the customs of their service." When **[p. 159]** *she had commanded thus to the priests, she arose and went to see those places and to hand over that place to Jacob and those who were with him. Afterwards she entered the tomb of Our Lord, and she found inside the tomb three crosses: one of Our Lord and two of those thieves who were crucified with him, one on his right and one on his left. As soon as the queen and her sons entered the tomb, her virgin daughter immediately fell down and died without disease, sickness, or malady of any kind. When Protonice saw that her daughter had died suddenly, she knelt down in prayer and weeping, and she prayed inside the tomb and spoke thus: "The Messiah who gave himself to death for all people and was crucified in this place and was placed in this tomb arose like God, the giver of life to all, and caused many to arise with him. Let not the crucifying Jews and lost pagans hear—those whose idols, carvings, and pagan fear I have renounced—and let them not rejoice in me and mock me and say that all this that has happened was because she renounced the gods she had worshiped and confessed a Messiah she knew not and went to honor the place of his tomb and crucifixion. If I am not worthy to be heard because I have worshiped creatures instead of You, have pity for the sake of your worshiped name lest they revile this place as they reviled you by crucifying you."*

And as she was saying these things in prayer, her elder son approached her and said to her, "Hear what I say to Your Majesty. I think in my mind and thought that the sudden death of this my sister is not in vain, but this is a marvelous deed by which God is praised and not something by which he is reviled, as those who heard of this thought. Here we have come into this tomb of Christ, and we have found three crosses. We do not know which of them is the cross on which Christ was raised. Now, by the death of this my sister **[p. 160]** *we are able to see and learn which is the cross of Christ. He does not neglect those who believe in him." Queen Protonice, whose soul was very bitter at that time, rejoiced in her mind and in her wisdom because her son had spoken these things in truth and righteousness. Suddenly she approached and picked one of the crosses up in her hands and placed it on the body of her daughter, which was lying before her. In prayer she said, "O Messiah who showed amazing powers in this place, as we have heard and believe, if this cross is yours, Lord, and upon this one was raised your humanity by the arrogant, show the great and increasing power of your divinity, which is one with your humanity, and bring* *this my daughter to life that she may arise and we may glorify your name through her when her soul returns to her body and so that your crucifiers may be confounded." She waited a long time after saying these things, and then she removed the cross from her daughter's body and placed another. Again she said in prayer, "O God, at whose sign worlds and creatures exist and who desires life for all people who turn to him, and who does not neglect the entreaty of those who entreat him, if this cross is yours, Lord, show the power of your victories as you are accustomed to do and bring to life this my daughter. Let her arise, let the pagans who worship creatures instead of you be confounded, and let the true believers confess as they open their mouths to praise you before those who disbelieve in you." And again she waited a long time, and then she removed the second cross from her daughter and placed on her the third. As she was about to raise her eyes to heaven and open her mouth in prayer, immediately and at once, in the twinkling of an eye, as soon as this cross came near her daughter's body, she came to life at once and stood up, praising Christ, who had brought her to life through his cross.*

When Queen Protonice saw how her daughter had come to life, she was very terrified and frightened, but she praised the Messiah in whom she believed, **[p. 161]** *who is the son of the living God. Her son said to her, "Did you see, my lady, that if this had not happened today, perhaps we would have left this the Messiah's cross, by which my sister has come to life, and taken and honored one of those thieving murderers. But now we see and rejoice in this one, and God, who has done this thing, is even more glorified thereby." Queen Protonice picked up Christ's cross and gave it to Jacob so that it could be kept in great honor, and she ordered that a great and glorious building be built over Golgotha and the tomb, that these places of the cross and tomb be honored and that there be there an assembly hall for the congregation of service. Then, when the queen saw that all the people of the city had gathered to see this thing, she commanded that her daughter go out with her openly without the veil of honor of queens to the palace of the king where she was staying, so that everyone could see and praise God. The Jews and pagans who had rejoiced at the beginning of this affair were saddened by the end of the affair. They would have been very happy had this not happened, for they saw many of them believing in the Messiah. Many were the signs and miracles that happened after his ascension—more than those that had happened before his ascension. The renown of this event went to far-away places and to all the apostles who were spreading the word of the Messiah. And there was peace in the church in Jerusalem and in the cities around it. Those who had not seen this sign praised God together with those who had seen it.*

And when Queen Protonice departed from Jerusalem for her city, Rome, [in] every city she entered people gathered to see her daughter. When she entered Rome she related to Claudius Caesar **[p. 162]** *all those things that had been done in her sight: how her daughter had died and then came to life. When Caesar heard these things, he ordered that all the Jews leave Rome and Italy. Since in every place this event was spoken of by many, and Protonice related this miracle to Simon Peter and everything that the apostles his friends had done, and they preached before everyone in order that those who had not heard or* *known might hear and know those things that Our Lord has done and does openly through our hands in order that the name of Our Lord may be praised by all people for ever and ever. Amen.*

These things that I have related to you are that you may know and reflect how great faith in the Messiah is for those who believe in him truly. Jacob, the leader of the church in Jerusalem, who saw this event with his own eyes, also wrote it and sent it to his friends the apostles in the cities in which they were. The apostles too wrote and made known to Jacob everything that the Messiah had done through their hands, and they were read out before every congregation of the church and before all the people. Peace.

The Teaching of the Apostle Thaddeus
Mallp̱ānūṯā ḏ-Adday Šliḥā

B-šattā tlāṯmā w-arb‘in wa-ṯlāṯ l-malkūṯā ḏ-Yawnāyē wa-ḇ-malkuṯeh d-Māran Ṭiberyos Qesar d-R(h)ōmāyē wa-ḇ-malkuṯeh d-Aḇgar malkā bar Ma‘nu malkā b-iraḥ tešri qḏēm b-yawm tre‘sar: šaddar (h)wā Aḇgar Ūḵāmā l-Māryaḇ w-la-Šmešgram: rêšānē wa-myaqqrē d-malkuṯeh: wa-l-Hannān Ṭabḇulārā šarrirā ‘amhon: **[p. 163]** *la-mḏittā aydā ḏ-meṯqaryā Elewṯerāpolis w-armā’iṯ dēn Bēṯ Guḇrin: lwāṯ myaqqrā Seḇinōs bar Ewsṭārgis Apiṭrāpā ḏ-māran Qesar: haw d-hu šliṭ (h)wā ‘al Suryā w-‘al Puniqē w-‘al Palesṭinē w-‘al aṯrā kolleh d-Ḇēṯ Nahrin. w-awbel(w) (h)waw leh eggrāṯā meṭṭul ṣeḇwāṯā ḏ-malkūṯā: w-ḵaḏ ezal(w) (h)waw lwāṯeh qabbel (h)wā ennon b-ḥezwāṯā w-ḇ-iqārā. wa-hwaw lwāṯeh yawmāṯā ‘esrin w-ḥamšā. wa-ḵtaḇ (h)wā l-hon peḥmā ḏ-eggrāṯā w-šaddar (h)wā ennon lwāṯ Aḇgar malkā. w-ḵaḏ npaq(w) (h)waw men lwāṯeh. ḥzaq(w) (h)waw w-eṯaw b-urḥā l-quḇal Ōrêšlem. wa-ḥzaw (h)waw nāšā saggi’ā ḏ-āṯeyn (h)waw men ruḥqā: d-neḥzōn la-Mšiḥā: meṭṭul da-npaq (h)wā ṭebbā ḏ-ṯeḏmrāṯā ḏ-neṣḥānaw b-aṯrawwāṯā maḇ‘ḏē. w-ḵaḏ ḥzaw l-nāšā hānon Māryaḇ wa-Šmešgram w-Ḥannān Ṭabbulārā: eṯaw (h)waw āp̱ hānon ‘amhon l-Ōrêšlem. w-ḵaḏ ‘al(w) (h)waw l-Ōrêšlem: ḥza’ū (h)waw la-Mšiḥā wa-ḥḏi(w) ‘am kenšē d-lāweyn (h)waw leh. w-ḥzaw (h)waw āp̱ l-y(h)uḏāyē: d-qāymin (h)waw kenšin kenšin: w-meṯḥaššbin (h)waw d-mānā ne‘bḏun leh. m‘āqin (h)waw gēr: d-ḥāzeyn (h)waw d-sugā ḏ-nāšūṯā d-mennhon mawdeyn (h)waw beh. wa-hwaw tamman b-Ōrêšlem yawmāṯā ‘esrē. w-ḵtaḇ (h)wā Ḥannān Ṭabbulārā kollmeddem d-ḥāzē (h)wā d-‘āsar (h)wā Mšiḥā: āp̱ šarkā ḏ-meddem da-‘ḇiḏ (h)wā leh tamman: (h)waw qḏām d-nêzlun l-ṯamman: wa-ḥzaq(w) (h)waw w-eṯaw (h)waw l-Urhāy. w-‘al(w) (h)waw qḏām Aḇgar malkā mārhon d-šaddar (h)wā ennon. w-yaḇ(w) (h)waw leh peḥmā ḏ-eggrāṯā d-awbel(w) (h)waw ‘amhon. w-men bāṯar d-eṯqri (h)way eggrāṯā: šarri(w) (h)waw d-nešta‘‘ōn qḏām malkā koll meddem da-ḥzaw: w-ḵoll meddem da-‘ḇaḏ (h)wā Mšiḥā b-Ōrêšlem. wa-qrā (h)wā Ḥannān Ṭabbulārā qḏāmaw koll meddem da-ḵtaḇ (h)wā w-ayti ‘ammeh. w-ḵaḏ šma‘ (h)wā Aḇgar malkā: tmah (h)wā w-eṯdammar: āp̱ rawrḇānaw d-qāymin (h)waw qḏāmaw. w-emar l-hon Aḇgar. hālēn ḥaylē lā hwaw da-bnay nāšā: meṭṭul d-layt d-naḥḥē miṯē ellā d-alāhā balḥoḏ. ṣāḇē (h)wā dēn Aḇgar: d-hu qnomeh ne‘bar (h)wā w-nêzal l-P̱alesṭinē w-neḥzē (h)wā b-‘aynaw koll meddem da-‘ḇaḏ (h)wā Mšiḥā. w-meṭṭul d-lā eškaḥ d-ne‘bar l-aṯrā* *ḏ-R(h)ōmāyē d-lāu dileh (h)wā: da-lmā* **[p. 164]** *‘ellṯā hāḏē teqrē (h)wāṯ la-ḇ‘eldḇāḇūṯā sniṯā: kṯaḇ (h)wā eggarṯā w-šaddar (h)wā la-Mšiḥā b-iḏeh d-Ḥannān Ṭabbulārā. wa-np̱aq (h)wā men Urhāy b-arba‘srē b-Āḏār. w-‘al (h)wā l-Ōrêšlem b-ṯarta‘srē b-nisān b-arb‘ā b-šabbā. w-ešḵḥeh (h)wā la-Mšiḥā bēṯ Gamaliel rabbā ḏa-y(h)udāyē. w-eṯqaryaṯ (h)wāṯ eggarṯā qḏāmaw aydā da-kṯiḇā (h)wāṯ hāḵannā. Aḇgar Ūḵāmā l-Išo‘ āsyā ṭāḇā d-eṯhzi b-aṯrā ḏ-Ōrêšlem. mār(y) šlām. šelmeṯ ‘layk w-‘al āsyūṯāḵ d-lā (h)wā b-sammānē wa-ḇ-‘eqqārē massē att: ellā b-mellṯāḵ m‘awwrē mp̱attaḥ att. wa-la-ḥg̱irē mhalleḵ att. wa-l-g̱arbē mḏakkē att. wa-l-ḥaršē mšamma‘ att. wa-l-ruḥē wa-l-bareggārē mappeq att wa-mšannqē bāh b-mellṯāḵ massē att. āp̱ miṯē mqim att. w-ḵaḏ hālēn tammihāṯā rawrḇāṯā šem‘eṯ d-‘āḇeḏ att: sāmeṯ b-re‘yān(y): d-aw alāhā att da-nḥeṯt men šmayyā wa-‘ḇaḏt hālēn: aw breh att d-alāhā: d-hālēn kolhēn ‘āḇeḏ att. meṭṭul hānā keṯbeṯ b‘êṯ mennāḵ: d-ṯêṯē lwāṯ(y) kaḏ sāg̱eḏ-nā lāḵ. w-ḵêḇā meddem d-iṯ li tassē ak d-haymneṯ bāḵ. āp̱ hāḏē tuḇ šem‘eṯ. da-y(h)udāyē rāṭnin ‘layk w-rāḏp̱in lāḵ: w-āp̱ d-nezqp̱unāḵ bā‘eyn: wa-l-mesraḥ bāḵ ḥāyrin. mḏittā ḥḏā z‘orṯā aḥiḏ-nā: w-la-ṯrēn sāp̱qā l-me‘mar bāh b-šelyā. w-ḵaḏ qabblāh (h)wā Išo‘ l-eggarṯā bēṯ kāhnē da-y(h)uḏāyē: emar leh l-Ḥannān Ṭabbulārā: zel w-emar leh l-mārāḵ d-šaddrāḵ ṣêḏ(y): ṭuḇayk d-ḵaḏ lā ḥzaytan hayment bi. kṯiḇ gēr ‘lay: d-aylēn d-ḥāzeyn li lā nhaymnun bi. w-ḏa-kṯaḇt li d-êṯē lwāṯāḵ: haw meddem d-eštaddreṯ ‘law l-hārkā mekkêl eṯtallaq leh. w-sāleq-nā li lwāṯ āḇ(y) d-šaddran: w-mā ḏ-selqeṯ lwāṯeh: mšaddar-nā lāḵ l-ḥaḏ men talmiḏay: d-ḵêḇā meddem d-iṯ lāḵ nassē w-naḥlem. wa-l-ḵoll man d-iṯ lwāṯāḵ. nap̱nē ennon l-ḥayyē da-l-‘ālam. w-ḵarkāḵ nehwē briḵ. wa-ḇ‘eldḇāḇā tuḇ lā neštalleṭ beh l-‘ālam. kaḏ dēn ḥzā (h)wā Ḥannān Ṭabbulārā: d-haḵannā emar (h)wā leh Išo‘. wa-ḇ-yaḏ d-ṣayyārā (h)wā ḏ-malkā. šqal (h)wā w-ṣār ṣalmeh d-Išo‘ b-semmānē g̱ḇayyā. w-ayti (h)wā Ḥannān* **[p. 165]** *Ṭabbulārā ‘ammeh l-Aḇgar malkā māreh. w-ḵaḏ ḥzay (h)wā Aḇgar malkā l-ṣalmā haw qabbleh (h)wā b-ḥezwāṯā rabbṯā: w-sāmeh (h)wā b-iqārā rabbā: b-ḥaḏ men bāttē d-āpadnā dileh. w-ešta‘‘i (h)wā leh kollmeddem da-šma‘ (h)wā men Išo‘: kaḏ ‘ḇiḏān (h)way leh mellaw ba-kṯābē. w-men bāṯar d-estallaq (h)wā Mšiḥā la-šmayyā: šaddar (h)wā Y(h)uḏā tōmā lwāṯ Aḇgar l-Adday šliḥā: haw d-iṯaw (h)wā men šaḇ‘in wa-ṯrēn šliḥin. w-ḵaḏ eṯā Adday l-ḵarkā ḏ-Urhāy. šrī (h)wā bēṯ Ṭoḇyā bar Ṭoḇyā y(h)uḏāyā: haw d-iṯaw (h)wā men Paleṣṭinē. w-eštma‘ (h)wā ‘law b-ḵolleh karkā. w-‘al (h)wā ḥaḏ men ḥêraw dileh d-Aḇgar w-emar (h)wā ‘law d-Adday: hu da-šmeh (h)wā ‘Aḇdu bar ‘Aḇdu: men rêšānē d-yāṯbay-wa‘dā dileh d-Aḇgar. d-hā eṯā izgaddā wa-šrā hārḵā: haw da-šlaḥ (h)wā lāḵ ‘law Išo‘: da-mšaddar-nā lwāṯāḵ ḥaḏ men talmiḏay. w-ḵaḏ šma‘ (h)wā Aḇgar hennēn hālēn w-g̱aḇrawwāṯā rawrḇāṯā d-‘āḇeḏ (h)wā Adday w-āswāṯā tammihāṯā ḏ-massē (h)wā: sām (h)wā b-re‘yāneh w-emar: d-šarrirā’iṯ haw hu da-šlaḥ (h)wā leh Išo‘: d-mā ḏ-selqeṯ la-šmayyā: ešaddar lāḵ l-ḥaḏ men talmiḏay: w-ḵêḇāḵ nassē. w-šaddar (h)wā dēn Aḇgar wa-qray l-Ṭoḇyā w-emar (h)wā leh: šem‘eṯ d-g̱aḇrā ḥaḏ ḥaylṯānā eṯā wa-šrā b-ḇaytāḵ. assqeh lwāṯ(y). ṭāḵ neštkaḥ li saḇrā šappirā ḏ-ḥulmānā men lwāṯāḵ. w-qaddem (h)wā Ṭoḇya l-yawmā ḥrênā w-ḏaḇreh (h)wā l-Adday šliḥā w-assqeh lwāṯ Aḇgar: kaḏ yāḏa‘ (h)wā hu Adday: da-ḇ-ḥaylā ḏ-alāhā mšaddar (h)wā lwāṯeh. w-ḵaḏ sleq (h)wā Adday w-‘al (h)wā lwāṯ Aḇgar: kaḏ qāymin ḥêraw lwāṯeh: beh b-ma‘lānā da-lwāṯeh ḥezwā tammihā eṯhzi (h)wā leh l-Aḇgar men parṣopeh d-Adday. w-ḇāh b-šā‘ṯā da-ḥzā (h)wā Aḇgar ḥezwā haw: np̱al (h)wā wa-sg̱eḏ (h)wā l-Adday. w-*

ṯemhā rabbā eḥaḏ (h)wā l-ḵollhon hānon d-qāymin (h)waw qḏāmaw. hennon gēr l_ā ḥzaw l-ḥezwā haw d-eṯḥzi (h)wā leh l-Aḇgar. haydēn emar leh Aḇgar l-Adday: d-šarrirā'iṯ talmiḏeh att d-Išo' haw gabbār ḥaylā breh d-alāhā: haw da-šlaḥ (h)wā li da-mšaddar-nā lāḵ l-ḥaḏ men talmiḏay l-asyūṯā wa-l-ḥayyē. emar leh Adday. meṭṭul d-men qḏīm hayment (h)wayt b-man **[p. 166]** *d-šaddran lwāṯāḵ: meṭṭul (h)u haw eštlaḥt ṣêḏayk: w-ḵaḏ ṭuḇ thaymen beh: koll meddem da-ṯhaymen beh nehwē lāḵ. emar leh Aḇgar. hāḵannā haymneṯ beh: d-la-y(h)uḏāyē hānon d-zaqp̱uy (h)waw: b'êṯ (h)wêṯ d-eḏabbar li ḥaylā: w-êzal eḥroḇ ennon. w-meṭṭul malkūṯā hay d-R(h)ōmāyē eṯnakkp̱eṯ ba-qyāmā ḏ-šaynā da-mqām li 'am māran Qesar Ṭiḇeryos ak āḇāhay qaḏmāyē. emar leh Adday. māran ṣeḇyānā (h)u d-aḇū šamli. w-ḵaḏ šlem ṣeḇyānā ḏ-yālōḏeh: ettrim lwāṯ aḇū: w-iṯeḇ 'ammeh ba-šmayyā: haw d-iṯaw (h)wā beh men 'ālam. emar leh Aḇgar āp̱ enā mhaymen-nā beh w-ḇ-aḇū. emar leh Adday. meṭṭul d-hāḵannā hayment: sā'em-nā iḏ(y) 'layk ba-šmeh d-haw d-hayment beh. w-ḇāh b-šā_'ṯā d-sām (h)wā iḏeh 'law: eṯassi men neḵyānā ḏ-ḵêḇā d-iṯ (h)wā leh nugrā. w-ṯmah (h)wā Aḇgar w-eṯdammar d-aykannā da-šmi' (h)wā leh 'al Išo': d-'āḇeḏ (h)wā w-massē: hāḵannā w-āp̱ hu Adday d-lā sammā meddem massē (h)wā ba-šmeh d-Išo'. w-āp̱ l-'Aḇdu bar 'Aḇdu peṭgārā iṯ (h)wā leh b-reglaw. w-āp̱ hu qarreḇ (h)wā leh reg̱law. w-sām (h)wā iḏeh 'layhēn w-assyeh (h)wā. w-ṯuḇ lā hwāṯ leh peṭgārā w-āp̱ ba-mḏittā kollāh aswāṯā rawrḇāṯā massē (h)wā. w-ḥaylē tammihē mḥawwē (h)wā bāh. emar leh Aḇgar. hāšā d-yāḏa' koll nāš: da-ḇ-ḥayleh d-Išo' Mšiḥā hālēn teḏmrāṯā 'āḇeḏ att: w-hā tammihīn ḥnan ba-'ḇādayk. bā'ē-nā hāḵēl mennāḵ: d-ṯešta''ē lan 'al meṯyāṯeh da-Mšiḥā d-aykannā hwāṯ: w-'al ḥayleh šḇiḥā w-'al teḏmrāṯā aylēn da-šmi' (h)wā li d-'āḇeḏ (h)wā. aylēn d-enā ḥzêṯ ennēn 'am šarkā ḏ-ḥaḇrayk. emar leh Adday. men hāḏē lā šāteq-nā d-aḵrez. d-meṭṭul hāḏē (h)u gēr eštaddreṯ l-hārkā d-êmar w-ellep̱. l-ḵoll man d-ṣāḇē da-nhaymen aḵwāṯāḵ. la-mḥār kanneš li kollāh mḏittā w-ezro' bāh mellṯā ḏ-ḥayyē b-ḵārozūṯā d-makrez-nā qḏāmayḵon. w-ḇāṭar yawmā haw pqaḏ (h)wā Aḇgar l-'Aḇdu bar 'Aḇdu haw d-eṯassi (h)wā men kêḇā marrirā ḏ-reglaw da-nšaddar (h)wā kārōzā: w-neqrē (h)wā b-ḵollāh mḏittā: w-ṯetkannaš (h)wāṯ nāšūṯā kollāh gaḇrē w-neššē l-ḏukkṯā hay d-meṯqaryā Ḇēṯ Ṯḇārā:* **[p. 167]** *l-aṯrā rawwiḥā ḏ-Ḇēṯ 'wiḏā: d-nešm'ūn (h)waw mallp̱ānuṯeh d-Adday šliḥā. w-ḵaḏ eṯkannšaṯ kollāh mḏittā gaḇrē w-neššē allep̱ l-hon Adday šliḥā 'al haymnūṯā ḏ-Māran Išo' Mšiḥā w-emar l-hon: aylēn d-qabbel(w) mellṯeh da-Mšiḥā nqawwōn ṣêḏayn: w-āp̱ aylēn d-ṣāḇeyn d-neštawtp̱un 'amman ba-ṣlōṯā: w-ḵen nêṯōn l-ḇāttayhon. w-ḥḏi (h)wā b-hāḏa (h)u Adday šliḥā: da-ḥzā (h)wā d-sug̱'ā ḏ-nāšūṯā ḏa-mḏittā pāšaṯ lāh lwāṯeh. w-ḏallilē (h)waw aylēn d-lā qawwi(w) (h)waw b-haw 'eddānā: kaḏ āp̱ hennon hālēn dallilē bāṯar yawmāṯā qallil qabbel(w) (h)waw l-mellaw w-haymen(w) (h)waw ba-sḇarṯā ḏ-ḵārōzūṯeh da-Mšiḥā. w-ḵaḏ ḥzā (h)wā Aḇgar malkā: d-ḵollāh mḏittā ḥeḏyaṯ (h)wāṯ b-mallp̱ānuṯeh. emar leh āp̱ hu Aḇgar malkā l-Adday šliḥā: mekkêl koll aykā ḏ-ṣāḇē att. bni 'êḏtā bēṯ-ṣawbā d-aylēn d-haymen(w) wa-mhaymnīn b-mellayk w-ak mā da-pqiḏ lāḵ men māran. hwayt mšammeš att b-'eddānē ṯkilā'iṯ. w-aylēn d-hāweyn 'amman mallp̱ānē ba-sḇarṯā hāḏē: rêšānē rawrḇē mṭayyeḇ-nā d-ettel l-hon. d-meddem 'am tešmešṯā lā nehwē l-hon 'ḇāḏā ḥrênā. w-ḵoll meddem d-meṯḇ'ē lāḵ l-nep̱qāṯeh d-ḇaytā enā yāheḇ lāḵ d-lā ḥušbān. kaḏ hāwyā mellṯāḵ šliṭā wa-mamlḵā b-ḵarkā hānā. wa-ḏ-lā nāš ḥrênā hwayt 'ā'el att lwāṯ(y) mšallṭā'iṯ l-āpadnā ḏ-iqāreh d-malkuṯ(y). w-ḵaḏ* *nḥeṯ (h)wā Aḇgar malkā. l-āpadnā ḏ-malkūṯeh ḥāḏē (h)wā hu w-rawrḇānaw ‘ammeh wa-ḇ-ḥaḏūṯā ḏ-lebbhon mšabbḥīn (h)waw āp̱ hennon l-alāhā: d-ap̱ni (h)wā re‘yānhon lwāṯeh: kaḏ kāp̱rīn (h)waw b-ḥanpūṯā d-qāymīn (h)waw bāh: w-mawdeyn (h)waw ba-sḇarṯeh da-Mšiḥā. w-ḵaḏ bnā (h)wā Adday ‘êḏtā: mqarrḇīn (h)waw bāh neḏrē w-qurbānē: hennon w-nāšūṯā ḏa-mḏittā. w-ṯamman mšammšīn (h)waw koll yawmay ḥayyayhon. Šwiḏā dēn wa-‘Ḇeḏnebbō rêšē d-ḵumrē d-ḵarkā hānā: kaḏ ḥzaw (h)waw āṯwāṯā d-‘āḇeḏ (h)wā Adday: rheṭ(w) (h)waw wa-‘qar(w) (h)waw ‘alawwāṯā: da-‘layhēn mḏabbḥīn (h)waw qḏām Nebbō w-Ḇêl allāhayhon l-ḇar men ‘lāṯā rabbṯā ḏ-meṣ‘aṯ karkā. w-qā‘eyn (h)waw w-āmrin. d-šarrirā’iṯ hānā d-haw rabbā mhirā wa-šḇiḥā. da-šma‘n (h)wayn koll rabbṯā d-‘āḇeḏ (h)wā b-aṯrā ḏ-P̱alesṭinē. w-ḵoll aylēn talmiḏē da-mhaymnīn (h)waw ba-Mšiḥā:* **[p. 168]** *mqabbel (h)wā l-hon Adday aylēn w-ma‘beḏ (h)wā l-hon b-šem aḇā wa-ḇrā w-rūḥā ḏ-quḏšā. āp̱ y(h)ūdāyē yāḏ‘ay l-Mūšē wa-nḇiyē aylēn d-rakkiḵē mzabbnin (h)waw: āp̱ hennon eṯp̱is(w) (h)waw w-eṯtalmaḏ(w) w-awdi(w) (h)waw ba-Mšiḥā da-ḇreh (h)u d-alāhā ḥayyā. lā dēn Aḇgar malkā w-lā Adday šliḥā ‘āṣē (h)wā l-nāš da-qtirā’iṯ* (by force) *nhaymen (h)wā beh ba-Mšiḥā. Aggay dēn ‘āḇeḏ šērāyē w-ḥewwārē d-malkā w-P̱allūṭ w-‘Aḇšlāmā w-Ḇar Semyā ‘am šarkā ḏ-ḥrānē ḥabrayhon naqp̱ū (h)waw l-Adday šliḥā. w-qabbel (h)wā ennon w-šawtep̱ ennon ‘ammeh b-ṯešmešṯā: kaḏ qāreyn (h)waw b-ḏiyaṯeqe ‘attiqṯā wa-ḥḏaṯṯā w-ḇa-nḇiyē wa-ḇ-su‘rānayhon da-šliḥē kollyawm b-hon meṯhaggeyn (h)waw.*

w-men bāṯar šnayyā da-ḇnā (h)wā Adday šliḥā ‘êḏtā b-Urhāy w-aṯqnāh (h)wā b-ḵoll meddem d-zāḏeq (h)wā lāh: w-ṯalmeḏ (h)wā l-sug̱‘ā ḏ-nāšūṯā ḏa-mḏittā w-āp̱ b-quryā ḥranyāṯā ḏ-raḥḥiqān wa-ḏ-qarriḇān bnā (h)wā ‘êḏāṯā w-ḵallel w-ṣabbeṯ wa-mšammšānē w-qaššišē aqim (h)wā b-hēn. wa-ḏ-qāreyn (h)waw kṯāḇē allep̱ (h)wā b-hēn. w-ṭaḵsē d-ṯešmešṯā l-g̱aww wa-l-ḇar allep̱ (h)wā. bāṯar hālēn kollhēn eṯkreh (h)wā kurhānā d-nāp̱eq (h)wā beh men ‘ālmā hānā. wa-qrā (h)wā l-Aggay qḏām kolleh kenšā ḏ-‘êḏtā w-qarreḇ (h)wā wa-‘aḇḏeh (h)wā qaššišā. wa-l-‘Aḇšlāmā d-sāp̱rā (h)wā. ‘aḇḏeh (h)wā mšammšānā. w-men bāṯar tlāṯā yawmin ḥrānin da-šma‘ (h)wā w-qabbel sāhḏūṯā ḏ-mallp̱ānūṯā ḏ-ḵārōzūṯeh men bnay tešmešṯeh qḏām ḥêrē kollhon np̱aq (h)wā leh men ‘ālmā hānā. w-iṯaw (h)wā yawmā ḥamšā b-šabbā. b-arb‘esrē b-ayyār yarḥā. w-ḇ-eḇlā rabbā wa-ḇ-ḥaššā marrirā hwāṯ ‘law kollāh mḏittā. lā (h)wā dēn krisṭyanē balḥoḏ m‘āqin (h)waw ‘law: ellā āp̱ y(h)uḏāyē w-ḥanpē d-iṯ (h)wā beh b-ḵarkā hānā. Aḇgar dēn malkā yattir men koll nāš m‘āq (h)wā ‘law. hu w-rawrḇānē d-malkūṯeh. wa-ḇ-ḵaryūṯā ḏ-re‘yāneh šāṭ (h)wā wa-šaḇqeh l-iqārā ḏ-malkūṯeh b-haw yawmā. wa-ḇ-ḏem‘ē ḥnigāṯā bāḵē (h)wā leh ‘am koll nāš. w-‘ammā kolleh da-mḏittā d-ḥāzē **[p. 169]** *(h)wā leh: meṯdammar (h)wā beh da-ḵmā ḥā’eš (h)wā ‘law. w-ḇ-iqārā rabbā wa-myattrā zayyaḥ (h)wā w-qaḇreh ak ḥaḏ men rawrḇānē mā ḏ-mā’eṯ (h)wā w-sāmeh (h)wā b-qaḇrā rabbā ḏa-glāp̱ē d-ṣeḇtē haw aynā ḏ-sīmīn (h)waw beh d-ḇēṯ Aryū aḇāhāṯā ḏ-aḇū d-Aḇgar malkā. tamman sāmeh (h)wā ḥaššišā’iṯ b-ḵaryūṯā wa-ḇ-‘āqṯā rabbṯā. w-‘ammā kolleh d-‘êḏtā ezal (h)wā men ‘eddānā l-‘eddānā wa-mṣallē (h)wā tamman ḥp̱iṭā’iṯ w-ḏuḵrānā ḏ-‘uhdāneh ‘āḇḏin (h)waw men šnā la-šnā ak puqdānā w-yulpānā da-mqabbel (h)wā l-hon men Adday šliḥā w-ak mellṯeh d-Aggay: d-hu hwā mḏabbrānā w-p̱āqōḏā w-yārṯā ḏ-ḵursyeh men bāṯreh b-iḏā ḏ-ḵāhnūṯā d-qabbel (h)wā menneh qḏām koll nāš.*

In the year 343 of the kingdom of the Greeks, in the reign of Our Lord Tiberius Caesar of the Romans, and in the reign of King Abgar, son of King Ma'nu, in the month of October on the thirteenth day, Abgar the Black sent Maryab and Shmeshgram, chiefs and honored men of his kingdom, and the trusted Hannan Tabularius with them **[p. 163]** *to the city which is called Heliopolis, or in Aramaic Beth Gubrin, to the honored Sevinus, son of Eustargis, the procurator of our lord Caesar who was governing over Syria, Phoenicia, and Palestine, and over all the land of Mesopotamia. They took to him letters concerning affairs of the kingdom, and when they came to him he received them with joy and honor. They were with him for twenty-five days. He wrote for them answers to the letters and sent them to King Abgar. When they departed from him, they set forth and came on the road to opposite Jerusalem. They saw many people coming from afar in order to see the Messiah because the fame of his victories had gone forth to far-away places. When Maryab, Shmeshgram, and Hannan Tabularius saw the people, they too went with them to Jerusalem. When they entered Jerusalem, they saw the Messiah, and they rejoiced with the crowds that followed him. They also saw the Jews who were standing in multitudes and plotting what they would do to him, for they were seeing that many people from among them were confessing him. And they were there in Jerusalem for ten days. Hannan Tabularius wrote down everything he saw the Messiah doing and also the rest of what had been done by him before they arrived there. They departed and came to Edessa, and they entered before King Abgar, their lord who had sent them. They gave him the replies to the letters they had brought with them. After the replies were read they began to relate before the king everything they had seen and everything the Messiah had done in Jerusalem. Hanna Tabularius read before him everything he had written and brought with him. When King Abgar heard, he was amazed and marveled, and so also his grandees who were standing before him. Abgar said to them, "These powers were not of humans because there is no one who can bring the dead to life other than God alone." Abgar then desired to go himself and descend to Palestine and see with his own eyes everything the Messiah had done, but because he was not able to cross into the territory of the Romans, which did not belong to him, lest* **[p. 164]** *this be considered a cause for odious enmity, he wrote a letter and sent it to the Messiah by the hand of Hannan Tabularius. He departed from Edessa on the fourteenth of March and entered Jerusalem on the twelfth of April on a Wednesday. He found the Messiah at the house of Gamaliel, the chief of the Jews. The letter was read out before him, as it was written thus: "Abgar the Black to Jesus, the good healer who has been seen in the place of Jerusalem. My lord, greetings. I have become a follower of yours and of your healing, for you do not heal through drugs or herbs, but by your word you cause to be opened [the eyes of] those who have been blinded, you cause the lame to walk, you make lepers whole, and you make the deaf hear, you cast out spirits and demons, and you heal with your word those who are in pain. You also raise the dead. Since I have heard of these great marvels that you are doing, I put it in my mind that either you are God come down from heaven and doing these things or your are the son of God that you you do all these things. For this reason I have written and summoned you that you come to me, for I worship you, and you will heal for me any sickness* *that I have because I have believed in you. Also this have I heard that the Jews are muttering against you and persecuting you, and they are seeking to crucify you and looking to do you harm. I hold this little city, and it is sufficient for two to live in it in tranquility." When Jesus received the letter in the house of the priests of the Jews, he said to Hannan Tabularius, "Go and tell your lord who sent you to me: Blessed are you that without seeing me you believed in me, for it is written: 'They who see me will not believe in me.' that you have written to me to come to you, the thing for which I was sent will be accomplished here henceforth, and I will ascend to my father who sent me. As soon as I ascend to him, I will send you one of my disciples to heal and cure whatever sickness you have. All those who are with you he will lead to life eternal. May your town be blessed, and may no enemy gain dominion over it ever." When Hannan Tabularius saw that Jesus spoke thus to him, and inasmuch as he was the king's portraitist, he took down and drew a picture of Jesus in choice pigments. Hannan brought [the picture]* **[p. 165]** *with him to his lord King Abgar. When King Abgar saw that portrait, he received it with great joy and set it in great honor in one of the rooms of his palace. And he (Hannan) related to him everything that he had heard of Jesus, as his words had been made into books. After the Messiah was taken up into heaven, Judas Thomas sent the apostle to Abgar Thaddeus, he who was one of the seventy-two apostles. When Thaddeus came to the town of Edessa, he took up residence in the house of Tobias son of Tobias the Jew, who was from Palestine. His reputation was heard of in the whole city, and one of Abgar's nobles, he whose name was Abdu son of Abdu and who was one of the chiefs of Abgar's pages, entered and said about Thaddeus, "Here an envoy has come and has taken up residence here. He is the one about whom Jesus sent (word) to you, (saying) 'I will send to you one of my disciples.' " When Abgar heard these words and the great deeds that Thaddeus was doing and the marvelous cures that he was effecting, he put it in his mind and said, "Truly this is he whom Jesus sent (when he said,) 'As soon as I ascend to heaven I will sent to you one of my disciples, and he will cure your sickness.' " Abgar then sent and summoned Tobias and said to him, "I have heard that a powerful man has come and taken up residence in your house. Have him come to me. Perhaps good patience will be found for me for health from you." The next day Tobias led Thaddeus the apostle to Abgar. Since Thaddeus knew that he had been sent to him by the power of God, and when he went and entered into Abgar's presence, with his companions standing around him, at his entrance unto him an astonishing vision was seen by Abgar from Thaddeus' countenance, and immediately Abgar saw that vision he fell down and worshiped Thaddeus, and great astonishment seized all those who were standing before him, for they did not see the vision that was seen by Abgar. Then Abgar said to Thaddeus, "Truly you are the disciple of Jesus, that mighty man of power, son of God, he who sent word to me (saying,) 'I will send to you one of my disciples for healing and for life.'" Thaddeus said to him, "Because you believed long ago in him* **[p. 166]** *who sent me to you, because of this was I sent to you. Since you believe in him, everything that you believe in will be yours." Abgar said to him, "Thus have I believed in him that I have sought to lead out a force and go to destroy the Jews who crucified him, but on account of the kingdom of the*

Romans I am ashamed of the peace treaty that has been concluded by me with our lord Caesar Tiberius as (did) my forefathers." Thaddeus said to him, "Our lord, the will of his father has been done. When the will of his father was accomplished he was raised to his father and sat with him in heaven, he who will be forever." Abgar said to him, "I have believed in him and in his father." Thaddeus said to him," Because you have thus believed, I will place my hand upon you in the name of him in whom you have believed." As soon as he placed his hand upon him he was healed of the pain of the illness he had had for a long time. Abgar was astonished, for just as it had been heard by him about Jesus, that he worked and healed, thus too was Thaddeus, who healed without any drug in the name of Jesus. So too Abdu son of Abdu had gout in his feet, and he too brought his feet near, and he placed his hand upon them and healed him, and he no longer had gout. So also did he effect great healings in all the city and showed astonishing powers there. Abgar said to him, "Now that everyone knows that you work these miracles through the power of Jesus Christ, and here we are astonished by your deeds, I request of you that tell us about the coming of the Messiah, how it was, about his glorious power and about the miracles which have been heard by me which he performed—these things which I have seen, along with the rest of your friends." Thaddeus said to him, "Of this I am not silent to preach, since for this I have been sent here in order that I speak and teach everyone who desires to believe like you. Tomorrow assemble for me all the city, and I will disseminate therein the word of life through the preaching that I will preach before you." After that day Abgar ordered Abdu son of Abdu, the one who was healed of the bitter disease in his feet, that he send a herald and summon the entire city, and that all the people, men and women, should be gathered in the place called Beth T'vara, **[p. 167]** *in the open space of Beth Awida, in order that they hear the teaching of Thaddeus the apostle. When all the city, men and women, were assembled, Thaddeus the apostle taught about faith in Our Lord Jesus Christ and said to them, "Those who have received the word of the Messiah will remain beside us, and also those who desire to share with us in prayer, and then they will go to their homes." And Thaddeus the aostle rejoiced in that he saw that many people of the city remained with him, and few were those who did not remain at that time. When even theose few, after a few days, accepted his words and believed in the tidings of his preaching of the Messiah, and when King Abgar saw that the whole city rejoiced in his teaching, King Abgar said to Thaddeus the apostle, "Henceforth, wherever you desire, build a church, a meeting place of those who have believed and believe in your words, and as you have been commanded by Our Lord, you will serve faithfully at [various] times. I am making preparations to give those who are teachers with us in these tidings great nobles so that they will have no other duty aside from service, and everything you require for household expenses I will give you without reckoning, for your word will be permitted and sovereign in this city, and to the exclusion of anyone else you will enter into my presence authoritatively in the palace of the honor of my kingdom." When King Abgar went down to the palace of his kingdom, he rejoiced, and his nobles with him, and in the joy of their hearts they too glorified God, who had turned their minds to Him. When they had disavowed the paganism in which they had stood and* *confessed the tidings of the Messiah, and when Thaddeus had built a church, they celebrated vows and oblations, they and the people of the city. And there they served all the days of their lives.*

Then Shwida and Ebednebbo, chiefs of the priests of this town, when they saw the signs that Thaddeus was producing, they ran and ripped up the altars upon which they had sacrificed to Nebbo and Baal, except for the great altar in the middle of the town, and they were crying out and saying, "Truly this is the great and glorious skilled one of whom we have heard every great thing he did in the land of Palestine." All those disciples who believed in the Messiah **[p. 168]** *Thaddeus received and put to work in the name of the Father, the Son, and the Holy Ghost. The Jews too who knew Moses and the prophets, they who sold silks, they too were persuaded and became disciples and confessed the Messiah who is the son of the living God. Neither King Abgar nor Thaddeus the apostle compelled anyone by force to believe in the Messiah.*

Then Aggai, the king's maker of silks and white stuffs, Pallut, Abshlama, and Bar-Semya, with the rest of their other friends, joined Thaddeus the apostle, and he received them and caused them to share with him in service. As they read the Old and New Testaments, the Prophets, and the Acts of the Apostles every day, they meditated upon them.

Years after Thaddeus the apostle built the church in Edessa and set it in order with everything that was appropriate to it, and after he had made disciples of many of the people of the city and had built churches in other villages that were far away and near-by, surrounded them with walls, set them in order, and established in them deacons and priests and those who read and taught books and the rites of service inside and outside—after all these things he was afflicted with the illness with which he would depart from this world. He summoned Aggai before all the congregation of the church, celebrated the liturgy, and made him priest. Abshlama, who was a scribe, he made deacon. After three days more, during which he heard and received testimony of the teaching of his preaching from the clergy before all the noblemen, he departed from this world. It was on the fifth day of the week, the fourteenth of the month of May. In great mourning and bitter sorrow was all the city; not only were the Christians distressed over him but also the Jews and pagans who were in this town. More than anyone was King Abgar distressed over him, he and his the grandees of his kingdom. With distress of mind he became deplorable and abandoned the honor of his kingship on that day, and with doleful tears he wept along with all the people. All the inhabitants of the city who saw **[p. 169]** *him were astonished by how he sorrowed over him. With great honor and dignity he went in procession and buried him as he would one of his grandees who had died, and he placed him in a large tomb with carved ornamentation, in which King Abgar's forefathers of the House of Aryu had been placed. There he placed him sadly with distress and great sorrow. And all the people of the church went from time to time and prayed there earnestly, and memorials of commemoration of him they made from year to year according to the commandment and doctrine they had received from Thaddeus the apostle and according to the word of Aggai, who was the leader, commander, and inheritor of his seat after him, by virtue of* *the priesthood he had received from him before everyone.*

The Martyrdom of St. Barbara

Sāhḏūṯā ḏ-Qaddišṯā Barbārā

B-zaḇnē hānon: da-ḇ-hon mamleḵ (h)wā Maksemyānos haw rašši‘ā w-‘annāṯā: b-heg̱mōnūṯā ḏ-Marqyānos heg̱mōnā: hwā rḏup̱yā rabbā ‘al kollhon kresṭyānē. iṯ (h)wā gaḇrā ḥaḏ rabbā b-aṯrā ḏ-Êliopolis ba-qriṯā da-šmāh Dālāsūn: w-p̱arriqā men Anṭyoḵyā mīlē tre‘sar: wa-šmeh iṯaw (h)wā Dyosquros. hānā ‘attir (h)wā ṭāḇ: bram dēn iṯaw (h)wā ḥanpā. iṯ (h)wā leh dēn barṯā ḥḏā iḥiḏiṯā: da-šmāh Barbārā: w-šappirā (h)wāṯ ṭāḇ. hu dēn aḇūh maḥḥeḇ (h)wā lāh saggi: wa-ḇnā lāh mag̱dlā ḥaḏ rabbā: w-ḥaḇšāh beh. aykannā ḏ-lā teṯhzē la-ḇnaynāšā: meṭṭul šup̱rāh rabbā: wa-hḏirūṯā ḏ-p̱arṣōpāh. etaw dēn nāšin men rawrḇānē: w-mellel(w) ‘am aḇūh meṭṭulṯāh: aykannā **[p. 170]** *d-nettlīh l-g̱aḇrā. hu dēn ‘al lwāṯāh w-emar lāh: barṯ(y): nāšin men rawrḇānē mallel ‘amm(y) meṭṭulṯeḵ: ettleḵ l-g̱aḇrā. aykannā ṣāḇyā att: barṯ(y) ḥḇiḇaṯ(y): emar(y) li. hi dēn kaḏ ḥāraṯ beh b-rugzā: arimaṯ ‘aynēh la-šmayyā w-emraṯ d-lā tallṣan āḇ(y): d-hāḏē es‘or. w-ellā hwayt yāḏa‘: d-enā nap̱š(y) l-mawtā yāhḇā-nā. hu dēn šanni: wa-np̱aq men lwāṯāh. meṯemen (h)wā dēn b-ḇalanay d-menneh ba-šmāh meṯbanyā (h)wāṯ. aqim (h)wā bāh dēn ūmānē sug̱’ā: aykannā ḏa-ḇa-‘gal w-qallilā’iṯ teštamlē. kaḏ dēn pqaḏ ennon l-ūmānē hu Dyosquros aḇūh: d-aykannā zāḏeq l-hon d-ne‘ḇdūn: w-yaḇ l-ḵollḥaḏ mennhon ag̱reh mšamlyā: šanni (h)wā l-aṯrā raḥḥiqā: w-ṯamman awḥar zaḇnā saggi’ā. neḥtaṯ dēn hi amṯeh da-Mšiḥā Barbārā: aykannā ḏ-ṯeḥzē benyānā dilāh d-ḇalanay. w-ḵaḏ ḥāraṯ ba-p̱niṯā taymnāyṯā: w-eṯbaqqyaṯ d-ṯartēn kawwin balḥoḏ pṯaḥ(w) bāh ūmānē. ‘nāṯ w-emraṯ l-hon l-ardeḵlē: l-mānā balḥoḏ tartēn kawwin pṯaḥton? ‘naw w-emar(w) lāh: d-aḇūḵ pqaḏ lan d-ne‘baḏ hāḵannā. w-emraṯ l-hon dēn sāhedṯeh da-Mšiḥā Barbārā: haw mā ḏ-āmrā-nā l-ḵon s‘or d-lā deḥlā: w-meḥdā ba-‘g̱al w-qallilā’iṯ aqim(w) li hārkā kawwṯā ḥrêṯā. w-emar(w) lāh hennon: mārṯā: dāḥlinan w-men d-ḏalmā kaḏ nêṯē aḇūḵ w-neḥzē: ḥnan lā meškḥīnan la-mqām qḏām ḥemmṯeh. āmrā l-hon amṯeh d-alāhā Barbārā: haw meddem d-enā āmrā-nā l-ḵon s‘or d-lā deḥlā. w-ḵaḏ nêṯē āḇ(y). enā mappisā-nā leh ‘alhāḏē. hennon dēn šam‘ūh: wa-‘ḇaḏ(w) āp̱ kawwṯā ḥrēṯā: aykannā ḏ-p̱eqdaṯ l-hon.*

kaḏ dēn maṭṭyaṯ hi qaddišṯā wa-ḏ-lā mūm l-wa‘deh d-uznā ḏ-šaḥḥinē: eṯpanyaṯ l-maḏnḥā w-rešmaṯ b-ṣeḇ‘āh ‘al šīšā ṭupseh da-ṣliḇā yaqqirā. w-qayyām haw rušmeh da-ṣliḇā ‘law d-šīšā ‘ḏammā l-yawmānā: l-ṯeḏmurṯā ḏ-aylēn d-ḥāzeyn: wa-l-ṯešbuḥṯā ḏ-alāhā. kaḏ dēn ‘allaṯ l-ḇalanay dilāh: āp̱ demwāṯā qaddišāṯā ḏ-‘eqbāṯāh: bāh b-ar‘ā hay eṯṯba‘. **[p. 171]** *w-men dukkṯā hay: kollnāš nāseḇ daḥḥiḥā l-ḥulmānā wa-l-‘uḏrānā. hāḏā (h)i masḥūṯā d-eṯdammyaṯ l-Yordnān: d-ḇāh hu Mārkoll Išo‘ Mšiḥā arken (h)wā rêšeh qaddišā: w-qabbel (h)wā ‘māḏā men Yōḥannān kārōzeh wa-m‘ammḏānā. hāḏā (h)i ma‘mōḏīṯā (pool) d-eṯdammyaṯ la-m‘īnā ḏ-Šiloḥā: b-ḇāh samyā ḏ-men kres emmeh ašig̱: l-ma‘mōḏīṯā ḏ-Ḇēṯhesdā: d-ḇāh mšarryā b-mellṯā eṯassi. hāḏā (h)i ma‘mōḏīṯā: d-iṯ bāh mayyā ḥayyē: hālēn d-šelaṯ men Māran atttā hay Šāmrāyṯā.*

tuḇ dēn b-ḥaḏ men yawmin: kaḏ ‘āḇrā (h)wāṯ d-ṯêzal lāh l-ḇalanay hi sāhedṯeh da-Mšiḥā Barbārā: ḥzāṯ pṯaḵrē (idols) da-l-hon sāg̱eḏ (h)wā aḇūh dawyā: w-

eṯmalyaṯ (h)wāṯ rūḥā ḏ-qudšā: haw mabbūʻā ḏ-ṯāḇāṯā w-yāhōḇā ḏ-šūkānē wam'aḏrānā ḏ-šarrirē: hi hāḏē sāheḏteh da-Mšiḥā: w-maprgā (h)wāṯ b-šuprā: dazḵāṯ w-ḏāšaṯ l-āḵelqarṣā. kaḏ hāḵêl ḥzāṯ la-ptaḵrē hānon ḥaršē: raqqaṯ bappayhon kaḏ āmrā l-hon: d-akwāṯḵon nehwōn 'āḇōḏayḵon: w-aylēn da-ṯkilin 'layḵon. w-kaḏ selqaṯ tuḇ l-magdlā ḏ-ḇeh hu 'āmrā (h)wāṯ: ba-ṣlōṯā ḏa-lwāṯ alāhā beh aminā'iṯ 'anyā (h)wāṯ.

kaḏ dēn eštamli benyānā w-eṯtaqqan dilāh d-ḇalanay: pnā men urḥeh haw rašši'ā aḇūh Dyosquros. w-'al (h)wā l-ḇalanay akman d-neḥzīh: wa-ḥzā tlāṯ kawwin qayyāmān. wa-'nā w-emar l-ūmānē: tlāṯ kawwin aqimton? āmrin leh ūmānē: barṯāḵ (h)u peqdaṯ lan d-hāḵannā ne'ḇad. w-eṯpni lwāṯ barṯeh w-emar: att pqaḏt ennon l-ūmānē: da-ṯlāṯ kawwin nepṯḥūn? 'nāṯ w-emraṯ leh: ên āḇ(y): šappir peqdeṯ. meṭṭul da-ṯlāṯ ennēn kawwin manhrān l-ḵoll barnāšā d-āṯē l-'ālmā: w-ṯartēn balḥoḏ 'ammūṯāṯa ennēn. w-nasḇāh (h)wā aḇūh wa-nḥeṯ l-ḇalanay. w-emraṯ leh: kmā yattir men tartēn manhrān naṣṣiḥā'iṯ hālēn tlāṯ. w-emraṯ tuḇ lwāṯeh amteh da-Mšiḥ_a Barbārā: eṯbayyan hāšā āḇ(y) wa-ḥzi: hā gēr [p. 172] aḇā: w-hā brā: w-hā rūḥā qaddišā.

w-kaḏ šmaʻ hālēn aḇūh: eṯmli ḥemmṯā w-rugzā saggi'ā. wa-šmaṯ saypā da-'law tlē (h)wā: akman d-neqṭlih. w-ṣallyaṯ dēn qaddišṯā Barbārā: w-eṯpaṯḥaṯ šennā hay d-lāh qarriḇā (h)wāṯ: w-qabblāṯāh b-gawwāh. w-meḥdā appqāṯāh (h)wāṯ lwāṯ ṯūrā haw d-ṯamman iṯ (h)wā la-mqabblūṯāh rā'awwāṯā trēn: d-rā'eyn (h)waw b-ṯūrā haw: w-ḥza'ūh kaḏ 'ārqā. w-kaḏ eṯqarraḇ aḇūh lwāṯhon: mša''el (h)wā l-hon: enhu da-ḥza'ūh l-ḇarṯeh. w-ḥaḏ mennhon: meṭṭul d-ṣāḇē (h)wā d-ṯeštawzaḇ: mawmāṯā yāmē (h)wā d-lā ḥzā lāh. w-haw ḥrênā dēn pāšeṭ (h)wā ṣeḇ'eh: w-l-aḇūh mḥawwē (h)wā lāh. kāḏ dēn ḥzāṯ qaddišṯā meddem da-'bad: lāṭāṯeh (h)wāṯ: w-meḥdā hwā hu w-'erbaw ḥaḇšušyāṯā. w-hā knišān ḥaḇšušyāṯā hālēn 'al qabrāh d-qaddišṯā 'dammā l-yawmānā. w-kaḏ sāleq (h)wā aḇūh bāṯrāh l-ṯūrā haw: w-eškḥāh (h)wā l-qaddišṯā w-naggḏāh marrirā'iṯ: w-aḥdāh b-saʻrā ḏ-rêšāh w-gā'ar (h)wā lāh. w-aḥḥtāh (h)wā men haw ṯūrā: w-a''lāh (h)wā w-ḥaḇšāh b-ḇaytā ḥaḏ šīṯā: w-eḥaḏ wa-ḥtam b-appēh b-'ezqteh. w-aqīm 'lēh nāṭōrā: aykannā ḏ-lā neškaḥ nāš ne''ol lwāṯāh: 'dammā ḏ-ezal w-awda' 'lēh l-Marqyānos hegmōnā: aykannā ḏ-nawbḏīh.

kaḏ dēn eṯā hegmōnā: pqaḏ d-naytōnāh lwāṯeh. kaḏ dēn eṯā aḇūh 'am Geranṭos Qomṭrisā appqūh men baytā haw d-ḇeh ḥḇišā (h)wāṯ: w-ašlmūh l-hegmōnā: kaḏ mawmē leh aḇūh b-allāhē: da-ḇ-šendē qšayyā nawbḏīh. haydēn iṯeḇ hegmōnā 'al bêm dileh: w-kaḏ ḥā'ar b-šuprāh emar lāh: mānā ṣāḇyā att? ḥus 'al napšeḵ: w-ḏabbaḥ l-allāhē. w-ellā ṯḏabbḥīn: l-negḏē marrirē mašlem-nā leḵ. 'nāṯ dēn w-emraṯ leh sāheḏteh da-Mšiḥā: d-enā mṭayybā-nā: d-enā qnōm(y) deḇḥā ḏ-tawdīṯā eṯqarraḇ l-alāhā pārōqā ḏ-ḵoll: haw [p. 173] da-'bad šmayyā w-ar'ā w-ḵoll da-ḇ-hon. meṭṭul dēn allāhayk nḇiyā dāwīḏ āmar: d-pumē iṯ l-hon w-lā mmallǝlīn: 'aynē iṯ l-hon w-lā ḥāzeyn: iḏē iṯ l-hon w-lā māysīn: reglē iṯ l-hon w-lā mhallḵīn: akwāṯhon nehwōn 'āḇōḏayhon: w-aylēn da-ṯkīlīn 'layhon: haydēn hegmōnā eṯmli ḥemmṯā: wa-pqaḏ d-nešlḥūnāh: wa-l-pagrāh d-lā-ḥawsān b-negḏē nḇasbsūn: wa-ḇ-mennē d-sa'rā neṯharkān maḥwāṯā ḏ-'al gušmāh. wa-'ḇad(w) lāh hāḵannā: 'dammā ḏ-ḵolleh gušmāh eṯpalpal ba-ḏmā. pqaḏ (h)wā ḏ-têzal l-ḇēṯ-ḥḇušyā: 'aḏ meṯḥaššaḇ da-ḇ-aynā mawtā nawbḏīh. b-pelgeh dēn d-lêlyā: dnaḥ (h)wā 'lēh nuhrā rabbā: w-eṯḥzi lāh pārōqan kaḏ *āmar: eṯhayyal w-eṯlabbaḇ sāheḏṯā dil(y) ḥḇīḇṯā. ‘ṯīḏā gēr d-meṭṭulṯeḵ: ḥaḏūṯā rabbṯā _ṯehwē ba-šmayyā w-ḇ-ar‘ā b-neṣḥāneḵ. lā teḏhlīn men lūḥāmaw da-trūnā hānā: enā gēr hāwē-nā ‘ammeḵ: w-ep̱aṣṣēḵ men lūḥāmaw. kaḏ hālēn emar lāh: assi la-maḥwāṯāh: w-lā eṯhzi menhēn ‘al pag̱rāh. ellā ḥāḏyā (h)wāṯ w-rāwzā hi sāheḏṯā qaddišṯā: b-lūḇāḇā da-hwā lāh men Māran.*

In the times during which Maximian, that impious and wicked one, was ruling, during the governorship of Marcian the governor, there was a great persecution of all Christians. There was a great man in the land of Heliopolis in a village named Dalasun—and it was thirteen miles distant from Antioch—and his name was Dioscorus. He was very rich, but he was a pagan. He had an only daughter whose name was Barbara, and she was very beautiful. Her father loved her greatly, and he built for her a great tower and closed her up in it so that she could not been seen by anyone on account of her great beauty and the comeliness of her visage. People from the nobles came and spoke for her with her father, that **[p. 170]** *he should give her to a husband. Therefore he went to her and said to her, "My daughter, people from among the nobles have spoken with me for you that I should give you to a husband. How do you desire, my beloved daughter? Tell me." She looked at him with hatred, raised her eyes to heaven, and said, "Do not force me, father, to do this. If you do, you may know that I will give myself to death." He then departed and left her. He was attending to a bath that was being built by him in her name. He established into many workers so that it would be finished quickly and swiftly. When then Dioscorus, her father, ordered the workers how it was right for them to do and gave every one of them his full wage, he departed for a far-away place, and there he tarried a long time. Then the maid of Christ, Barbara, went down to see the bath building of hers, and when she looked in the southern direction and discerned that the workmen had opened only two apertures in it, she said to the master builders, "Why have you opened only two apertures?" They replied to her, saying, "Your father ordered us to do thus." The martyr to Christ, Barbara, said to them, "This is what I am telling you: act without fear and quickly and swiftly make for me another aperture." They said to her, "We are afraid that when your father comes and sees, we will not be able to stand before his anger." The handmaiden of God Barbara said to them, "This is what I tell you: do it without fear, and when my father comes I will convince him of this." They then heard her and made another apertures as she had ordered them.*

When the holy and spotless [maid] arrived at the location of the cistern of hot [waters], she turned to the east and drew with her finger on the marble the sign of the honored cross, and that sign of the cross remains on it until today to the wonder of those who see it and to the glory of God. When she entered the bath belonging to her the blessed prints of her heels were imprinted in the ground. **[p. 171]** *From this place everyone takes some dust for healing and aid. This is the bathing that resembles the Jordan, in which the Lord of All Jesus Christ lowered his holy head and received baptism from John, his preacher and baptizer. This is a pool that resembles the pool at Siloah in which the man blind from his mother's womb washed, the pool at Bethesda in which the paralyzed man was* *healed by a word. This is the pool in which is the water of life, that which the Samaritan woman asked of Our Lord.*

Then one day, when the Martyr to Christ Barbara was going to the bath, she saw the idols which her wretched father worshiped, and this Martyr to Christ, who was shining with beauty, who overcame and trampled on the Devil, was filled with the Holy Spirit, that source of good things, giver of grace, and help to those who are true. When she saw those mute idols thus, she spat in their faces while saying to them, "Like you be your makers and those who trust in you." And when she departed to the tower in which she lived, in her prayer with God she was constantly responded to.

When her bath building was finished and made ready, her wicked father Dioscorus returned from his trip and entered the bath as one who would see it and saw three apertures existing, he said to the workmen: "Have you made three apertures?" The workmen said to him, "Your daughter ordered us to do so." And he turned to his daughter and said, "Did you order the workmen to open three apertures?" She replied and said to him, "Yes, father. Indeed I ordered it because three are the apertures shining for every human being who comes into the world, and two alone are dark." Her father took her and went into the bath, and she said to him, "How much more brilliantly than two are these three shining!" Then the handmaiden of Christ, Barbara, said, "Consider now, father, and see: here is the Father, **[p. 172]** *and here the son, and here the Holy Ghost."*

When her father heard these words, he was filled with great anger and rage, and he drew the sword that was hung about him as though to kill her. Then the holy Barbara prayed, and the mountain top near which she was opened up and took her inside, and it put her out on a mountain where there were two shepherds tending their flocks to receive her, and they saw her fleeing. When her father approached them, he asked them if they had seen his daughter. One of them, because he wanted her to escape, swore oaths that he had not seen her. The other, however, pointed his finger and indicated her to her father. When the blessed woman saw what he did, she cursed him, and immediately he and his sheep became beetles—and thus these beetles are gathered over the saint's tomb until today. When her father went after her on the mountain and found her, he scourged her bitterly and grabbed her by the hair on her head and dragged her. He took her down from the mounain and put her in prison in a mean room, and he stopped up and sealed her mouth with his signet and stationed a guard over her so that no one could go in to her while he went and informed Marcian the governor, how to put her to death.

When the governor came he ordered them to bring her to him. When her father came with Gerontius Comtris (?), they took her out of the room in which she was imprisoned and turned her over to the governor. When her father swore by the gods that he should put her to death with cruel tortures, the governor sat on his seat of judgment. When he looked upon her beauty, he said to her, "What do you desire? Have mercy upon yourself and sacrifice to the gods. If you do not sacrifice, I will turn you over to bitter scourges." The martyr to Christ replied and said to him, "I am prepared, for I myself am a sacrifice of confession I sacrifice to God, the savior of all, he **[p. 173]** *who made the heavens and the* *earth and all who are in them. For the sake of your gods did the prophet David say, 'Mouths they have, and they do not speak. Eyes they have, and they do not see. Hands they have, and they do not touch. Feet they have, and they do not walk.' Like them be their makers and those who trust in them." then the governor was filled with anger and ordered them to strip her and tear her flesh to pieces with scourges without pity, and to burn the wounds that were on her body with strands of hair. Thus they did to her until all her body was drenched in blood. He ordered her to go to the prison while he considered by what sort of death he should put her to death. However, in the middle of the night a great light shone upon her, and Our Savior appeared to her, saying, "Be strong and take heart, my beloved martyr, for prepared it is that for you there shall be great joy in heaven and earth for your victory. Do not fear the threats of this tyrant, for I shall be with you and I shall save you from his threats." When he said these things to her, he healed her wounds, and none of them could be seen on her body, but she, this holy martyr, rejoiced and was glad in the encouragement that she had from Our Lord.*

From the Tale of Sindban the Wise

Men Taš'īṯā ḏ-Sindḇān Ḥakkīmā

Iṯ (h)wā malkā ḥaḏ da-šmeh (h)wā Kūreš. w-men yawmay ḥayaw brā lā hwā leh w-iṯ (h)wā leh neššē šḇa'. w-qām w-ṣalli wa-nḏar neḏrā. wa-mšaḥ nap̱šeh. wa-ṣḇā alāhā. w-yaḇ leh brā ḥaḏ. wa-rḇā ṭalyā w-šwaḥ ak arzā. w-yaḇeh [l-sāp̱reh] **[p. 174]** *d-nallep̱ ḥeḵmṯā. wa-hwā tlāṯ šnīn lwāṯ sāp̱reh w-meddem lā ilep̱. w-emar dēn malkā. d-hānā ṭalyā en nehwē ṣêḏ sāp̱reh rebbō šnīn. meddem lā ilep̱. ellā ettlīw l-Sindḇān ḥakkīmā. meṭṭul d-iṯaw gaḇrā ḥakkīmā. wa-myattar men kollhon p̱ilosop̱ē. wa-qrā malkā l-Sindḇān w-emar leh: aykannā ṣāḇē-tt d-ṯallp̱īw l-ṭalyā emar li. wa-'nā Sindḇān w-emar l-malkā. mallep̱-nā l-ṭalyā b-yarḥē eštā. 'ḏammā ḏ-neḏroš 'am koll p̱ilosop̱ d-iṯ ṯḥēṯ uḥdānāḵ. w-enhu d-lā mšamlē-nā meddem d-emreṯ nêḇḏūn ḥayyay men ar'ā. w-ḵoll d-qānē-nā lāḵ nehwē. yelpeṯ gēr d-malkē ak nūrā iṯayhon. w-emaṯ d-ṯemṭē l-nāš awqḏ_āṯeh. eḥawwē lāḵ d-mallep̱-nā la-ḇrāḵ mār(y) malkā w-ḵaḏ nšamlē yulpāneh. tettel li hu meddem d-eṯba' mennāḵ.*

w-emar malkā haw d-ḇā'ētt ettel lāḵ. āmar Sindḇān kollmeddem d-lā rāḥem att d-nes'or nāš lwāṯāḵ. lā tes'rāy lwāṯ ḥrênā. wa-ḵtaḇ(w) kṯāḇā baynāṯhon. w-yaḇ Sindḇān yamminā l-malkā. w-ašlem ṭalyā l-Sindḇān. w-p̱aqḏeh w-emar leh. d-men bāṯar štā yarḥīn w-ṯartēn šā'īn. nêṯē ṭalyā lwāṯ aḇū w-lā nḵattar šā'ṯā ḥḏā ellā nešqol rēšeh d-Sindḇān.

w-eḥaḏ Sindḇān b-iḏeh d-ṭalyā. w-awbleh l-ḇayteh wa-ḇnā leh baytā rawwiḥā. w-ḵallšeh w-ḥawwreh wa-ḵtaḇ 'al essaw. w-iṯeḇ Sindḇāddēn [= Sindḇān dēn] lwāṯeh. w-mallep̱ (h)wā leh. w-ḇeh b-ḇaytā iṯ (h)wā l-hon meklā w-meštyā w-lā 'ḇar 'eddānā ḥaḏ men protesmiā d-sāmeh baynāṯhon. w-ḇāṯar štā yarḥīn ilep̱ ṭalyā **[p. 175]** *haw meddem d-lā mṣā nāš men bnaynāšā d-nêlap̱ akwāṯeh. w-men meddem yawmā ḥaḏ šaddar malk_ā lwāṯ Sindḇān w-emar leh. mānā iṯ lwāṯāḵ w-p̱anni hu w-emar leh. haw meddem d-rāḥem-att. la-mḥār maytē-nā leh l-ṭalyā lwāṯāḵ b-'eddānā ḏ-ṯartēn šā'īn en māryā neṣbē. wa-ḥḏi malkā w-eṯp̱saḥ wa-*

hp̱aḵ Sindḇān lwāṯ ṭalyā w-emar leh. ṣāḇē-att da-ḇ-hānā lêlyā. eṯhaššaḇ ʻal malwāšāḵ. b-hay d-ḇāʻē-nā d-awblāḵ lwāṯ aḇūḵ.

w-men bāṯar d-ḥār b-malwāšeh d-ṭalyā. ḥzā d-lā zāḏeq da-nmallel ʻḏammā l-šaḇʻā yawmīn. meṭṭul d-ḏāḥel (h)wā ʻlaw d-lā nmūṯ. w-ḵaḏ ḥzā Sindḇān arʻel iḏaw w-reg̱law w-eṯʻassaq ʻlaw. wa-ḥzā ṭalyā l-rabbeh d-ettʻiq w-emar leh. mā lāḵ d-eṯqašši ʻlayk hānā suʻrānā. meṭṭul d-en pāqeḏ-att li d-lā emallel yarḥā ḥaḏ ʻāḇeḏ-nā ellā pqoḏ li haw meddem d-rāḥem-att. w-emar Sindḇān: kaḏ aqīmeṯ qyāmā ʻam aḇūḵ d-la-mḥār nêṯē brāḵ lwāṯāk. w-lā zāḏeq li d-ehpoḵ beh. w-lā bāʻē-nā d-ehwē lwāṯ aḇūḵ daggālā. enā mekkêl enā meṯtaššē-nā. ḥzi att bar(y) lā tmallel ʻḏammā ḏ-ʻāḇrīn štā yawmīn. wa-l-yawmā ḏ-la-mḥār pqaḏ leh l-ṭalyā d-nêzal lwāṯ aḇū.

aḇū dēn men rḥemṯeh lwāṯ breh. kanneš leh ḥaḇrē aylēn d-yāṯḇīn (h)waw ʻammeh. wa-ʻḇaḏ leh mšaṯyā. haydēn qrāy aḇū w-qarrḇeh lwāṯeh w-našqeh. w-mallel ʻammeh. hu lā mallel ʻam aḇū. w-šarri mešal leh w-hu lā panni peṯgāmā. haydēn emar malkā l-aylēn da-ḥḏāraw. mānā iṯaw šarbeh d-ḇer(y).

wa-ʻnā ḥaḏ w-emar d-ʻeqqārā mšaḥ leh rabbeh da-nsatteṯ beh **[p. 176]** *yulpāneh w-men haw ʻeqqārā pḵīr l-šenneh. w-eṯkši šarbeh d-ṭalyā ʻal malkā. w-ḵaḏ ḥzā men neššaw d-malkā. emraṯ leh šḇoqāy aykā ḏ-yāṯḇā-nā. enā w-haw balḥoḏ kḇar mawdaʻ li šarbeh. meṭṭul da-ṯḵīl (h)wā ʻlay men qaddim. w-meddem d-l-emmeh lā mḥawwē (h)wā. li dēn mḥawwē w-g̱ālē. meṭṭul d-emmeh d-ṭalyā mʻīqā (h)wāṯ ʻal šeṯqeh. w-šqalṯeh attṯā l-ṭalyā w-awblāṯeh l-ḇaytāh. w-šarryaṯ tmallel ʻammeh. hu lā mallel ʻammāh. w-lā panni lāh peṯgāmā. haydēn emraṯ leh d-lā yāḏʻā-nā lāḵ saḵlā. w-āp̱ lā iṯayk malkā. w-lā pāleṭ att men ʻenyān(y). āmrā-nā lāḵ meddem. w-lā šāḇqā-nā lāḵ ʻḏammā ḏa-sʻart leh. w-en ṭalyā iṯayk. w-en ṣāḇē att ʻḇaḏ meddem d-āmrā-nā lāḵ. yāḏʻā-nā d-aḇūḵ sāʼeḇ w-eṯmaḥḥal w-eṯrappi w-enā qāṯlā-nā leh l-aḇūḵ. w-hāwē att malkā ḥlāp̱aw. w-šāqel att li b-neššē. w-hwêṯ enā lāḵ attṯā. w-men bāṯar d-emraṯ l-ṭalyā hālēn eštaḥḥaq šaḥqā rabbā. w-emar lāh: daʻ d-lā mmallel-nā ʻammeḵ w-lā ʻam nāš hrênā ʻḏammā ḏ-ʻāḇrīn šaḇʻā yawmāṯā. w-meḥdā šāmʻā att pūnāy-peṯgāmā menn(y) ʻal mellayk. w-men bāṯar d-šemʻaṯ hālēn yedʻaṯ d-nep̱laṯ men iqāreh. w-ḏeḥlaṯ w-eṯhaššḇaṯ. d-mānā teʻbaḏ leh.*

haydēn arīmaṯ qālāh ṭāḇ. wa-mḥāṯ ʻal appēh. w-ṯelḥaṯ mānēh. wa-šmaʻ malkā qālāh wa-qrāh. w-šalāh w-emar lāh mā leḵ. haydēn emraṯ leh enā āmrā (h)wêṯ la-ḇrāḵ da-nmallel ʻamm(y). haydēn menšel(y) np̱al ʻlay wa-ṣḇā d-neḇzaḥ bi. w-ḥāreṭ ennēn l-appay w-yāḏʻā (h)wêṯ d-kollhon mūmē iṯ beh. w-hānā mūmā lā yāḏʻā (h)wêṯ beh. **[p. 177]**

w-ḵaḏ hālēn emraṯ l-malkā. psaq ṭāḇṯā men breh. wa-p̱qaḏ d-neṯqtel. g̱ḏaš dēn w-iṯ (h)wā leh l-malkā mālōḵē p̱ilosop̱ē lā ak da-ḇ-surhāḇā sāʻar (h)wā meddem. ʻḏammā ḏ-meṯmleḵ (h)wā b-hon. w-ḵaḏ šmaʻ(w) hālēn. da-p̱qaḏ malkā d-neṯqtel breh. w-lā eṯmleḵ b-hon. eṯhaššaḇ(w) b-napšhon. d-haw meddem da-p̱qaḏ malkā ba-šḥāqā ʻḇaḏ d-haymen l-attṯeh. w-emar(w) p̱ilosop̱ē lā zāḏeq d-neṯqtel. w-lā zāḏeq l-malkā d-neqtol la-ḇreh. meṭṭul da-l-ḥarṯā l-napšeh ʻāḏel. w-lan marḥeq men lwāṯeh. ellā neṯparras aykannā ḏa-nšawzeḇ l-ṭalyā men mawtā. haydēn emar ḥaḏ mennhon d-ḵollḥaḏ mennan nqūm. nšawzeḇ beh. yawmā ḥaḏ. w-ezal haw w-ʻal lwāṯ malkā wa-sg̱eḏ leh w-emar d-lā zāḏeq d-neʻbḏūn malkē meddem. ʻḏammā ḏ-qāymīn ʻal šrārā.

p̱ilosop̱ā qaḏmāyā emar mār(y) malkā ḥyi da-šmīʻ li: d-iṯ (h)wā ba-zḇan malkā ḥaḏ. d-lā rḥīm (h)wā ʻlaw meddem ak reḥmaṯ-neššē w-aḏīq wa-ḥzā b-ḥaḏ men yawmīn attṯā šappīrṯā. w-ʻallaṯ reḥmṯāh b-lebbeh w-aḥḥḇāh. w-šaddar b-ḥaḏ men yawmāṯā w-qrā l-g̱aḇrāh b-suʻrānā. haydēn ezal malkā lwāṯ attṯā hay. wa-ḇʻā mennāh d-neznē bāh. hi dēn b-ḥemmṯāh emraṯ l-malkā. mār(y) emṯāḵ iṯ(y). w-ḵoll mā ḏ-ṣāḇē att ʻḇaḏ. w-iṯ (h)wā kṯāḇā ḥaḏ l-ḇaʻlāh da-mzahhar (h)wā ʻal zānyūṯā saggi. emraṯ l-malkā. qri b-hānā kṯāḇā. wa-nsaḇ malkā wa-qrā wa-ḥzā da-mzahhar saggi ʻal zānyūṯā. haydēn qām malkā rhīḇāʼiṯ w-ezal. w-nep̱laṯ ʻezqṯeh ṯḥēṯ ʻarsā: w-hu np̱aq w-attṯā eštawzḇaṯ: eṯā gaḇrāh w-iṯeḇ ʻal ʻarsā. wa-ḥzā l-ʻezqṯā w-eštawdʻāh w-hay attṯā lā rgīšā hwāṯ bāh. w-emar gaḇrā b-nap̱šeh: d-malkā ʻal wa-np̱al ʻam attaṯ. w-zāʻ men malkā. w-lā ʻal ʻlēh zaḇnā **[p. 178]** *saggīʼā. haydēn šaddraṯ attṯā lwāṯ aḇūh w-awdʻāṯeh. d-gaḇrā dil(y) eṯnaḵri menn(y). w-ezal aḇūh lwāṯ malkā. w-emar: arʻā iṯ (h)wā li. wa-l-hānā yaḇṭāh d-nep̱lḥīh wa-p̱laḥ bāh zaḇnā. w-hāšā eṯnaḵri mennāh w-lā pālaḥ bāh w-šāḇeq lāh. emar malkā l-g̱aḇrā ḏ-attṯā: att mānā āmar att? wa-ʻnā haw w-emar: šarrirāʼiṯ mār(y) arʻā yaḇ li. w-lā mahmay li men tūqānāh kmā ḏ-meṣyaṯ ḥaylā. wa-g̱ḏaš b-ḥaḏ men yawmīn ʻalleṯ lāh wa-ḥzêṯ bāh šḇīlā ḏ-p̱arsṯā ḏ-aryā. w-ḏeḥleṯ men aryā d-ehpoḵ eʻʻol lāh. emar malkā l-g̱aḇrā: šarrirāʼiṯ ʻal lāh ella lā sraḥ bāh meddem. zel ʻol l-arʻāḵ ploḥāh ṭāḇāʼiṯ w-lā teḏhal.*

w-ṭuḇ iṯ (h)wā gaḇrā ḥaḏ wa-zḇan pāraḥṯā da-mmalləlā b-leššānā ḏ-nāšā. w-sāmāh b-qap̱sā ḥaḏ. wa-ṯlāh b-ḇaytā dileh. wa-p̱aqḏāh d-ṭawdaʻ leh kollmeddem d-sāʻrā attṯeh. wa-np̱aq w-ezal b-urḥā. w-eṯā rāḥmāh d-hay attṯā wa-np̱al ʻammāh. w-ḵaḏ ḥzāṯ hay pāraḥṯā yeḏʻaṯ kollmeddem d-sāʻrīn (h)waw. w-men bāṯar d-eṯā gaḇrā d-hay attṯā. emraṯ leh pāraḥṯā koll meddem d-seʻraṯ attṯā. w-lā šeḇqaṯ da-ḥzāṯ d-lā emraṯ. wa-np̱aq men lwāṯāh w-eṯḥaššaḇ ʻlēh. w-emraṯ attṯā b-nap̱šāh emraṯ awdʻaṯ l-g̱aḇrā. w-emraṯ l-amṯāh: att emart l-g̱aḇrā dil(y) meddem d-seʻreṯ? w-imāṯ amṯā d-lā emreṯ leh. haydēn attṯā bʻāṯ pursā d-teʻḇaḏ l-p̱āraḥṯā daggālṯā. haydēn šeqlaṯ l-qap̱sā. w-sāmṯeh kolleh lêlyā lwāṯāh. wa-mkarrḵā (h)wāṯ raḥyā b-iḏāh zḇan zḇan. wa-mqarr_ḇā (h)wāṯ meḥzīṯā mennāh. w-aḏlqaṯ qeryōnā wa-zḇan mḥawwyā (h)wāṯ leh wa-zḇan mḵassyā (h)wāṯ leh. w-rāssā hwāṯ mayyā ʻal qap̱sā. wa-mḥawwyā (h)wāṯ hāḵan kolleh lêlyā. ʻḏammā ḏ-emraṯ pāraḥṯā b-nap̱šāh barqā dēn **[p. 179]** *w-raʻmē w-meṭrā hwā kolleh lêlyā. w-mā ḏ-eṯā gaḇrā b-ṣap̱rā eṯāh l-p̱āraḥṯā w-šalāh d-mānā ḥzayt b-hānā lêlyā .ṭiṭikos. āmrā leh pāraḥṯā. d-ḇarqē w-meṭrē w-raʻmē lā šaḇqūn d-eḥzē meddem. w-men da-šmaʻ gaḇrā hālēn men pāraḥṯā. iḏaʻ koll d-emraṯ pāraḥṯā ʻal attaṯ baṭṭilā iṯaw. meṭṭul d-meṭrā lā (h)wā kolleh lêlyā hānā. wa-ḇa-ṣnīʻūṯā w-ḇīšūṯā seʻraṯ hālēn attṯā w-ʻeḇdaṯ l-p̱āraḥṯā daggālṯā. w-appqāh mārāh w-qaṭlāh w-raʻʻi l-attṯā.*

There was a king whose name was Cyrus. In (all) the days of his life he had no son, but he had seven wives. He arose, prayed, made a vow, and anointed himself. God so desired and gave him a son. The child grew and shot up like a cedar. He gave him [to his scribe] **[p. 174]** *for him to teach (him) wisdom. He was with the scribe for three years, and he learned nothing. Then the king said, "If this child were with the scribe for many years, he wouldn't learn anything. Rather, give him to Sindban the Wise because he is a wise man and is honored* *by all philosophers." So the king summoned Sindban and said to him, "Tell me how you wish to teach the child." Sindban replied and said to the king, "I will teach the child in six months so that he will be able to dispute with every philosopher under your jurisdiction. If I do not carry out what I have said, may my life cease to exist in the world, and all that I have acquired will be yours, for I have learned that kings are like fire: when it touches anyone it burns him. I will show you that I will teach your son, my lord king, and when his instruction is completed you will give me whatever I ask of you."*

The king said, "That which you ask I will give you." Sindban said, "Everything that you do not desire people to do to you, do not do to another." And they concluded a pact between themselves, and Sindban made an oath to the king, and he turned the child over to Sinban and ordered him, saying, "After six months and two hours let the child come to her father, and let him not delay one hour, or else we will remove Sindban's head."

Sindban took the child by the hand and led him to his house, and there he built him a spacious chamber, and he plastered it, whitewashed it, and wrote on the walls. Then Sindban sat with him and taught him. There were in the house food and drink for them, and not once did any appointed time ever pass that he placed between them (?). After six months the child had learned **[p. 175]** *what no human being had ever been able to learn as he had. One day the king sent to Sindban and said to him, "What do you have?" And he replied and said to him, "That which you desire. Tomorrow I will bring you the child at the time of two hours, if the Lord wills." The king rejoiced and was glad, and Sindban returned to the child and said to him, "Do you desire that this night I calculate your horoscope, for I am seeking to take you to your father?"*

After he looked at the child's horoscope, he saw that it was incumbent that he not speak for seven days because he feared for him lest he die. When Sindban saw this, it made his hands and feet tremble, and he was vexed for his sake. The child saw that his master was troubled, and he said to him, "What is wrong with you that this thing is grievous upon you? If you command me not to speak for a month, I will do it, but order me what you like." Sindban said, "Since I made a promise to your father, [saying that] tomorrow your son will come to you, it is incumbent upon me that I not break it, and I do not seek to be deceitful with your father. Henceforth I will be concealed. You see to it, my son, that you do not speak for six days." And the next day I ordered the child to go to his father.

Out of his love for his son, his father gathered for him friends, those who were sitting with him, and made a banquet for him. then his father summoned him and drew him close and kissed him. He spoke to him, but he did not speak to his father. He began to ask him (questions), but he did not address a word to him. then the king said to whose who were around him, "What is wrong with my son?"

One answered and said, "His master annointed him with an herb so that he would plant his instruction firmly, **[p. 176]** *and from this herb his teeth are locked. This was burdensome for the king. When he saw one of the king's wives, she said, "Leave him [with me] as I am sitting. [When] he and I are alone, doubtless he will make his story known to me because he has trusted me for a* *long time, and what he would not reveal to his mother he will reveal openly to me." Because the child's mother was distressed over his silence, the woman picked the child up and took him to her room. She began to speak with him, but he did not speak to her and did not address a word to her. Then she said to him, "I know you are not a fool, and you are not the king. Neither will you escape from conversing with me. I will tell you somehting, and I will not let you go until you have done it, even if you are a child. If you want, do what I tell you. I know that your father is growing old, feeble, and weak. I am going to kill you father, and you will be king in his stead. You will take me to wife, and I will be your wife." After she said these things to the child, he was greatly troubled and said to her, "Know that I will not speak to you or anyone else until seven days have passed, and immediately [thereupon] you will hear an answer from me to your words." After she heard these things, she knew that she had fallen from his respect, and she was afraid and calculated what she should do to him.*

Then she gave out a loud cry and smote her face and rent her clothes. The king heard her cry and summoned her. He asked her what was wrong with her. Then she said, "I was talking to your son so that he would speak with me. All of a sudden he fell upon me and wanted to penetrate me. He made these scratches on my face. I knew that he possessed all flaws, but this flaw I did not know in him." **[p. 177]**

When she said these things to the king, he abandoned his good opinion of his son and ordered him to be killed. It happened that the king had philosopher advisors so that he would not do anything in haste without being advised by them. When they heard these things, that the king had ordered that his son be killed without being advised by them, they thought among themselves that this thing the king had ordered in adversity he had done because he believed the woman. The philosophers said, "It is not right that he should be killed, and it is not right that the king should kill his son because in the end he will find fault with himself and drive us away from himself. But we should plan how we can save the child from death." Then one of them said, "Each of us will undertake to save him for one day." This one went to the king, bowed to him, and said, "It is not right for kings to do anything until they are standing upon the truth."

The first philosopher said, "My lord king, it has been heard by me that once upon a time there was a king to whom nothing was as beloved as the love of women. He looked out and saw one day a beautiful woman, and love for him entered his heart and he loved her. One day he sent and summoned her husband on an errand. Then the king went to the woman and asked her to commit adultery with him. In her wrath she said to the king, "My lord, I am your servant. Do what you wish." There was a book belonging to her husband that warned greatly against adultery, so the king arose hastily and departed, but his signet ring fell under the bed. He left, and the woman was saved. Her husband came and sat on the bed. He saw the ring and recognized it, but the woman was not aware of it. The man said to himself, "The king entered and slept with my wife." He was terrified of the king, and he did not go to her for a long time. **[p. 178]** *Then the woman sent to her father and informed him, [saying,] "My husband has become estranged from me." Her father went to the king and said,*

"I had a plot of land, and I gave it [to someone] to till, and he tilled it for a time. Now he is estranged from it, does not till it, and he abandoned it." The king said to the woman's husband, "What say you?" He replied and said, "Truly, my lord, he gave me land, and its cultivation was not neglected by me insofar as possible. But it happened one day that I went to it and saw on it a lion's paw print. I was too afraid of the lion to return and enter it." The king said to the husband, "Truly he went to her, but he did her no harm. Go, enter your land, till it well, and fear not."

Again there was a man who bought a bird that talked in the language of people. He set it in a cage and hung it in his house. He ordered it to inform him of everything his wife did, and he departed an went on a journey. The wife's lover came and slept with her. When the bird saw, it knew everything they were doing. After the husband of the woman came, the bird told him everything his wife had done, and it did not omit anything it had seen without telling it. He departed from it and thought about it. The wife said to herself, "My maid has informed the man." She said to the maid, "Did you tell my husband what I did?" The maid said, "I did not tell him." then the woman sought for a plan to do to the treacherous bird. Then she took out the cage and put in before herself all night long. She turned a gristmill with her hand from time to time, and brought a mirror close to (the bird) and lit a lamp, and sometimes she showed such things all through the night until the bird said to itself, "There have been lightning, **[p. 179]** *thunder, and rain all night." When the man came in the morning, he went to the bird and asked it, "What did you see during the night, parrot?" The bird said to him, "The lightning, rain,, and thunder did not let me see anything." Inasmuch as the man heard these things from the bird, he realized that all the bird had said about his wife was false because there had been no rain during all that night. In cunning and evil did the woman do these things and did [thus] to the treacherous parrot. The [bird's] master took it out and killed it, and he appeased the woman.*

From *The Cave of Treasures*
men Kṯāḇā ḏa-M'arraṯ-Gazzē

W-armi alāhā šenṯā 'al Āḏam wa-ḏmeḵ: wa-nsaḇ ḥḏā el'ā men gabbeh d-yamminā w-'aḇdāh l-Ḥawwā menneh. w-ḵaḏ ett'ir Āḏam men šenṯeh wa-ḥzāh l-Ḥawwā ḥḏi bāh saggi. wa-hwaw Āḏam w-Ḥawwā b-g̱aww pardisā lḇīšīn šuḇḥā w-map̱rg̱īn b-ṯešboḥṯā tlāṯ šā'īn: haw dēn hānā pardisā l'al iṯaw wa-m'allay men kollhon ṭūrē rāmē. tlāṯīn zartīn ba-mšoḥṯā ḏ-rūḥā ḏ-quḏšā wa-ḥāḏar l-ḵollāh ar'ā.

emar dēn Mōšē nḇiyā aykannā ḏa-nṣaḇ māryā alāhā ḥaylṯānā pardisā b-g̱aww 'ḏen: w-sām tamman l-Āḏam da-g̱ḇal. 'ḏen dēn iṯēh ṭup̱sā ḏ-'êḏṯā ba-šrārā w-'êḏṯā iṯēh mraḥḥmānūṯeh d-alāhā: hay da-'ṯīḏ (h)wā alāhā d-nep̱ros 'al **[p. 180]** *kollhon bnaynāšā: meṭṭul d-iḏa' alāhā ak mqaddmūṯ-iḏa'ṯeh meddem d-eṯẖaššaḇ Sāṭānā 'al Āḏam b-g̱aww 'ubbā ḏa-mraḥḥmānūṯeh qaddem sāmāh. ak da-mzammar (h)wā ṭūḇānā Dāwīḏ: d-māryā bēṯ-ma'mrā hwêṯ lan l-ḏār dārīn. hānaw dēn da-ḇ-g̱aww mraḥḥmānūṯāḵ 'ḇaḏt lan. w-ḵaḏ mappis leh l-alāhā ḥlāp̱* *purqānā ḏa-ḇnaynāšā emar eṯdakkar ‘êḏṯāḵ d-qanyā men qḏīm. hānaw dēn. l-hay mraḥḥmānūṯā ḏa-‘ṯīḏatt d-tep̱ros ‘al gensan mḥayylā.*

‘ḏen iṯēh ‘êḏṯā qaddišṯā. w-p̱ardisā da-ḇ-g̱awwāh aṯrā ḏa-nyāḥṯā w-yārṯūṯā ḏ-ḥayyē hay d-̣tayyeḇ alāhā l-ḵollhon bnaynāšā qaddīšē.

w-meṭṭul d-iṯaw (h)wā Āḏam kāhnā w-malkā wa-nḇiyā a‘‘leh alāhā l-p̱ardisā da-nšammeš b-g̱aww ‘ḏen ak kāhnā b-‘êḏṯā qaddišṯā: ak d-masheḏ ‘law ̣tūḇānā Mōšē. d-nep̱lḥū lam l-alāhā b-yaḏ tešmešṯā kāhnāyṯā b-ṯešboḥṯā. wa-neṭṭrīw l-p̱uqdānā haw d-eṯg‘el leh b-yaḏ mraḥḥmānūṯeh d-alāhā. w-ašri ennon alāhā l-Āḏam w-Ḥawwā b-p̱ardisā wa-nṣaḇ alāhā ilānā ḏ-ḥayyē ba-mṣa‘ṯeh d-p̱ardisā. w-šarrira (h)y mellṯā hāḏē w-maḵrzaṯ-šrārā d-haw ilānā ḏ-ḥayyē ba-mṣa‘ṯeh d-p̱ardisā la-ṣlīḇ pārōqānā mqaddam-ṣā’ar (h)wā. eṯnṣeḇ tamman ba-mṣa‘ṯeh d-p̱ardisā w-hānā hu d-eṯqḇa‘ ba-mṣa‘ṯāh d-ar‘ā. **[p. 181]**

God cast sleep upon Adam, and he slept. And He took a rib from his right side and made Eve from it. When Adam awoke from his sleep and saw Eve, he rejoiced in her greatly, and Adam and Eve were inside paradise clothed in glory and shining with praise for three hours. This paradise is above and raised above all the high mountains, by three cubits of the measurement of the Holy Ghost, and surrounding all the earth.

The Prophet Moses told how the Lord God Almighty planted paradise inside Eden, and he placed there Adam, whom he had made. Eden is a symbol of the church truly, and the church is God's mercy, which God is prepared to spread over **[p. 180]** *all people because God knew with his foreknowledge within the bosom of his mercy what Satan plotted against Adam before he placed him there, as the Blessed David has sung: "Lord, thou hast been our dwelling-place in all generations." These things, which were inside your mercy, you did for us. And when God was persuaded to save people, he said, "Remember your church, which is redeemed from long ago." Theses are the things, then, for this mercy, that you are prepared to spread over our comforted species."*

Eden is the Holy Church, and paradise, which is inside it, is a place of rest and inheritance of life, which God has prepared for all holy people.

Because Adam was priest, king, and prophet, God raised him to paradise so that he would serve inside Eden as priest in the holy church, as the Blessed Moses testifies: "Let them work for God through priestly service in praise, and let them keep this commandment, which was made for him through the mercy of God." And God caused Adam and Eve to dwell in paradise, and God planted the tree of life in the middle of paradise, and true is this word and the preaching of the truth that this tree of life in the middle of paradise was a prefiguration of the savior's cross. It was planted there in the middle of paradise, and this is the one that was set up in the middle of the earth. **[p. 181]**

From *Kalilag and Demnag*
men *Kṯāḇā ḏ-Ḵalīlag w-Ḏemnag*

Tāg̱rā meskênā iṯ (h)wā. w-ezal ba-ṯg̱urṯā l-aṯrā ḥrênā. w-iṯ (h)wā leh mā manyān parzlā. meṭṭul d-nāš baytāyā layt (h)wā leh: ašlmeh l-gaḇrā yāḏʻeh d-nezdahhar beh wa-ḥzaq. w-kaḏ ṭap̱ bʻāy l-p̱arzlā men yāḏʻeh. w-p̱arzlā zabbneh w-appeq ʻal nap̱šeh w-āmar l-ṯāg̱rā d-p̱arzlā aḵlū ʻuqbrē. w-ṯāg̱rā b-hay d-lā naqneṭ yāḏʻeh w-naḏhel emar leh. māḏēn šarrirā hay d-āmrīn d-layt b-arbʻaṯ reg̱lē: w-lā b-ṯartēn: d-ḥarrip̱īn šennaw men d-ʻuqbrā. ellā kaḏ hāḏē hwāṯ: eškḥeṯ d-att ḥlim att. ḥusrānā da-ʻḇaḏ(w) ʻuqbrē meṯṯʻē. w-hu ḥḏi b-hay d-ṯāg̱rā leh eṯṯpis. w-kaḏ zammneh d-nelʻas l-yawmā b-ḇayteh. w-ḏḇar tāg̱rā l-ḇar yāḏʻeh w-ezal ṭaššyeh. emar leh yāḏʻeh. kaḏ ḏḇartāy l-ḇer(y) mānā ʻḇaḏt leh? āmar leh tāg̱rā d-enā brāḵ lā deḇreṯ. ellā hu eṯā (h)wā bāṯar(y): wa-ḥzêṯ da-nḥeṯ bāz w-ḥaṭp̱eh. w-yāḏʻeh aylel wa-qrā b-g̱enn malkā: kaḏ mḥabbeṭ rêšeh w-ḥaḏyeh w-āmar. aykā eṯhazyaṯ aw eštamʻaṯ d-ḇāz mṣā d-neḥṭop̱ ṭalyā? w-ṯāg̱rā emar leh. aykā ḏ-ʻuqbrē eṯmṣi d-neklūn mā manyē parzlā. māḏēn āp̱ bāz da-l-p̱īlā ḥāṭep̱ law saggi rabbā. haydēn emar yāḏʻeh: āḥ(y): parzlāḵ enā eḵalṯeh w-eḵleṯ mrārē: ṭimaw saḇ: w-haḇ li ber(y). **[p. 182]**

There was a poor merchant, and he went to another place on a business trip. He had a hundred pounds of iron. Because he had no household member, he turned it over to a man he knew to watch over it, and he departed. When he came back, he asked for the iron from his acquaintance. He had sold the iron and spent [the proceeds] on himself. So he said to the merchant, "The iron was eaten by mice." The merchant, in order not to make his acquaintance anxious or frighten him, said, "How true is what they say that there is nothing with four feet, or with two, with teeth as sharp as those of mice. However, since this has happened, I have found that you are correct. The loss the mice have made is negligible." The [other person] rejoiced in that the merchant had been convinced by him. When he invited him to partake of food that day in his house, the merchant led his acquaintance's son away and went off and hid him. His acquaintance said to him, "When you led my son away, what did you do with him?" the merchant said to him, "I did not lead your son away, but he came after me, and I saw a hawk come down and snatch him off." The acquaintance wailed and called for the king's protection, as he was beating his head and breast and saying, "When has it ever been seen or heard that a hawk was able to snatch a child?" The merchant said to him, "Just as mice were able to eat a hundred pound of iron, so too is it not much greater for a hawk to snatch an elephant." The acquaintance then said, "My brother, I stole your iron and was galled. Take its price and give me my son." **[p. 182]**

From a Metrical Sermon by Ephraem Syrus

Men Mêmrā d-ʻal Maḵsānūṯā wa-Ṣlōṯā

dileh d-Ṭūḇānā Mār(y) Ap̱rim

Men rawmā rāḏeyn raḥmē.
kollan neḥur la-mrawmā.
men šmay šmayyā (h)u purqānā.
nawdē l-ʻāmar ba-šmayyā.

ba-zmirṯeh emar Dāwīḏ
mellṯā ḏa-ṣlōṯa (h)y kollāh:
da-lwāṯāḵ mār(y) arimeṯ
‘aynay ‘āmar ba-šmayyā
w-makkeḵ nap̱šeh d-akwāṯeh
ḥnan neṯmakkaḵ ba-šrārā
ak ‘aynay ‘aḇdē da-lwāṯ
mārayhon talyān kollšā‘
d-neḥzōn enhu da-ḵmirin
nehwōn zhirē wa-ḵmirē.
w-enhu da-p̱siḥin ennon
āp̱ ‘aḇdē b-ḥezwā nehwōn.
w-awsep̱ tuḇ Dāwīḏ w-rattem **[p. 183]**
peṯgāmā ak qaḏmāyā
d-ak ‘aynēh d-amṯā lwāṯāh
d-mārṯāh ḥāyrān koll‘eddān
d-enhu da-p̱siḥa (h)y qerbaṯ
lwāṯ parṣōp̱āh ḥaḏyā’iṯ
w-en mārṯā tehwē kmirā
amṯā dāḥlā w-meṯtaššyā
da-ḥzāṯ da-ḵmirān appēh
mestarrḏē men z‘ip̱ūṯāh.
hāḵannā lam āp̱ ‘aynay
lwāṯāḵ māryā allāhan
d-lā mṣē-nā emar Dāwīḏ
d-eḏūṣ w-eḥdē qḏām appayk
‘ḏammā ḏa-ṯraḥḥem ‘alayn
da-ḥzêṯ da-z‘ip̱ parṣōp̱āḵ.
wa-ḥnan hay hāḏē ḏ-Ḏāwīḏ
neṯḥaššaḇ nernē w-nêmar:
raḥḥem ‘alayn alāhā
w-att māryā raḥḥem ‘alayn. **[p. 184]**

From on high arise mercies.
All of us are looking at the height.
From the heaven of heavens is salvation.
We acknowledge him who lives in heaven.
In his psalm David said
a word that is all prayer:
“Unto thee Lord I lifted
my eyes, [O you who] dwell in heaven.”

And he humbled himself so that like him
we may be humbled truly.
As the eyes of servants to the presence of
their lords are always fixed
that they may see if they are gloomy,
they (the servants) will be wary and sad.
But if they are happy
the servants too will be [happy] in their sight.
And David continued and said gently **[p. 183]**
a word like the former:
As the eyes of the maid in the presence of
the mistress are looking always.
If she is happy, she (the maid) approaches
near her countenance joyfully.
And if the mistress is gloomy,
the maid fears and hides herself
since she has seen that her [mistress's] face is gloomy,
she is terrified by her anger.
Thus also my eyes
to the Lord our God
I am not able, said David,
to exult and rejoice before your face
until you have mercy upon us,
for I have seen that your countenance is angry,
and this [saying] of David
we contemplate, meditate, and say:
have mercy upon us, God,
and you, Lord, have mercy upon us. **[p. 184]**

From the Syriac *Book of Medicines*

Rêšā da-Ṯlāṯā

'al Kurhānē Kollhon d-Hāweyn b-Rêšā

Chapter Three

On All Diseases that Occur in the Head

W-qaḏmā'iṯ 'al neḵyānē w-ma'bḏānwāṯā mlilāṯā: eṯhawwyaṯ gēr men q̱ḏim: d-ḵollhēn ma'bḏānwāṯā d-p̱agrā: la-ṯrēn puršānē meṯpallg̱ān. l-nap̱šānyāṯā w-la-ḵyānyāṯā:: w-hāneyn nap̱šānyāṯā: meṯpallg̱ān la-mlilāṯā wa-l-margšānyāṯā w-la-mzī'ānyāṯā. w-eṯamraṯ tuḇ da-l-nap̱šānyāṯā haw muḥḥā sā'ar l-hēn. menhēn b-yaḏ meṣ'āyūṯā ḏ-haddāmē ḥrênē. menhēn (h)u qnomeh sā'ar l-hēn. d-iṯayhēn hānēn mlilāṯā::

'ṯiḏīnan dēn d-nallep̱ b-rêšā hānā. 'al neḵyānē ḏ-g̱āḏšīn l-ma'bḏānwāṯā hānēn mlilāṯā:: hānaw dēn: l-hānēn d-metta'bḏān men tlāṯā 'ubbaw d-muḥḥā:: qaḏmāyṯā iṯēh: hay d-meṯhaggəg̱ā w-meṯqarryā panṭasiyā: wa-ḏ-ṯartēn hay d-meṯhaššḇā w-meṯkannyā suḵlā:: w-ḏa-ṯlāṯ: hay d-meṯ'ahhḏā: w-meštammhā 'uhdānā:: hu dēn muḥḥā: l_a hwā organon margšānā balḥoḏ eṯtaqqan men

kyānā: ellā rāg̱šā ḏ-reg̱šē (h)wā men beršiṯ. w-hay da-ḇ-yaḏ gyāḏē: hu muḥḥā mšaddar ḥaylā margšānā l-ḵollhon haddāmaw d-p̱ag̱rā: iḏi‘a (h)y galyā’iṯ: men hay d-ḵaḏ nestappaq gyāḏā aynā d-hu: bar šā‘ṯā ḏ-lā rg̱ešṯā hwā haddāmā haw. b-yaḏ d-meṯklē ḥaylā haw d-nāḥeṯ (h)wā leh: men muḥḥā w-meṯpallag̱ beh:: galyā (h)y dēn tuḇ iḏi‘ā’iṯ: w-āp̱ men hay da-ḇ-šennṯā. aw la-g̱mār baṭṭālīn **[p. 185]** *reg̱šē: aw .ṭāḇ ‘ammūṯā’iṯ ma‘bḏīn:: iḏi‘a (h)y hāḵêl d-qallil (h)u rāḏē haydēn ḥaylā w-nāḥeṯ men rêšā l-haddāmē. w-hāḏē meṯamrā ba-‘yāḏā: ‘ammiqā’iṯ w-lā ‘ammiqā’iṯ. iṯēh kmāyūṯāh šennṯā lp̱uṯ d-mardīṯā:: hāḏē dēn gaḏšā ḏ-ḏ-ak hāḵannā gēr rāḏē w-nāḥeṯ āp̱ kmā ḏ-iṯēh āp̱ šennṯā b-‘ammiqūṯā:: dāmē hāḵêl da-ḇ-zaḇnā kolleh d-šennṯā: hāwē mnāḥ ḥaylā haw nap̱šānā’iṯ: w-ma‘baḏ taqqip̱ā’iṯ haw kyānāyā:: meṯyaḏ‘aṯ dēn hāḏē: men hay d-mā ḏ-lā’ē ḥaylā hānā: ‘am d-ḏāmeḵ bar šā‘ṯeh meṯhayyal. w-yattirā’iṯ mā ḏ-ḇāṯar saybarṯā mmaššaḥṯā neḏmaḵ. w-men hay tuḇ d-ḇa-zḇan šennṯā: hāwē pšārā šappirā’iṯ b-ḵolleh pag̱rā. law b-ḵarsā lḥoḏ:: ellā zāḏqā’iṯ haydēn mettniḥ: āp̱ haddāmā haw d-ḇeh iṯaw rêšāh d-nap̱šā mlilṯā. lebbā gēr meṯhazyā d-qallil qallil sā‘ar (h)wā. ak d-lā nestneq zaḇnā naggirā la-nyāḥṯeh:: muḥḥā dēn law hāḵannā: ellā b-‘irūṯā ma‘baḏ b-ḵollzḇan. b-šennṯā dēn šālē:: w-ḇadgon šennṯā ‘ammiqtā nāp̱lā ‘al aylēn d-meṯdarršīn saggi’ā’iṯ. ak man d-yattirā’iṯ rāḏē ḥaylā. w-eṯpawšaš men rêšā kaḏ meṯdarršīn (h)waw. meṭṭul sup̱āqā hāḵêl d-ḥaylā haw d-eštammar men muḥḥā: w-meṭṭul leūṯā ḏ-lay b-ma‘bḏānwāṯā saggi’āṯā. ‘al nyāḥṯā sniq akḥaḏ ‘al ḥuyālā:: akznā hāḵêl d-men bāṯar duršā dāmḵīn pšiqā’iṯ w-‘āsqā’iṯ. w-hāḵannā w-āp̱ kaḏ nqabblūn saybarṯā: w-āp̱ kollmā ḏ-tehwē raṭṭiḇā ba-ḵyāneh: d-ak hāḵannā dāmḵīn yattir bāh ba-ḏmūṯā w-āp̱ kaḏ neštōn ḥmārā yattirā: āp̱ kaḏ nesḥōn masḥwāṯā ḏ-mayyā šaḥḥinē ḏ-meṯnaṣlīn ‘al rêšayhon: dāmḵīn yattirā’iṯ:: kollhēn gēr hālēn d-meṯhazyān d-mālyān leh l-muḥḥā da-‘lēh d-hāḏē malyūṯā sniq: mā ḏa-‘mil wa-myabbeš b-ma‘bḏānūṯā saggiṯā. w-men hālēn kollhēn meṯyaḏ‘ā: d-muḥḥā* **[p. 186]** *mā ḏ-‘mal .ṭāḇ w-neṣṭḇē d-nettniḥ: haydēn ‘āḇeḏ šennṯā kyānāyṯā w-yattirā’iṯ enhu d-ḥaylā haw mṯarsyānā d-ḇeh: māšaḥ leh raṭṭiḇūṯā aw men qarrirūṯā saggiṯā neqqar. haydēn šennṯa (h)y da-ḇ-tulā‘ē wa-ḇ-meṯnaššyānūṯā hāwyā. w-ḵollhon ḥāššē ḥrênē d-ḏ-ak hālēn.*

First on injuries and mental functions. It has been shown previously that all functions of the body are divided into two divisions, the psychological and the natural. The psychological ones are divided into those pertaining to the mind, those pertaining to the senses, and those pertaining to motion. It has also been said that it is the brain that performs the operations of the mind, some through the intermediary of other members, and some, which pertain to the mind, it performs itself.

We are ready then to teach in this chapter about injuries that happen to these mental functions, which are caused by the three cavities of the brain. First is the one that imagines, and it is called imagination; second is the one that thinks, and it is called intelligence; and third is the one that remembers, and it is called memory. The brain was not constituted by nature to be an organ of perception only, but it has been the principal sensor of sensations from the beginning. Through nerves the brain sends the power to feel to all members of the body. This is known clearly from the fact that when a nerve is severed, wherever it is, immediately the member it serves becomes without feeling because the power that descended to it from the brain and was distributed throughout it has been withdrawn from it. This is obviously clear from the fact that during sleep the senses either are utterly idle **[p. 185]** *or they work obscurely. It is thus known that the power that ascends and descends from the head to the body does so in a small quantity. These [two kinds of sleep] are customarily said to be [sleeping] "deeply" and [sleeping] "lightly." The amount of sleep varies in proportion to the amount of power that comes down [from the head]. It happens that as the power that ascends and descends [varies], so does sleep in depth. It seems therefore that during the whole period of sleep the psychological power is at rest, and the natural (power) works intensely. This then is known. When this power is weary, as soon as [one] lies down it is immediately made strong again, even more so if [one] lies after moderate nourishment. Moreover, during the time of sleep, digestion takes place nicely throughout the whole body and not in the belly only; and moreover, very properly, that member also in which [is seated] the chief of the rational soul is rested. Now it is seen that the heart works very slowly [during sleep], since it has no need of a lengthy period for its rest; with the brain, however, it is not so, for it works without cessation always in wakefulness, and during sleep it is drawn out. For this reason deep sleep falls upon those who exercise greatly, because the power ascends more and is wasted away from the head while they are exercising. Because of the emptying thus of the power that is sent from the brain and because of the fatigue caused by excessive exertions, he is in need of rest as well as of strength. Likewise therefore after exertion [people] sleep easily and heavily, and so also when they have received nourishment—and more so when it (the nourishment) is moist in its nature. They also sleep more in form and also when they drink much wine, and when they bathe with hot water poured over their heads they sleep more. All these things are seen to fill the brain, which is need of this fullness when it is overworked and dried up by great exertion. From all these things it is known that when the brain* **[p. 186]** *has worked much and needs to rest, then it creates a natural sleep, more especially if it has within itself the power for nourishment, [or if] it has anointed itself with moisture or [if] it is very cold, then the sleep is as in a stupor and senselessness. All other senses are like these.*

A Flood in Edessa

Tuḇ men Taš'yāṯā ḏ-Su'rānā ak da-ḇ-P̱āsiqāṯā

From the Stories of Events in Brief

Ba-šnaṯ ḥammešmā wa-ṯlāṯa'srē b-malkūṯeh d-Seweros wa-ḇ-malkūṯeh d-Aḇgar malkā bar Ma'nu malkā b-iraḥ tešrin ḥrāy 'šen (h)wā mabbu'ā ḏ-mayyā da-np̱aq men āpadnā rabbā d-Aḇgar malkā rabbā wa-'šen wa-sleq ak 'yāḏeh qaḏmāyā wa-mlā (h)wā wa-šp̱a' l-ḵoll gabbīn. w-šarri (h)waw dārāṯā w-eṣṭwē w-ḇāttē ḏ-malkūṯā d-neṯmlōn mayyā. w-ḵaḏ ḥzā Aḇgar malkā. sleq (h)wā leh l-ṯaqnā ḏ-ṭūrā da-l'el men āpadnā dileh aykā ḏ-yāṯḇīn w-'āmrīn 'āḇḏay 'ḇāḏā dilāh d-malkūṯā. w-ḵaḏ ḥakkimē meṯḥaššḇīn (h)waw: d-mānā ne'bḏūn l-hon l-mayyā yattirē d-ettawsap̱ (h)waw. gḏaš wa-hwā meṭrā rabbā w-'aššinā b-lêlyā.

w-etā Dayṣān d-lā b-yawmeh wa-d-lā b-yarḥeh. w-etaw mayyā nukrāyē. w-eškaḥ ennon l-qaṭaraqtē kad aḥidīn b-parzlē rawrbē da-qrimīn (h)waw wa-b-moklē d-parzlā da-mšarrərīn (h)waw. wa-d-lā eštkaḥ l-hon ma'lānā l-mayyā. hwā leh yammā rabbā l-bar men šurēh da-mdittā. w-šarri (h)waw mayyā nāḥtīn men bēt yā'yātā d-šurā la-mdittā. w-Abgar malkā kad qā'em (h)wā b-purkāsā rabbā d-metqrē d-pārsāyā. ḥzā (h)wā b-lampêdē d-nurā l-mayyā. wa-pqad (h)wā. w-eštqel (h)waw tar'ē w-qaṭaraqtē tmānyā d-šurā ma'rbāyā da-mdittā men aykā da-npaq nahrā. w-bāh b-šā'tā tar'aw (h)waw mayyā l-šurā ma'rbāyā wa-'qar(w) l-āpadnā rabbā w-payā da-mdittā. w-'al l-gaww mdittā d-māran malkā. wa-šqal (h)waw koll meddem d-eštkaḥ (h)wā qdāmayhon benyānē rgigē w-payā da-mdittā. koll meddem d-qarrib (h)wā l-nahrā men taymnāyāh w-garbyāyāh. wa-sraḥ **[p. 187]** *(h)waw tub b-hayklā d-'êdtā da-kristyānē. w-mit (h)waw b-hānā 'bādā yattir men trēn alpīn da-bnaynāšā. saggi'ē dēn mennhon. kad dāmkīn (h)waw b-lêlyā 'al 'layhon mayyā men šelyā w-ethneq (h)waw. kad malyā (h)wāt mdittā qālā d-yallātā. w-kad ḥzā Abgar malkā surḥānā hānā da-hwā (h)wā. pqad (h)wā d-kollhon umānē da-mdittā narḥqūn (h)waw ḥānwāthon men lwāt nahrā. w-nāš lwāt nahrā lā nebnē leh ḥānūtā. wa-b-ḥekmtā d-māšōḥē w-yādō'ē ettsim ḥānwātā da-kmā nehwē ptāyā d-nahrā. w-awsep (h)waw 'al mušḥāteh qadmāytā. āpen gēr mayyā saggi'īn (h)waw w-'aššīnīn. ellā āp hu ptāyeh d-nahrā z'or (h)wā. d-mayyā d-reglātā 'esrīn w-ḥammeš mqabbel (h)wā ba-knišūthēn d-men koll gabbīn. wa-pqad (h)wā Abgar malkā. d-kollhon hānon d-yātbīn b-eṣtwā w-pālḥīn luqbal nahrā. d-men tešrin qdēm wa-'dammā l-nīsān lā hwaw bāytīn b-ḥānwāthon. ellā gzirāyē d-nāṭrīn mdittā. ḥamšā mennhon hwaw bāytīn b-šurā l'el men dukktā d-'āllīn bāh mayyā la-mdittā kolleh zabnā d-satwā. w-mā d-argeš b-lêlyā wa-šma' qālā d-mayyā nukrāyē d-šarri d-ne''lūn la-mdittā... w-kollman d-šāma' qālā w-mahmē w-lā nāpeq. hā mayyā tāb'īn menneh besyānā d-šāṭ puqdāneh d-malkā. w-ettsim (h)wā hānā puqdānā men hānā zabnā da-hwā beh hākannā 'dammā l-yawmāt 'ālmā. māran dēn Abgar malkā pqad (h)wā w-etbni leh benyānā l-ma'mrā d-malkūteh bēt satwā Bēt Tbārā. w-tamman 'āmar (h)wā kolleh zabnā d-satwā. wa-b-qaytā nḥet (h)wā leh l-āpadnā ḥdattā d-etbni (h)wā leh 'al rêš mabbu'ā. w-āp hennon ḥêrē dileh bnaw l-hon benyānē l-ma'marhon ba-šbābūtā d-hāwē bāh malkā b-šuqā rāmā d-metqrē Bēt Saḥrāyē. w-meṭṭul d-netqayyam (h)wā šaynāh da-mdittā qadmāyā. pqad (h)wā Abgar malkā w-eštbeq ḥawbātā da-tba'tā men gawwāyē da-mdittā. w-men aylēn d-'āmrīn b-quryā w-b-agorsē w-etkalyat tba'tā mennhon ḥammeš šnīn. 'dammā d-'etrat* **[p. 188]** *mdittā b-nāšūtā w-etkalləlat ba-bnaynāšā.*

In the year 513 of the kingdom of Severius and during the reign of King Abgar, the son of King Ma'nu, in the month of November the water source erupted and went out from King Abgar's great palace, and it gained strength, going beyond its former custom, and it filled and overflowed its banks. The courtyards, porches, and houses of the kingdom began to be filled with water. When King Abgar saw this, he went out to the tableland that was above his palace, where the workers of the kingdom dwelt and lived. While the wise men were considering what they should do about the great waters, which were increasing, it happed that a great and violent rain came during the night. The Daisan (river) came out of season, and there was unheard-of water. It found the cataracts closed with large [pieces of] iron, which were overlaid with bars of iron that were reinforcing. Since no entrance for the water was found, there was formed a large sea outside the wall of the city. The water began to go down into the city over the battlements. While King Abgar was standing on the great tower called the Persian (Tower), he saw the water by lamp light, and he gave an order, and the gates and the eight cataracts of the western wall of the city were removed from where the river went out. Immediately the water broke through the western wall and destroyed the great and beautiful palace of the city. It entered the city of our lord the king and carried away everything that was found before the delightful and lovely buildings of the city., everything that was near the river on its southern and northern sides, and it damaged **[p. 187]** *also the church of the Christians. During this event more then three thousand people died. While many of them were asleep during the night, the water entered upon them suddenly, and they drowned, as the city was filled with cries of distress. When King Abgar saw this damage that was being done, he ordered that all the workmen of the city should remove their shops from next to the river and that no one should build a shop by the river, and with the wisdom of surveyors and experts the shops were placed so that however much the river's breadth was, they increased its former measurement. Even if the water was great and violent, except where the breadth of the river was small, it would accommodate the water of twenty-five floods in its total on all sides. And King Abgar ordered that all those who dwelt in the portico and worked opposite the river should not spend the night in their shops from October until April, excepting the policemen who guarded the city, five of whom would spend the night on the wall above the place at which the water entered the city throughout the winter. Whenever they perceived (anything) during the night and heard the sound of unusual water that was starting to enter the city, all who heard the sound and was negligent and did not go out, the water would exact from him a fine for having treated the king's command with contempt. This command was placed from this time such that it has remained thus for all the days of the world. Our lord King Abgar then gave an order, and a building was built for him for an abode in the winter at Beth T'vara, and there he dwent all the time during the winter. In the summer he went down to the new palace that was built for him at the head of the spring. So also did his companions build for themselves buildings for dwelling in the neighborhood in which the king was in the high market that is called Beth Sahraye. Because the former prosperity of the city was re-established, King Abgar gave an order, and tax debts were forgiven for those inside the city and for those who were living in the villages and fields, and they were exempted from taxes for five years until* **[p. 188]** *the city was enriched by humanity and adored with people.*

From the *Chronicle of Times* by Barhebraeus
On the Taking of Babylon
Men Kṯāḇā ḏ-Maḵṯḇānūṯ Zaḇnē ḏ-Ḇar ʿEḇrāyā
Meṭṭul Mešqlā ḏ-Ḇāḇel

Nḥeṯ mleḵ malkē Hūlākū ʿal Bag̱dāḏ: wa-mṭā āp̱ Bājū men Bēṯ R(h)ōmāyē. wa-np̱aq ḥaylawwāṯā ḏ-Ḇag̱dāḏāyē l-ḇar d-nep̱g̱ʿūn b-Ṯāṯārāyē. w-iṯayhon (h)waw d-qāymīn b-rêšayhon: amīrā rabbā kurdāyā d-meṯqrē Bar Kūrār: w-Ḏāwīṯdār zʿorā ʿaḇḏā ḏ-ḵālīp̱ah. w-p̱āš trayhon gabbē luqbal ḥḏāḏā: kaḏ lā ārʿīn: ʿesrīn wa-ṯlāṯā yawmīn: meḥdā b-yōm arbʿā tmānāyā b-yarḥā qaḏmāyā ḏ-Ṭayyāyē: šnaṯ šeṯmā w-ḥammšīn w-šeṯ: d-hi šnaṯ ANSṬ d-Yawnāyē: eṯqarraḇ qaḏmāʾiṯ Bājū Nōyān w-ḥaylawwāṯeh l-ḏukkṯā ḏ-meṯqaryā qaḇrā d-Aḥmaḏ b-g̱abbā maʿrḇāyā ḏ-Ḇag̱dā_ḏ: w-qreḇ āp̱ Bag̱dāḏāyē. wa-p̱g̱aʿ(w) ba-ḥḏāḏē: w-eṯṯbar gabbā ḏ-Ḇājū Nōyān: w-eṯnaṣṣaḥ b-zāḵūṯā Bag̱dāḏāyē. w-iṯaw (h)wā amīrā Sulaymān Šāh ʿam ḥaylā dileh ʿal šurē ḏ-Ḇag̱dāḏ. **[p. 189]**

w-ḵaḏ hwā ramšā: emar Bar Kūrār sāḇā l-Ḏawītdār.talyā: d-hāšā d-alāhā yaḇ lan zākūṯā: zāḏeq d-neʿʿol l-ḇāttayn w-neṯtnīḥ: w-ḵen neppoq mendrêš w-nep̱g̱aʿ. haw dēn eštaʿli w-lā ṣḇā d-neʿʿol: w-ḇāṯ kollhon l-ḇar. w-meṭṭul da-ḇ-ḏukkṯā mmakkeḵṯā šāreyn (h)waw hennon Bag̱dāḏāyē: ezal Tāṯārāyē wa-ṯraʿ ʿlayhon turʿṯā ḏ-rgelṯā rabbṯā ḏ-mayyā men Deqlaṯ: w-aṭip̱ ennon mayyā b-p̱algeh d-lêlyā. w-šarri ʿārqīn men gaww mayyā: wa-ṯri āp̱ qeštāṯhon w-g̱êrayhon w-ṯīqē ḏ-saypayhon. w-ḵaḏ nhar ṣap̱rā: pnaw ʿlayhon Tāṯārāyē bnay gabbā ḏ-Hūlākū: w-aggar qrāḇā ʿḏammā la-ṯšaʿ šāʿīn d-yōm ḥammšā: w-ḥaḇ w-awḥel gabbā ḏ-Ḇag̱dāḏāyē: w-eṯqtel Bar Kūrār: wa-ʿraq Dawīṯdār w-ʿal la-mḏittā.

haydēn Bājū w-ḥaylawwāṯeh eṯaw šraw b-g̱abbā maʿrḇāyā ḏ-Ḇag̱dāḏ. w-Hūlākū šrā b-g̱abbā maḏnḥāyā: b-yōm trēn tlāṯaʿsar b-yarḥā qaḏmāyā: w-aqīm qrāḇā qašyā ʿlēh da-mḏittā: luqbal tāg̱ā ḏ-ḏārṯā ḏ-ḵālīp̱ah. w-ḵaḏ psaq saḇrā hu Mustaʿṣem ḵālīp̱ah dāwyā: qrā l-Ḇar ʿAlqamī wazīrā dīleh: wa-l-Najm-aldīn ʿAḇd-alganī bar Darnūs wa-l-Mār(y) Makkīḵā qāṯōlīqā: wa-p̱qaḏ l-hon d-nessḇūn sug̱ʾā ḏ-ḏahḇā: w-ʿellāṯā malkāyāṯā: w-raḵšē arāḇiqo: w-nappqūn l-izgaddē ḏ-Ṯāṯārāyē men ḥḇušyā: w-nalbšūn ennon: w-nettlūn l-hon mawhḇāṯā šappirāṯā: w-nêzlūn ʿammhon lwāṯ mleḵ malkē. w-neṯbʿōn melltā l-ḥayyaw d-ḵālīp̱ah w-ḏa-ḇnaw wa-ḏ-ḇaytāyaw: wa-nappqūn rawḥā: d-hānon d-hway: b-yaḏ mālōḵē bišē hway. w-en neḥḥōn mekkêl w-nettel l-hon ḥayayhon: ʿaḇdē hāweyn wa-mšaʿḇḏē w-yāhḇay maḏaṯā. w-ḵaḏ np̱aq hennon hālēn lwāṯ mleḵ malkē: w-šamli izgaddūṯhon: ʿakkar ennon w-lā appes l-hon d-nehpḵūn lwāṯ ḵālīp̱ah. w-aʿšneh **[p. 190]** *la-qrāḇā: wa-ṯraʿ Tāṯārāyē turʿṯā rabbṯā b-ḇurgā ḏ-ʿajamāyā: wa-ʿal(w) la-mḏittā: b-yōm ʿruḇtā ʿesrīn w-ḥammšā b-yarḥā qaḏmāyā. w-eṯhayyal ʿlayhon bnay mḏittā: w-appeq ennon mendrêš l-ḇar. w-ṯuḇ taqqen Tāṯārāyē: wa-l-yawmā ḏ-ḇāṯreh: kemaṯ b-yōm šabbṯā: eštallaṭ ʿal kollhon šurē. wa-ʿraq Bag̱dāḏāyē: w-eṯtašši b-ḇāttē w-ḥulānē ḏa-ṯhoṯ arʿā. w-ḇeh b-yōm šabbṯā: np̱aq trayhon bnaw d-ḵālīp̱ah l-ḇar ṣēḏ mleḵ malkē: w-ḇāṯar šāʿṯā np̱aq āp̱ hu ḵālīp̱ah. wa-p̱qaḏ mleḵ malkē: w-armi beh parzlē: w-qām ʿlaw nāṭōrē b-ḥdā men yārīʿāṯā šaḇʿā yawmīn. ʿḏammā ḏ-ʿal hu mleḵ malkē qnōmāʾiṯ l-ḏārṯā ḏ-ḵālīp̱ah. wa-ḇaṣṣi l-gazzē wa-mṭaššyāṯā w-simāṯā ʿattiqāṯā w-ḥaḏtāṯā: w-galli kollhēn w-appeq. wa-šmaṭ mōglāyē saypayhon: wa-qṭal l-ḵolleh ʿammā ḏ-Ḇag̱dāḏāyē rebbwāṯā ḏa-ḇnaynāšā: yattirāʾiṯ Iberāyē ʿḇaḏ qaṭlā saggiʾā. w-*

qāṯōlīqā kanneš la-ḵresṭyānē kollhon l-ʻêḏṯā ḏ-šuqā ḏa-ṯlāṯā: w-ṯamman naṭṭar ennon: w-lā nāš men kresṭyānē etakki. āp̱ ʻattirē d-Ṭayyāyē sug̱ʼā d-neḵsayhon lwāṯ qāṯōlīqā ayti: d-ḏam en neštawzḇūn nqaddōn dilhon: w-ḵollhon eṯqtel.

bāṯarken dēn kaḏ eṯbhel qallil mleḵ malkē: qarrḇeh l-ḵālīp̱ah dāwyā qḏāmaw: w-ḏāneh w-ḥayyḇeh l-mawtā. wa-p̱qaḏ w-sāmū b-saqqā w-ḥaṭ ʻlaw: wa-ḇ-rep̱sē ḏ-reg̱layhon qaṭlū. b-hay d-nāšīn Ṭayyāyē aḏḥlū la-mleḵ malkē kaḏ āmrīn: d-en neṯešeḏ men dmeh d-hānā ʻal arʻā: lā ṭuḇ nāḥeṯ meṭrā: ʻlēh āp̱ gumrē ḏ-nurā neḥḥḇān mennāh. w-harkā nesbaṯ šulmā malkūṯā ḏ-ʻAbbāsāyē: āp̱ šarkā ḏ-malkūṯā ḏ-Ṭayyāyē šarri l-mezdʻzāʻū. w-qāmaṯ w-eṯnaṣṣḥaṯ malkūṯā ḏ-Mōg̱lāyē b-aṯrawwāṯā hālēn da-l-ḇar: ak d-āp̱ b-aṯrawwāṯā hānon da-l-g̱aww. **[p. 191]**

The King of Kings Hülägü descended upon Baghdad, and also Baju arrived from Anatolia, and the forces of the Baghdadis went out to fight the Tatars. Standing at their head were the great Kurdish amir called Ibn Kurar and the younger Dawitdar, the servant of the caliph. Both sides remained facing each other, not meeting for twenty-three days. Suddenly on Wednesday, the eighth of the first month of the Arabs, the year 656, which is the year 1569 of the Greeks, Baju Noyan and his forces approached the place called Ahmad's Tomb on the western side of Baghdad, and the Baghdadis also drew near, and they attacked each other. Baju Noyan's side was broken through, and the Baghdadis were triumphant in victory. Amir Sulayman Shah was with his force on the walls of Baghdad. **[p. 189]**

When it was evening, the aged Ibn Kurar said to the young Dawitdar, "Now that God has given us victory, it is appropriate that we go to our houses and rest, and then we will go out anew and attack." The other, however, was arrogant and did not want to go in, so they all spent the night outside. Because the Baghdadis were staying in a low-lying place, the Tatars went down and caused a great flood of water from the Tigris to break in upon them, and the water overwhelmed them in the middle of the night. They began to flee through the water, and their bows, arrows, and the scabbords of their swords got wet. When morning broke, the Tatars who were on Hülägü's side returned, and the battle continued for nine hours on Thursday, and the side of the Baghdadis burned out and became exhausted. Ibn Kurar was killed, and Dawitdar fled and entered the city.

Then Baju and his forces came and camped on the western side of Baghdad. Hülägü camped on the eastern side on Monday the thirteenth of the first month, and he initiated a fierce battle against the city opposite the crown of the caliph's courtyard. When the wretched caliph Mustaʻsim lost hope, he called Ibn ʻAlqami, his vizier, and Najm al-Din Abd al-Ghani Ibn Darnus and the Catholicos Mar Makkika, and he ordered that they should set out a lot of gold, regal implements, and Arabian horses, set free the ambassadors of the Tatars from prison, clothe them, and give them beautiful gifts, and that they should go with them to the King of Kings and request a promise for the life of the caliph, his sons, and his household and for them to escape with their lives, because the things that had taken place had happened because of bad advice. If they lived henceforth and [Hülägü] granted them their lives, they would be servants, reduced to servitude, and givers of tribute. When these persons went out to the King of Kings and fulfilled their mission, he detained them and did not allow them to return to the caliph. And he intensified **[p. 190]** *the battle, and the Tatars made a huge breach in the Ajamiyya Tower and entered the city on Friday, the twenty-fifth of the first month. They overwhelmed the people of the city and sent them outside again. The Tatars got ready, and on the next day, i.e. Saturday, they gained dominion over all the walls. The Baghdadis fled and hid in houses and holes beneath the earth. On Saturday both the caliph's sons went out to the presence of the King of Kings, and after a while the caliph also went out himself. The King of Kings gave and order and had iron [shackles] thrown on him, and guards stood over him in one of the tents for seven days until the King of Kings himself entered the caliph's courtyard and sought for the treasuries, hidden things, and treasures old and new. He revealed them all and had them taken out. The Mongols drew their swords and killed all the people of Baghdad, myriads of people. Mostly the Georgians did the great killing. The catholicos gathered all the Christians in the Church of the Tuesday Market, and their he kept them under guard, and none of the Christians was harmed. The rich of the Arabs too brought much of their wealth to the catholicos, thinking if they escaped they would retain possession of them, but they were all killed.*

Then, when the King of Kings calmed down a little, he had the wretched caliph brought near in his presence, and he judged him and condemned him to death. He gave an order, and they placed him in a sack and sewed him up in it, and with kicks of their feet they killed him because Arab people had frightened the King of Kings when they said that if any of the blood of this person was shed upon the ground, the rain would not fall again but rather upon it (the ground) burning coals of fire would burn from it. Here the kingdom of the Abbasids came to an end, and so also did the kingdom of the Arabs begin to totter. The kingdom of the Mongols arose and was victorious in those places outside, as also in these places which were within. **[p. 191]**

From the Reign of Baidu Khan

W-meṭṭul da-ḇ-zaḇnā hānā kollhon Mog̱lāyē rawrḇē w-ḏaqdqē b-ḵollāyūṯhon ahgar(w): w-menkaḏū eṯgzar(w): w-ḇa-šyāg̱āṯā wa-ṣlawwāṯā ḏ-ḏilānīn l-mašlmānē.tāḇ etmahhar(w): hu ṯuḇ Baydū kaḏ šp̱ar l-hon ahgar: wa-ḥḏi(w) beh .tāḇ .tāḇ kollhon rawrḇānē ḏ-malkūṯeh. ellā men ʻenyān kreṣtyānē lā meṯmṣē (h)wā d-neṯqp̱es: w-neṯṯḵel ʻal nāš barnāšā b-ḵollhon pursānē ḏ-malkūṯā ṣtar mennhon lā meṯdnē (h)wā. w-men hānā šarri maḥgar ʻal trayhon qup̱sē. la-ḵreṣtyānē man āmar (h)wā da-ḵreṣtyāna (h)u: wa-ṣlīḇā tlē b-ṣureh. l-Ṭayyāyē dēn mḥawwē (h)wā d-mašlmāna (h)u: ellā law meṯmṣē (h)wā l-mêlap̱ tawdiṯhon w-qāymīn la-ṣlōṯā: hu Baydū la-ḇreh mšaddar (h)wā da-nṣallē ʻammhon. wa-ḇ-hāḏē mšayyen (h)wā tarʻiṯhon: wa-mrayyaḥ rug̱zhon. bram lā meṯhappē (be hidden from) (h)wā ʻlayhon d-Ṭayyāyē d-la-p̱niṯ kreṣtyānē yattir meṣtlē w-meṯhannē (rely). w-qarribūṯā ḏ-yarḥē ḥammšā b-hūp̱āḵē d-ak hālēn dḇar malkūṯeh.

Because at this time all the Mongols, great and small, in their entirety had become Muslim and were already circumcised and were quite skilled in the ablutions and prayers of the Muslims, Baidu too, as it seemed to them, had become Muslim, and all the grandees of his kingdom rejoiced in him greatly. However, from the society of Christians he was not able to withdraw, and he would not assent to trust anyone in all the affairs of the kingdom aside from them. From this he began to stumble on two pebbles: for the Christians there were those who said that he was Christian and a cross was hung on the wall; to the Arabs, however, he showed himself as a Muslim, but he was not able to learn their confession, and when they were standing for prayer Baidu would send his brother to pray with them. By this he would appease their minds and calm their rage. However, it was hidden from the Arabs that he was more inclined in the direction of the Christians and relied [more on them]. For nearly five months with manners like these he led his kingdom.

Aaron ܐܗܪܘܢ *ahrōn*

abandon (verb) ܫܒܩ *šbaq/nešboq*; Ethpe *eštbeq* to be abandoned (see "leave")

Abbasid ܥܒܐܣܝܐ *ᶜabbāsāyā*

Abd al-Ghani (pr n) ܥܒܕܐ ܠܓܢܝ *ᶜabd algani*

Abdnebo ܥܒܕܢܒܘ *ᶜabdnebō*

Abgar ܐܒܓܪ *abgar* (pr n)

Abijah ܐܒܝܐ *abiyā*

able ܡܫܟܚ *meškaḥ* (*l-* + inf or *d-* + impf, to do); ܡܨܐ *mṣā/nemṣē*; pass part *mṣē/maṣyā* able; Ethpe *etmṣi* to be able

ablution ܫܝܓܬܐ *šyāgtā*

abode ܐܘܢܐ *awwānā*; ܡܥܡܪܐ *maᶜmrā*

above ܠܥܠ *lᶜel*

Abshlama ܥܒܫܠܡܐ *ᶜabšlāmā*

abundant ܫܦܝܥ *špiᶜ*; abundance ܡܠܝܘܬܐ *malyutā*

accompany (verb) ܠܘܐ *lwā/nelwē*; accompany in procession (verb) ܙܘܚ Pa *zayyaḥ*

according to ܡܛܠ *meṭṭul* ; *meṭṭul d-* for, because; ܡܛܘܠ variant spelling of *meṭṭul*; ܡܛܠܠܬ *meṭṭlāt* – form of *meṭṭul* when followed by enclitic pronouns II; ܠܦܘܬ *lput*

accurate ܚܬܝܬ *ḥattit*

accuse (verb) ܩܪܨܐ *qarṣā*

accustomed ܡܥܕ *mᶜād*

acknowledge (verb) ܝܕܐ Aph *awdi*

acquaintance ܝܕܥܐ *yād'ā*

acquire (verb) ܩܢܐ *qnā/neqnē*

act ܣܘܥܪܢܐ *suᶜrānā*

Adam ܐܕܡ *ādām*

add (verb) ܝܣܦ Aph *awsep*

Addai (=Thaddaeus) ܐܕܝ *adday*

admonition ܡܟܣܢܘܬܐ *maksānutā*

adorned (to be adorned with) (verb) Ethpa *etkallal b-*

adultery (verb) ܙܢܝܘܬܐ *zānyutā*; ܓܘܪ *gār/ngur*

advent ܡܐܬܝܬܐ *metitā*

adventure ܢܨܚܢܐ *neṣḥānā*

adversity ܫܚܩܐ *šḥāqā*

advise ܡܠܟ *mlak/nemlok*; Ethpe *etmlek b-* to be advised by; advisor ܡܠܘܟܐ *mālokā*

affair ܦܘܪܣܢܐ *pursānā*

afraid (verb) ܕܚܝܠ *daḥḥil*; ܕܚܠ *dḥel/nedḥal;* Aph *adḥel* to make afraid

after ܒܬܪ *bātar*; afterwards ܒܬܪܟܢ *bātarken*

again ܡܢ ܕܪܫ *men d-rêš* (see "head"); ܬܘܒ *tub*

against (to go against) (verb) ܢܚܬ *nḥet/neḥḥat* +*ᶜl* ; preposition ܥܠ *ᶜal* (with pron encl II, *ᶜl-*)

Aggai (pr n) ܐܓܝ *aggay*

agree (verb) ܕܢܐ Ethpe *etdni*; ܩܨ *qaṣ/neqqoṣᶜam*

Ahmad (pr n) ܐܚܡܕ *aḥmad*

aid ܥܘܕܪܢܐ *ᶜudrānā*

Alexander ܐܠܟܣܢܕܪܘܣ *aleksandros*

alive ܚܝ *ḥayy*

all (+ emph or pron encl) ܟܠ *koll*; all around ܠܚܘܕܪܐ *l-ḥudrā*; all the more *yattirā'it* (see "more than")

allow ܦܣܣ Aph *appes*

alone ܠܚܘܕ *lḥod*; ܒܠܚܘܕ *balḥod* (takes pron encl II)

already ܡܢܟܕܘ *menkadu*

altar *ᶜlātā* pl *ᶜlawwātā* (see "cause," "reason," "thing," "article"); ܡܕܒܚܐ *madbḥā*; ܬܪܘܢܘܣ *trōnos*

although ܐܦ ܐܢ *āp en*

always ܟܠܫܥ *kollšāᶜ*; ܐܡܝܢܐܝܬ *aminā'it*

ambassador ܐܝܙܓܕܐ *izgaddā*

amen ܐܡܝܢ *āmên*

among (preposition) ܒܝܬ *bēt*; ܒܝܢ *bayn* (+ pron encl II); ܒܝܢܬ *baynāt* (+ pron encl I)

Amoros ܐܡܘܪܘܣ *amoros*

amount ܟܡܝܘܬܐ *kmāyutā*

ancient ܩܕܝܡ *qaddim* ; *men qdim* of old, long ago, from eternity; ܩܕܡܝ *qadmāy*

and ܘ *w(a)*-; and so ܟܢ *ken*; and then ܟܢ *ken*

angel ܡܠܐܟܐ *malakā*

anger ܙܥܝܦܘܬܐ *z'iputā*; angry ܙܥܝܦ *z'ip*

animal ܚܝܘܬܐ *ḥayyutā* pl – *ywātā* ; living things, life (collective)

announce ܟܪܙ Aph *akrez*; announcer ܟܪܘܙܐ *kārōzā*

anoint ܡܫܚ *mšaḥ/nemšaḥ*; anointed ܡܫܝܚ *mšiḥ*; *mšiḥā* the Christ

answer (verb) Pa *panni* (see "return," "come back"); ܥܢܐ *ᶜnā/neᶜnē*; *punāy-pet-gāmā* (see "return"); answer to a letter ܦܚܡܐ *peḥmā*

Antioch ܐܢܛܝܘܟܝܐ *anṭyokyā*

anxious (to make anxious) (verb) ܩܢܛ Aph *aqneṭ*

anything ܡܕܡ *meddem*

aperture ܟܘܬܐ *kawwtā* pl *kawwē* (abs *kawwā* pl *kawwin*) (f)

apostle ܫܠܝܚܐ *šliḥā*

appearance ܐܣܟܝܡܐ *eskêmā*

appease (verb) Pa *raᶜᶜi* (see "tend," "keep," "rule"); ܫܝܢ Pa *šayyen*

appoint (verb) ܛܝܒ Pa *ṭayyeb*

appointed place ܘܥܕܐ *wa'dā*

approach (verb) ܩܪܒ *qreb/neqrab l-* ; Ethpa *etqarrab l-* to approach

appropriate to ܕܝܠܢܝ *dilānāy l-*

April ܢܝܣܢ *nisān*

Arab ܛܝܝܐ *ṭayyāyā*

Arabian (horse) ܐܪܒܝܩܘ *arābiqo*

Aramaic (in Aramaic) ܐܪܡܐܝܬ *ārāmā'it*

arc ܩܫܬܐ *qeštā* pl *–ē/-ātā*

archangel *rêš-malakē* (see "head")

arise (verb) ܩܡ *qām*; ܩܘܡ *qām/nqum*

arm ܕܪܥܐ *drā'ā* (f)

aroma ܒܣܡܐ *besmā*

aromatic spice ܗܝܪܘܡܐ *hêrōmā*

around about *l-appay* (see "countenance")

arrive (verb) ܡܛܐ *mṭā/nemṭē* Pa *maṭṭI* *l-* to arrive at

arrogant (to be arrogant) Eshtaph *ešta^{c}li* (see "exalt," "raise"); arrogant ܡܪܚ *marrāḥ*

arrow ܓܐܪܐ *gêrā*

article ܥܠܬܐ *^{c}elltā* pl ܥܠ̈ܠܬܐ *^{c}ellātā*

as (conj) ܟܕ *kad*

ascension ܣܘܠܩܐ *sulāqā*; ܡܣܣܩܬܐ *massaqtā*

ashamed (verb) ܒܗܬ *bhet/nebhat*

aside from ܣܛܪ *sṭar men*

ask (verb) ܫܐܠ *šel/nešal* ; Pa *ša''el l-* to ask questions of

ass ܚܡܪܐ *ḥmārā*

assembly ܟܢܘܫܬܐ *knutšā*; ܥܕܬܐ *^{c}êdtā*; assembly hall ܒܝܬܘܥܕܐ *bēt-wa'dā*

assent (verb) ܕܢܐ Ethpe *etdni*

assiduous ܚܦܝܛ *ḥpiṭ*; earnestly *ḥpiṭā'it*

assistance (to be of assistance) (verb) ܥܕܪ *^{c}dar/ne^{c}dar*

astonished ܕܡܪ Ethpe *etdammar*; ܬܡܝܗ *tammih*; ܬܡܗ *tmah/netmah*; astonishment ܬܡܗܐ *temhā*; ܬܗܪܐ *tahrā* and *tehrā*

astonishing ܬܡܝܗ *tammih*

astray (to go astray) (verb) ܛܥܐ *ṭ'ā/neṭ'ē*; *ṭ'ē/ṭa'yā*

at ܒ *b(a)-*; at (time) ܒ *b(a)-*; at hand (to be at hand) Ethpa *eṭṭayyab* (see "prepare"); at once ܫܠܝܐ *šelyā, men šelyā, men-šel(y)*; at such time as ܡܐ ܕ *mā d-*; at the same time ܗܝܕܝܢ *haydēn*

attack (verb) ܦܓܥ *pga^{c}/nepga^{c}*

attention ܥܝܪܘܬܐ *^{c}irutā*

attire ܐܣܟܝܡܐ *eskêmā*

audacious, bold ܠܒܝܒ *lbib*

Augustus ܐܓܘܣܛܘܣ *āgusṭos*

author ܡܟܬܒܢܐ *maktbānā*

authoritative, in authority ܡܫܠܛ *mšallaṭ*

authority (to put in authority) (verb) ܫܠܛ Pa *šalleṭ*

aware ܪܓܝܫ *rgiš*

baby ܥܘܠܐ *^{c}wellā*

Babylon ܒܒܠ *bābel*

backslide (verb) ܩܪܨܐ *qarṣā*

bad ܒܝܫ *biš*

Baidu Khan, Ilkhan ruler, AD 1295 ܒܝܕܘ *baydu*

Baju (pr n) ܒܐܓܘ *bāju*

band ܓܘܕܐ *gudā*

bank ܣܦܪܐ *spārā*

banquet ܡܫܬܝܐ *maštyā* ; ܫܪܘܬܐ *šārutā*; ܡܫܬܘܬܐ *meštutā* pl –*twātā*; banquet hall ܒܝܬܡܫܬܘܬܐ *bēt-meštutā*

Baptist (the) ܡܥܡܕܢܐ *maʿmmdānā*

baptize (verb) ܥܡܕ Aph *aʿmed*

bar ܡܘܟܠܐ *moklā* μοχλός

Barbara ܒܪܒܪܐ *barbārā*

barren woman ܥܩܪܬܐ *ʿqartā*

bath ܒܠܢܝ *balanay* (f); bathe (verb) ܣܚܐ *sḥā/nesḥē*; bathing ܡܣܚܘܬܐ *masḥutā*

battle (to do battle with) Aph *aqreb ʿam* (see "approach," "draw near to"); battle ܩܪܒܐ *qrābā*; battlement ܝܥܝܬܐ *yāʿitā* pl *yāʿyātā*

be (to be) (verb) ܗܘܐ *hwā/nehwē*

bear (verb) ܝܠܕ *iled/nêlad*; bearing ܫܩܝܠ *šqil*

beat (verb) ܚܒܛ *ḥbaṭ/neḥboṭ*; ܢܓܕ Pa *negdā* ; Pa *ḥabbeṭ* to keep on beating

beat against (verb) ܛܪܐ Ethpa *eṭṭarri*

beauty ܫܘܦܪܐ *šuprā*; beautiful ܫܦܝܪ *šappir*; beatified ܛܘܒܢ *ṭubān*

because *ʿal d-* (see "over")

become aware of (verb) ܪܓܫ Aph *argeš*

bed ܥܪܣܐ *ʿarsā*

Beelzebub ܒܥܠܙܒܘܒ *b'elzbob*

beetle ܚܒܫܘܫܐ *ḥabšušā* pl –*šyātā*

befall ܡܛܐ *mṭā/nemṭē*; *mṭāy* it fell his lot (*d-* to do something)

before ܩܘܒܠ *qubal, l-qubal*; ܩܕܡ *qdām* (+ pron encl II); ܠܘܩܕܡ *luqdam*

beget (verb) ܝܠܕ *iled/nêlad*

begin (verb) Pa *šarri* to begin (with *l-* + inf or with impf or part) (see "stop," "camp"); beginning (in the beginning) ܒܪܫܝܬ *b-rāšit*; beginning ܫܘܪܝܐ *šurāyā*

behind ܒܣܬܪ *bestar* (pron encl I)

behold ܗܐ *hā*

Beit-Jubrin (pr n) ܒܝܬܓܘܒܪܝܢ *bēt-gubrin*

Bel, supreme god of the Babylonians ܒܝܠ *bêl*

believe in (verb) ܗܝܡܢ *haymen/nhaymen b-*

belly ܟܪܣܐ *karsā* (abs/const *kres*)

belonging to ܕܝܠ *dil* (+ pron encl I); *dilānāy l-*

beloved ܚܒܝܒ *ḥabbib*

below ܬܚܬ *taḥt, l-taḥt*; ܬܚܝܬ *tḥēt*

belt ܩܡܪܐ *qamrā/qmārā*

bequeathe to (verb) Aph *awret* (see "inherit")

beside *ʿal-yad* (see "over"); *ṣêd* (+ pron encl II; also spelled ܨܝܕ); ܥܠܝܕ *ʿalyad*

besides ܣܛܪ *sṭar men*

Beth Awida ܒܝܬܥܘܝܕܐ *bēt-'widā*

Beth Sahray (pr n) ܒܝܬܣܚܪ̈ܝܐ *bēt-saḥrāyē*

Beth T'vara ܒܝܬܬܒܪܐ *bēt-tbārā*

Bethesda ܒܝܬܚܣܕܐ *bēt-ḥesdā*

Bethlehem ܒܝܬܠܚܡ *bēt-lḥem*

betray (verb) Aph *ašlem* (see "finished," follow")

betrothed ܡܟܝܪ *mkir*

between ܒܝܢ *bayn* (+ pron encl II); ܒܝܢܬ *baynāt* (+ pron encl I)

beware of (verb) Ethpa *ezdahhar b-* to beware of, watch over (see "warn against")

big ܪܒ *rabb* pl *rawrbin*;

bind (verb) ܦܟܪ *pkar/nepkor*; ܐܣܪ *esar/nesor*

bird ܦܪܚܬܐ *pāraḥtā* pl *pārḥātā*

birth ܡܘܠܕܐ *mawlādā*

bitter ܡܪܝܪ *marrir*; bitterness ܡܪܪܐ *mrārā*; *ekal* ~ to be galled

black ܐܘܟܡ *ukām*

blame ܥܕܠܝܐ *ʿedlāyā*

blameless *dlāʿ edlāy* (see "blame")

blemish ܡܘܡܐ *mumā*; *mawmē* see ܡܐ

bless (verb) ܒܪܟ Pa *barrek* to bless; Ethpa *etbarrak* to be blessed; blessed ܒܪܝܟ *brik*; ܛܘܒܢ *.tubān*; blessing ܒܘܪܟܬܐ *burktā*

blind (verb) Pa *ʿawwar* (see "wake," "watch"); blind ܣܡܝܐ *smē/samyā*;

blood (noun) ܕܡܐ *dmā* (abs *dem*)

blow (verb) ܢܫܒ *nšab/neššob*

boat ܣܦܝܬܐ *spittā* pl *–ē/spinātā*

body ܓܘܫܡܐ *gušmā* (abs *gšum*); ܦܓܪܐ *pagrā*

bodyguard ܢܛܪܚܨܐ *nāṭar-ḥaṣṣā*; *nāṭar-ḥaṣṣā* (see "rear")

bold ܠܒܝܒ

bolt ܡܘܟܠܐ *moklā* μοχλός

book ܟܬܒܐ *ktābā*

border ܬܚܘܡܐ *tḥumā*

bosom ܥܘܒܐ *ʿubbā*

bother (verb) ܗܪܪ Aph *ahhar*

bow ܩܫܬܐ *qeštā* pl *–ē/-ātā*

brain ܡܘܚܐ *muḥḥā*

breach ܬܘܪܥܬܐ *turʿtā*

bread ܠܚܡܐ *laḥmā*

breadth ܦܬܝܐ *ptāyā*

break (verb) ܬܒܪ *tbar/netbar*; Ethpe *ettbar* to be broken; break (bread) (verb) ܩܨܐ *qṣā/neqsē*; Ethpe *etqṣI* to be broken; break through (verb) ܬܪܥ *traʿ/netroʿ*

breast ܚܕܝܐ *ḥadyā*

bride ܟܠܬܐ *kalltā*

bridegroom ܚܬܢܐ *ḥatnā*

briefly ܦܣܝܩܬܐ *pāsiqātā, b-*

bright (to be bright) (verb) ܢܗܪ *nhar/nenhar*; brightness (of fire, e.g.) ܙܗܪܐ *zahrā* brilliant ܢܨܝܚ *naṣṣiḥ*

bring down (verb) ܬܚܬܝ Pali *taḥti*; Ethpali *ettaḥti* to be brought down, sent down, brought low

bring low (verb) ܬܚܬܝ Pali *taḥti*; Ethpali *ettaḥti* to be brought down, sent down, brought low

bring together (verb) Pa *kanneš* (see "gather")

broadcast (to be broadcast) (verb) Ethpe *etkrez* (see "proclaim," "announce," "preach"); Pa *sabbar* (see "think," "imagine")

brother ܐܚܐ *aḥā*

build (verb) ܒܢܐ *bnā/nebnē*; Ethpe *etbni* to be built

building ܒܢܝܢܐ *benyānā*

burden ܝܘܩܪܐ *yuqrā*; ܡܘܒܠܐ *mawblā* (abs/const *mawbal*, f); burdened ܫܩܝܠ *šqil* ; burdensome (to be burdensome) (verb) ܟܫܐ Ethpe *etkši*

burn (int) (verb) ܝܩܕ *iqed/nêqad*; Aph *awqed* to burn (trans); ܚܒܒ *ḥab/neḥḥob*; ܚܪܟ *ḥrak/neḥrok*; Ethpe *etḥrek* to be burned, singed

burning coal ܓܡܘܪܬܐ *gmurtā*

bury (verb) ܩܒܪ *qbar/neqbor*

but ܓܝܪ *gēr* (postpositive); ܐܠܐ *ellā;* for *en lā* if…not

buy (verb) ܙܒܢ *zban/nezben* Pa *zabben* to sell

by ܝܕ *yad*, *b-yad*; by means of (see *idā*) ܝܕ *yad*, *b-yad*; by day ܐܝܡܡܐ *imāmā*

Caesar ܩܣܪ *qesar*

cage ܩܦܣܐ *qapsā*

Caiaphas ܩܝܦܐ *qaypā*

calculation ܡܚܫܒܬܐ *maḥšabtā*

caliph ܟܠܝܦܗ *kālipāh*

call (verb) ܩܪܐ *qrā/neqrē*; Ethpe *etqri* to be called, be read out; called (to be called) (verb) ܟܢܐ Ethpa *etkanni*

calm ܢܝܚܐ *nyāḥtā;* calm down (verb) ܒܗܠ Ethpe *etbhel*; calm, at rest ܢܝܚ *niḥ*; *niḥā'it* calmly

camel ܓܡܠܐ *gamlā*

camp (verb) ܫܪܐ *šrā/nešrē* (ʿ*al* at, near)

candle ܩܪܝܘܢܐ *qeryōnā*

carnelian ܣܪܕܝܘܢ *sardyon*

carry (verb) ܝܒܠ Aph *awbel*

carve (verb) ܓܠܦ *glap/neglop*; carving ܓܠܦܐ *glāpā*; ܓܠܝܦܐ *glipā*

cast (verb) Aph *armi* (see "cast down," "fallen," "prostrate")

cast down (verb) ܫܕܐ *šdā/nešdē*; ܪܡܐ *rmē/ramyā*; Aph *armi* to cast

cast out (verb) Aph *appez* (see "go forth")

cataract ܩܛܪܩܛ *qaṭaraqṭā*

catch fire (verb) ܝܩܕ *iqed/nêqad*; Aph *awqed* to burn (trans)

catholicos ܩܬܘܠܝܩܐ *qātoliqā*

cause ܥܠܬܐ ʿ*elltā* pl ܥܠ̈ܠܬܐ ʿ*ellātā*

cave ܡܥܪܬܐ *m*ʿ*arrtā*

cavity ܥܘܒܐ ʿ*ubbā*

cedar ܐܪܙܐ *arzā*

censure ܥܕܠܝܐ ʿedlāyā

census ܡܟܬܒܢܘܬܐ maktbānutā

centurion ܩܢܛܪܘܢܐ qenṭrōnā

chapter ܪܫܐ rêšā; ܩܦܠܐܘܢ qepāle'on pl ܩܦ̈ܠܐܐ qepāle'ā

cheerful ܦܨܝܚ pṣiḥ

Chesroës ܟܘܣܪܘ kosraw

chest ܚܕܝܐ ḥadyā

chick ܦܪܘܓܐ parrugā

chief priest ܪܒ ܟܗܢܐ rabb-kāhnē

child ܛܠܝܐ ṭalyā/ṭlitā pl ṭlāyē/ṭalyātā (abs ṭlē pl ṭleyn)

childhood ܛܠܝܘܬܐ ṭalyutā

choke (verb) ܚܢܩ ḥnaq/neḥnoq; Ethpe etḥneq to be drowned, choked

choose (verb) ܓܒܐ gbā/negbē ; chosen gbē/gabyā (see "choose")

Christian ܟܪܣܛܝܢܐ kresṭyānā

church ܟܢܘܫܬܐ knutšā; ܥܕܬܐ ʿêdtā

circumcised (to be circumcised) (verb) ܓܙܪ Ethpe etgzar

cistern ܐܘܙܢܐ uznā

citizens ܓܘ̈ܝܐ gawwāyē

city wall ܫܘܪܐ šurā

city ܡܕܝܢܬܐ mdittā pl mdinātā; men mdinā la-mdinā from city to city

clad ܥܛܝܦ ʿṭip

clarion ܫܝܦܘܪܐ šipōrā

Claudius ܩܠܘܕܝܘܣ qlawdios

clearly idi'ā'it (see "known," "evident")

close ܩܪܝܒ qarrib

closet ܬܘܢܐ tawwānā

clothe (verb) Aph albeš (see "wear," "put on"); Pa ʿaṭṭep to clothe (see "return"); Pa kassi to clother, cover over, hide ܟܣܐ ksā/neksē; clothed ܠܒܝܫ lbiš; ܥܛܝܦ ʿṭip; clothing ܠܒܘܫܐ lbušā; ܐܣܛܠܐ esṭlā (f)

cloud ܥܢܢܐ ʿnānā (f)

cock ܬܪܢܓܠܐ tarnāglā (abs tarnāgul) cock

cold (to get cold) (verb) ܩܪ qar/neqqar; cold ܩܪܝܪܘܬܐ qarrirutā; ܩܪܝܪ qarrir

collapse ܡܦܘܠܬܐ mappultā

collate (verb) ܦܚܡ Pa paḥḥem

come (verb) ܐܬܐ etā/nêtē; Aph ayti to bring, take, lead; come back (verb) ܦܢܐ pnā/nepnē; Aph apni to lead back; coming ܡܐܬܝܬܐ metitā

comely ܦܐܐ pē/ܦܝܐܐ; comely ܗܕܝܪ hdir; comeliness hdirutā

comfort ܢܝܚܬܐ nyāḥtā; comfort (verb) ܚܝܠ Pa ḥayyel

command ܦܩܕ pqad/nepqod ; commander ܦܩܘܕܐ pāqodā; commandment ܦܘܩܕܢܐ puqdānā

commemoration ܥܘܗܕܢܐ ʿuhdānā

commerce ܬܓܘܪܬܐ tgurtā

commit adultery with (verb) ܙܢܐ znā/neznē b-committed (to be committed) (verb) ܓܥܠ Ethpe *etg'el* (*l-* to)

common people *daqdqē* (see "small")

community ܐܘܡܬܐ *ummtā*

companion ܚܒܪܐ *ḥabrā*

company ܓܘܕܐ *gudā*; ܚܝܠܘܬܐ *ḥaylutā* pl – *lawwātā*

compare (verb) ܦܚܡ Pa *paḥḥem*

compassion ܡܪܚܡܢܘܬܐ *mraḥḥmānutā*

compel (verb) ܐܠܨ *elaṣ/neloṣ*; ܥܨܐ *ᶜṣā/neᶜṣē*

complete (verb) Shaph *šamli* (see "full")

compose (verb) ܙܩܪ *zqar/nezqor*

compulsion ܩܛܝܪܐ *qṭirā*

conceal (verb) ܛܫܐ Pa *ṭašši*; (see "hide")

conceive (child) (verb) ܒܛܢ *bṭen/nebṭan*; conception ܒܛܢܐ *baṭnā*; to become pregnant *qabbel baṭnā*

concerning ܡܛܠ *meṭṭul* ; *meṭṭul d-* for, because; ܡܛܘܠ variant spelling of *meṭṭul*; ܡܛܠܬ *meṭṭlāt* – form of *meṭṭul* when followed by enclitic pronouns II

condemn (to condemn) (verb) Pa *ḥayyeb* (see "succumb," "conquered")

confession ܬܘܕܝܬܐ *tawditā*; confess (verb) ܝܕܐ Aph *awdi*

confirm (verb) Aph *aššar* (see "fix firmly"); ܚܝܠ Pa *ḥayyel*

confused (verb) ܒܗܬ *bhet/nebhat*

conquer (verb) ܙܟܐ *zkā/nezkē*; to be conquered ܚܒ *ḥāb/nḥub*

consider (verb) ܒܝܢ Ethpa *etbayyan*

constantly ܟܠܫܥ *kollšāᶜ*; ܐܡܝܢܐܝܬ *aminā'it*

constituted (to be constituted) (verb) Ethpa *ettaqqan* (see "right," "get ready," "prepare")

contemptible ܫܝܛ *šiṭ*

contest ܬܟܬܘܫܐ *taktōšā*

contract (to make a contract) (verb) *qyāmā* (see "rise up," "arise"); contract (verb) ܩܝܡܐ *qyāmā*; *aqim* ~ to make a contract

conversation ܥܢܝܢܐ *ᶜenyānā*

convert (verb) ܗܦܟ Pa *happek*; Ethpa *ethappak* to be converted

convince (verb) ܦܝܣ Aph *apis* (see "persuade")

cool ܩܪܝܪ *qarrir*; coolness ܩܪܝܪܘܬܐ *qarrirutā*

copy ܦܚܡܐ *peḥmā*

corpse ܫܠܕܐ *šladdā*

correct ܬܪܝܨ *triṣ*; ܚܠܝܡ *ḥlim*

couch ܥܪܣܐ *ᶜarsā*

counsel (verb) ܡܠܟ *mlak/nemlok*; Ethpe *etmlek b-* to be advised by

count (verb) ܚܫܒ *ḥšab/neḥšob*

countenance ܐܦܐ *appē* (pl only)

country ܐܬܪܐ *atrā* pl *–rē/-rawwātā*

course ܡܪܕܝܬܐ *marditā*

court *traᶜ –malkutā* (see "gate," "doorway")

courtyard ܕܪܬܐ *dārtā*

cover (verb); Pa *kassi* to clother, cover over, hide ܟܣܐ *ksā/neksē*

cover over Pa *kassi* ܟܣܐ *ksā/neksē*

coward(ly) ܫܦܠ *špal* and *špel/šaplā*

craft ܐܘܡܢܘܬܐ *umānutā*

craftsman ܐܘܡܢܐ *umānā*

create (verb) ܒܪܐ *brā/nebrē*; Ethpe *etbri* to be created, come into existence

creature ܒܪܝܬܐ *britā* pl *brayyā/beryātā*

crippled ܚܓܝܪ *ḥgir*

cross (verb)(*ᶜal*) ܥܒܪ *ᶜbar/neᶜbar*; cross ܨܠܝܒܐ *ṣlibā*; ܙܩܝܦܐ *zqipā*

crossing ܡܥܒܪܬܐ *maᶜbartā*

crowd (verb) ܚܒܨ *ḥbaṣ/neḥboṣ*; crowd ܟܢܫܐ *kenšā*

crown (verb) ܟܠܠ Pa *kallel*; crown ܬܓܐ *tāgā*; ܟܠܝܠܐ *klilā*

crucify (verb) ܨܠܒ *ṣlab/neṣlob* ; Ethpe *eṣṭleb* to be crucified; ܙܩܦ *zqap/nezqop* ; Ethpe *ezdqep* to be crucified; crucified ܙܩܝܦܐ *zqipā*; crucifier ܙܩܘܦܐ *zāqōpā*; crucifixion ܨܠܝܒܘܬܐ *ṣlibutā*

cry out ܝܠܠ Aph *aylel*

cry (verb) ܒܟܐ *bkā/nebkē*; ܝܠܠܬܐ *illtā* pl *yallātā*

crystal ܩܪܘܣܛܠܘܣ *qrosṭelos*

cube ܩܘܦܣܐ *qupsā*

cultivation ܬܘܩܢܐ *tuqānā*; ܫܝܢܐ *šaynā*

cunning ܨܢܝܥܘܬܐ *ṣniᶜutā*

cure (verb) ܚܠܡ Aph *aḥlem*

cure ܐܣܝܘܬܐ *āsyutā* (pl)

curse (verb) ܠܛ *lāṭ/nluṭ*

custom ܥܝܕܐ *ᶜyādā*

cut off (verb) ܦܣܩ *psaw/nepsoq*

Cyrenius ܩܘܪܝܢܘܣ *qewrinos*

Cyrus ܟܘܪܫ *kureš*

Daissan (river) ܕܝܨܢ *dayṣān*

Dalason (pr n) ܕܠܣܘܢ *dālāson*

damage ܚܘܣܪܢܐ *ḥusrānā*; ܣܘܪܚܢܐ *surḥānā*

Darius ܕܪܝܘܫ *daryuš*

dark (to grow dark; verb) ܚܫܟ *ḥeškā/neḥšak* (used impersonally in 3rd fem sing); dark ܥܡܘܛ *ᶜammuṭ*; darkness ܚܫܟܐ *ḥeškā*; ܚܫܘܟܐ *ḥeššōkā*

Darnus (pr n) ܕܪܢܘܣ *darnus*

dash (verb) ܛܪܐ Ethpa *eṭṭarri*

daughter ܒܪܬܐ *bartā* (constr *bat-*) pl ܒܢܬܐ *bnātā*; daughters ܒܢܬܐ *bnātā*

David ܕܘܝܕ *dāwid*

Dawitdar (pr n) ܕܘܝܬܕܐܪ *dāwitdār*

day ܝܘܡܐ *yawmā* pl *–ē/-ātā* (abs/constr *yōm*)

deacon ܡܫܡܫܢܐ *mšammšānā*

dead ܡܝܬ *mit*; death ܡܘܬܐ *mawtā*

deaf *ḥreš/ḥaršā* (see "silent")

debt ܚܘܒܬܐ *ḥawbtā*

deceitful ܕܓܠܐ *daggāl*

decoration ܨܒܬܐ *ṣebtā* pl –*tē*

deed ܣܘܥܪܢܐ *suʿrānā*; deeds of renown ܓܒܪܘܬܐ *gabrutā* pl –*rwātā*

deep ܥܡܝܩ *ʿammiq*

delay ܐܘܚܪ Aph *awḥar*; Eshtaph, *eštawḥar* ; ܬܘܚܪܬܐ *tawḥartā*; delaying ܡܚܝܪ *mḥir* (Aph act part, from confusion between ܚܘܪ and ܐܘܚܪ q.v.)

delight ܪܓܝܓ *rgig*

deliver (verb) ܦܨܐ Pa *paṣṣi*

deluge (verb) ܛܘܦ Aph *aṭip*

demand (verb) ܫܐܠ *šel/nešal*

demon ܒܪܐܓܪܐ *bar-eggārā* pl *bar-eggārē*; ܫܐܕܐ *šêdā*

deny (verb) ܟܦܪ *kpar/nekpor b-*

depart (verb) ܫܢܐ Pa *šanni*; ܦܪܩ *praq/neproz*

depict (verb) ܨܘܪ *ṣār/nṣur* (pass part ܨܝܪ *ṣir*)

depth ܥܘܡܩܐ *ʿumqā*; ܥܡܝܩܘܬܐ *ʿammiqutā*

deptrived (to be deprived) ܣܦܩ Ethpa *estappaq*

descend (verb) ܢܚܬ *nḥet/neḥḥat* ; Aph *aḥḥet* to send/bring down

desiccated ܡܝܒܫ *myabbaš*

design ܪܘܫܡܐ *rušmā*

desire (verb) ܬܒܥ *tbaʿ/netbaʿ*

desolate ܚܪܒ *ḥreb/ḥarbā*

despise (verb) ܒܣܐ *bsā/nebsē* (*b-* or *'al*)

detain ܥܟܪ Pa *ʿakkar*

devil ܕܝܘܐ *daywā*; ܫܐܕܐ *šêdā*

Devil, the ܐܟܠܩܪܨܐ *ākelqarṣā*

die (noun) ܩܘܦܣܐ *qupsā*

die (verb) ܡܘܬ *mit/nmut* ; Aph *amit* to put to death, cause to die

difficult ܥܛܠ *ʿṭel/ʿaṭlā*; ܥܣܩ *ʿseq/ʿasqā*; *ʿasqā'it* with difficulty; difficulty ܥܣܩܘܬܐ *ʿasqutā*; difficult for (to be difficult for) (verb) ܩܫܐ Ethpa *etqašši ʿal*

digestion ܦܫܪܐ *pšārā*

dinar ܕܝܢܪܐ *dênārā*

Dioscurus ܕܝܘܣܩܘܪܘܣ *diosquros*

direction ܦܢܝܬܐ *pnitā*

direct-object marker (non-obligatory) ܠ *l(a)*

dirt ܕܚܝܚܝܚܐ *daḥḥiḥā*

discharge ܣܘܦܩܐ *supāqā*

disciple ܬܠܡܝܕܐ *talmidā*; to make a disciple (trs verb) ܬܠܡܕ *talmed*; Ethpal *ettalmad* to become a disciple

discovery ܫܟܚܬܐ *škāḥtā*

disease ܚܫܐ *ḥaššā*; ܟܘܪܗܢܐ *kurhānā*; ܢܟܝܢܐ *nekyānā*

dismount (verb) ܢܚܬ *nḥet/neḥḥat*

disown (verb) ܢܟܪ Pali *nakri*

dispatch (verb) ܫܠܚ *šlaḥ/nešlaḥ*

dispute with (verb) ܕܪܫ *draš/nedroš*

disregard (verb) ܗܡܐ Aph *ahmi men*

distant ܦܪܝܩ *parriq*; ܪܚܝܩ *raḥḥiq*; distance ܪܘܚܩܐ *ruḥqā*; *men ruḥqā* from/at a distance

distress ܥܩܬܐ *ᶜāqtā*; ܟܪܝܘܬܐ *karyutā*; distress (verb) ܥܝܩ Aph *aᶜiq*; Ettaph *ettᶜiq* to be distressed

disturbed (verb) ܫܓܫ Ethpe *eštgeš*

divide (verb) ܦܪܫ Pa *parreš*; ܦܠܓ Pa *palleg*; Ethpa *etpallag* to be divided

divinity ܐܠܗܘܬܐ *alāhutā*

division ܦܠܓܐ *pelgā*; ܦܘܪܫܢܐ *puršānā*; ܦܠܓܘܬܐ *pelgutā*

do (verb) ܥܒܕ *ᶜbad/neᶜbed*; ܣܥܪ *sᶜar/nesᶜar*; Ethpe *estᶜar* to be done

doctrine ܝܘܠܦܢܐ *yulpānā*; ܡܠܦܢܘܬܐ *mallpānutā*

doleful ܚܢܝܓ *ḥnig*

dominion ܐܘܚܕܢܐ *uḥdānā*; dominion (to gain dominion over) (verb) Ethpa *eštallaṭ b-* (see "authority")

donkey ܚܡܪܐ *ḥmārā*

doorway ܬܪܥܐ *tarᶜā* (abs *traᶜ*)

doubtless ܟܒܪ *kbar*

drag (verb) ܓܪܪ *gar/neggor*

draught ܡܫܬܝܐ *meštyā*

draw (verb) ܫܡܛ *šmaṭ/nešmoṭ*; ܪܫܡ *ršam/neršom*

draw near to (verb) ܩܪܒ *qreb/neqrab l-*; Pa *qarreb* to put near, bring near

draw out (verb) ܫܠܐ *šlā/nešlē*

drawing ܪܘܫܡܐ *rušmā*

dried out ܡܝܒܫ *myabbaš*

drink ܡܫܬܝܐ *meštyā*; drink (verb) ܐܫܬܝ *ešti/neštē*; ܐܫܬܐ *ešti/neštē*; give to drink (verb) ܫܩܐ Aph *ašqi*

drive out (verb) ܪܕܦ *rdap/nerdop*

drown (trs) (verb) ܚܢܩ *ḥnaq/neḥnoq*; Ethpe *etḥneq* to be drowned, choked

drug *sammā* pl *sammānē* (see "blind")

dry (trs verb) ܝܒܫ Pa *yabbeš*; dry land ܝܒܫܐ *yabšā*

dumb *ḥreš/ḥaršā* (see "silent")

dust ܕܚܝܚܐ *daḥḥiḥā*

dwell (verb) ܝܬܒ *iteb/netteb*; *yāteb-waʿdā* page; ܥܡܪ *ᶜmar/neᶜmar*; dwell (to make dwell) (verb) Aph *ašri* (see "stop," "camp"); dwelling ܡܥܡܪܐ *maᶜmrā*

eagle ܢܫܪܐ *nešrā*

ear ܐܕܢܐ *ednā* (f)

early morning ܫܦܪܐ *šaprā*

earnest ܚܦܝܛ *ḥpiṭ*; earnestly *ḥpiṭā'it*

earth ܐܪܥܐ *arʿā* (abs *araʿ*) pl *arʿē/arʿawwātā*

easily *pšiqā'it* (see "easy")

east ܡܕܢܚܐ *madnḥā* (abs/constr *madnaḥ*)

easy ܕܠܝܠ *dlil*; ܦܫܝܩ *pšiq*

eat (to eat) (verb) ܐܟܠ *ekal/nekol*; ܠܥܣ *lʿes/nelʿas*

Eden ܥܕܢ *ʿden*

Edessa ܐܘܪܗܝ *urhāy*

edge ܣܦܪܐ *spārā*

edifice ܒܢܝܢܐ *benyānā*

eight ܬܡܢܐ *tmānē* (f)/*tmānyā* (m)

Either… or ܐܘ…ܐܘ *aw… aw*

elder ܩܫܝܫ *qaššiš*

elephant ܦܝܠܐ *pilā*

Eleutherapolis ܐܠܘܬܪܦܘܠܝܣ *elewṯerāpolis*

Elijah ܐܠܝܐ *eliyā*

Elizabeth ܐܠܝܫܒܥ *elišbaʿ*

emanate (verb) ܪܕܐ *rdā/nerdē*

embassy ܐܝܙܓܕܘܬܐ *izgaddutā*

emerald ܙܡܪܓܕܐ *zmargdā*

emir ܐܡܝܪܐ *amirā*

emptying ܣܘܦܩܐ *supāqā*

encounter ܐܘܪܥܐ *urʿā* (abs *uraʿ*);

encounter(verb) ܐܪܥ *eraʿ/neroʿ*

encouragement ܠܘܒܒܐ *lubābā*

end ܫܘܠܡܐ *šulāmā*; *nsab* ~ to come to an end; ܣܘܦܐ *sawpā* (abs *sōp*); end (to be at an end) (verb) Eshtaph *eštamli* (see "full"); end (in the end) ܚܪܬܐ *ḥartā, b-*

enemy ܒܥܠܕܒܒܐ *b'eldbābā*

engraving ܓܠܦܐ *glāpā*

enrolled ܡܟܬܒܢܘܬܐ *maktbānutā*

enter (verb) ܥܠ *ʿal/neʿʿol*; Aph *aʿʿel* to have enter, allow in

entirely ܓܡܪ *gmār, la-*

entrance ܡܥܠܢܐ *maʿlānā*

entrusted (verb) ܓܥܠ Ethpe *etg'el* (*l-* to)

envoy ܐܝܙܓܕܐ *izgaddā*

Ephraem ܐܦܪܝܡ *aprim*

epistle ܐܓܪܬܐ *eggartā*

equate (verb) ܫܘܐ Aph *ašwi*

erase (verb) ܓܪܪ *gar/neggor*

errand ܣܘܥܪܢܐ *suʿrānā*

escape ܦܘܠܛܐ *pulāṭā*; to escape ܦܠܛ *plaṭ/neplaṭ*

especially *yattirā'it* (see "more than")

espoused ܡܟܝܪ *mkir*

established (to be established) (verb) Ethpa *etqayyam* to be established (see "rise up," "arise")

estate ܐܓܘܪܣܐ *agorsā*

estranged (to be estranged) (verb) Ethpali *etnakri* (see "disown")

eternal *dalʿālam* (see "world")

Eustargis (pr n) ܐܘܣܛܪܓܝܣ *ewsṭārgis*

evangelize (verb) Pa *sabbar* (see "think," "imagine")

Eve ܚܘܐ *ḥawwā*

even if ܐܦܢ *āp en*

evening ܪܡܫܐ *ramšā*

event (see "word")

every (+ abs) ܟܠ *koll*; every moment ܟܠܥܕܢ *kollʿeddān*

everybody ܟܠܢܫ *kollnāš*

everything ܟܠܡܕܡ

evident ܝܕܝܥܐ *idiʿ*; *idiʿāʾit* clearly, evident

evil ܒܝܫ *biš*; ܒܝܫܘܬܐ *bišutā*

evil spirit ܕܝܘܐ *daywā*

evildoer ܚܝܒܐ *ḥayyābā*

exact (verb) ܬܒܥ *tbaʿ/netbaʿ*

exalt (verb) ܥܠܐ Pa *ʿalli*; Shaph *šaʿli* to exalt; exalted ܥܠܝ *ʿellāy*

excellent ܡܝܬܪ *myattar*

excelling ܡܝܬܪ *myattar*

except that ܐܠܐ ܐܢ *ellā en*

exercise ܕܘܪܫܐ *durāšā*; exercise (verb) Ethpa *etdarraš* (see "dispute with")

exertion ܡܥܒܕܢܘܬܐ *maʿbdānutā*

exhausted (to become exhausted) (verb) ܚܝܠ Aph *awḥel*

existing ܩܝܡ *qayyām*

expect (verb) ܣܟܐ Pa *sakki*; expectation ܣܒܪܐ *sabrā*

expedient ܦܩܚ *paqqāḥ*

expense ܢܦܩܬܐ *nepqtā* & *npaqtā*

expert ܝܕܘܥܐ *yādoʿā*

exploit ܢܨܚܢܐ *neṣḥānā*

exult (verb) ܕܘܨ *dāṣ/nduṣ*

eye ܥܝܢܐ *ʿaynā* (f); eye (of a needle) ܚܪܘܪܐ *ḥrōrā*

face ܐܦܐ *appē* (pl only); ܦܪܨܘܦܐ *parṣōpā*

fair ܦܐܐ *pē*/ܦܐܝܐ

faith ܗܝܡܢܘܬܐ *haymānutā*

faithful ܫܪܝܪ *šarrir*; faithful to ܬܟܝܠ *tkil ʿal*; *tkilāʾit* faithfully

fall ill (verb) ܟܪܗ Ethpe *etkrah*

fall ܡܦܘܠܬܐ *mappultā*; to fall ܢܦܠ *npal/neppel*; Aph *appel* to make fall; fallen (verb) ܪܡܐ *rmē/ramyā*; Aph *armi* to cast, lay down, lay before, offer

false ܕܓܠܐ *daggāl*

falsehood ܫܘܩܪܐ *šuqrā*

fame ܛܒܐ *ṭebbā*

far off ܡܒܥܕ *mabʿad*

far ܪܚܝܩ *raḥḥiq*

farm ܐܓܘܪܣܐ *agorsā*

fashion (verb) ܓܒܠ *gbal/negbol*

fast ܨܘܡܐ *ṣawmā*

fasten (verb) ܩܒܥ *qbaʿ/neqboʿ*; Ethpe *etqbaʿ* to be set up (cross, e.g.); ܐܣܪ *esar/nesor*

fasting ܨܘܡܐ *ṣawmā*

father ܐܒܐ *abā* pl *abāhē/abāhātā*

fatigued *lē* pl *leyn* (emph ܠܐܝܐ *layā* pl ܠܐܝ̈ܐ *layyā*) (see "toil")

favor ܪܚܡܐ *raḥmā*; ܛܝܒܘܬܐ *ṭaybutā*

fear ܕܚܠܬܐ *deḥltā*; ܪܬܝܬܐ *rtêtā*; to make fear ܩܢܛ Aph *aqneṭ*

fearful ܕܚܝܠ *daḥḥil*

feast ܫܪܘܬܐ *šārutā*; ܡܫܬܘܬܐ *meštutā* pl *–twātā*

feeble (to grow feeble) (verb) ܡܚܠ Ethpa *etmaḥḥal*

feel (verb) ܪܓܫ Aph *argeš*; ܡܘܫ *māš/nmuš*

feeling ܪܓܫܬܐ *rgeštā*

few *dallil* (see "easy")

fierce ܩܫܐ *qšē/qašyā*

fill (see "full")

finally ܚܪܬܐ *ḥartā, b-*

find fault with (verb) ܥܕܠ *^{c}dal/ne^{c}dol*

find out (verb) ܒܨܐ *baṣṣi* Pa

fine for negligence ܒܣܝܢܐ *besyānā*

finger ܨܒܥܐ *ṣeb^{c}ā*

finished (to be finished) (verb) Eshtaph *eštamli* (see "full"); ܬܠܩ Ethpa *eṭṭallaqu*; ܫܠܡ *šlem/nešlam*; Pa *šallem* to finish (trs), fulfill; Ethpa *eštallam* to be finished, fulfilled

fire ܢܘܪܐ *nurā* (f)

firm ground ܫܘܥܐ *šō^{c}ā*

first (to do first) (verb) ܩܕܡ *qdam/neqdam* ; Pa *qaddem* to precede, go before

first ܩܕܡܝ *qadmāy*; first of all ܠܘܩܕܡ *luqdam*; first-born ܒܘܟܪ *bukar*; firstly ܩܕܡܐܝܬ *qadmā'it*

fit ܙܕܩ *zādeq*

five ܚܡܫ *ḥammeš* (f), *ḥammšā* (m)

fix (verb) ܩܒܥ *qba^{c}/neqbo^{c}* ; Ethpe *etqba^{c}* to be set up (cross, e.g.)

fix firmly (verb) ܫܪܪ Pa *šarrar*

flame up (verb) Ethpal *etnabraš* (see "kindle")

flaw ܡܘܡܐ *mumā*; *mawmē* see ܡܘܡܐ

flee (verb) ܥܪܩ *^{c}raq/ne^{c}roq*

flock ܡܪܥܝܬܐ *mar^{c}itā* pl *-^{c}yātā*

flood ܪܓܠܬܐ *rgeltā*

fly (verb) ܦܪܚ *praḥ/nepraḥ*

follow (verb) ܠܘܐ *lwā/nelwē*; ܫܠܡ *šlem/nešlam*; ܪܕܦ *rdap/nerdop*; ܢܦܩ *npeq/neqqap*; follower ܫܠܡܐ *šālmā*

font ܐܘܙܢܐ *uznā*

food ܡܐܟܠܐ *meklā*; ܠܚܡܐ *laḥmā*

foolish ܣܟܠ *skal* and *skel/saklā*

foot ܪܓܠܐ *reglā* (f); ܦܪܣܬܐ *parstā*

footprint ܥܩܒܬܐ *^{c}eqbtā*

for ܐܟܡܢ *akman;* ܐܝܟ ܡܢ *ak man* like one who, like him who, as though; for (prep) ܠ *l(a)* ; for ܡܛܠ *meṭṭul* ; *meṭṭul d-* for, because; ܡܛܘܠ variant spelling of *meṭṭul*; for ܓܝܪ *gēr* (postpositive); ܡܛܠܬ *meṭṭlāt –*

form of *meṭṭul* when followed by enclitic pronouns II; ܐܝܢܘ *aynaw; aynā-(h)u* which is?; ܕܝܢ *dēn* (postpositive)

for all generations ܕܪ *dār: l-dār-dārin*

for ever and ever ܕܪ *dār: l-dār-dārin*

for that reason ܒܓܕܘܢ *bagdon*

for the sake of ܚܠܦ *ḥlāp* (+ pron enc II)

forbid (verb) ܟܠܐ *klā/neklē*

force ܥܨܐ *^{c}ṣā/ne^{c}ṣē*; ܩܛܝܪܐ *qṭirā*; *qṭrā'it* by force

ford ܡܥܒܪܬܐ *ma^{c}bartā*

fore- ܡܩܕܡܘܬ *mqaddmut*

fore ܩܕܡܝ *qadmāy*

foreigner ܐܟܣܢܝܐ *aksnāyā*

forever *l-^{c}ālam, l-^{c}ālam ^{c}ālmin* (see "world")

forget (verb) ܢܫܐ *nšā/neššē*; Ethpa *etnašši* to forget

forgetfulness ܡܬܢܫܝܢܘܬܐ *metnaššyānutā*

forgive (verb) ܫܒܩ *šbaq/nešboq*; Ethpe *eštbeq* to be forgiven (see "leave")

forgotten (to be forgotten) (verb) Ethpe *eṭṭ'i* (see "wander," "astray")

form (verb) ܓܒܠ *gbal/negbol*; ܙܩܪ *zqar/nezqor*

form ܕܡܘܬܐ *dmutā*

former ܩܕܡܝ *qadmāy*

fortune ܓܕܐ *gaddā*

foundation ܫܬܐܣܬܐ *šatestā* pl *šatesē* (f); ܬܪܡܝܬܐ *tarmyātā* (f pl)

fount ܡܥܝܢܐ *m^{c}inā* (f)

four ܐܪܒܥ *arba^c* (f), *arb^{c}ā* (m)

fourth ܪܒܝܥܝ *rbi^{c}āy*

fox ܬܥܠܐ *ta^{c}lā*

freeze (verb) ܓܠܕ Aph *agled*

Friday ܥܪܘܒܬܐ *^{c}rubtā*

friend ܪܚܡܐ *rāḥmā*; ܚܒܪܐ *ḥabrā*

from here ܡܟܐ *mekkā*

from ܡܢ *men*; *mān*

fruit ܦܐܪܐ *pêrā*

fulfill Pa *šallem*; Ethpa *eštallam* fulfilled (see "finished," "follow")

full (to be full) ܡܠܐ *mlā/nemlē*; *mlē/malyā* full; Pa *malli* to fill (trs); Ethpe *etmli* to be filled; Ethpa *etmalli* to be filled, fulfilled

fullness ܡܠܝܘܬܐ *malyutā*

function ܡܥܒܕܢܘܬܐ *ma^{c}bdānutā*

futile ܣܪܝܩ *sriq*

Gabriel ܓܒܪܝܐܠ *gabryêl*

gain dominion over (verb) Ethpa *eštallaṭ b-* (see "authority")

Galilean ܓܠܝܠܝܐ *glilāyā*

Galilee ܓܠܝܠܐ *glilā*

gall ܡܪܪܐ *mrārā*; *ekal* ~ to be galled

Gamaliel (pr n) ܓܡܠܝܐܠ *gamaliel*

garment ܠܒܘܫܐ *lbušā*; ܡܐܢܐ *mānā*

gate ܬܪܥܐ *tar^{c}ā* (abs *tra^c*)

gather (verb) Ethpa *etkannaš* to be gathered together ܟܢܫ *knaš/neknoš*

gaze at (verb) ܚܘܪ *ḥāar/nḥur l-*

Gedaliah (pr n) ܓܕܠܝܐ *gdalyā*

Gehenna ܓܗܢܐ *gehhannā*

generation ܫܪܒܬܐ *šarbtā*

gentle ܪܟܝܟ *rakkik*

Georgian ܐܝܒܪܝܐ *iberāyā*

Gerontius ܓܪܢܛܘܣ *geranṭos*

gesture ܪܡܙܐ *remzā*; to make gestures ܪܡܙ *rmaz/nermoz*; with gesture, by signs ܡܪܡܙ *mermaz*

get ready (verb) ܬܩܢ Pa *taqqen*

get ܩܒܠ Pa *qabbel*

gift ܡܘܗܒܬܐ *mawhabtā*; ܕܫܢܐ *dāšnā*

give (verb) ܝܗܒ *yab* (perf only; impf *nettel*); ܢܬܠ *nettel* (impf only)

give back (verb) (see "return")

give birth to (verb) ܝܠܕ *iled/nêlad*

giver ܝܗܘܒܐ *yāhōbā*

glad (to be glad) (verb) ܚܕܐ *ḥdi/neḥdē*

glad (to be glad) (verb) ܦܨܚ Ethpe *etpṣaḥ*

gladness ܚܕܘܬܐ *ḥadutā* (abs *ḥadwā*); ܪܘܙܐ *rwāzā*

glass ܙܓܘܓܝܬܐ *zgōgitā*

gloomy ܥܡܘܛ ^{c}*ammuṭ*; ܟܡܝܪ *kmir*

glory ܐܝܩܪܐ *iqārā*; ܫܘܒܚܐ *šubḥā* (abs *šbuḥ*); glorification ܬܫܒܘܚܬܐ *tešboḥtā*

go away ܦܪܩ *praq/neproz*

go back on (verb) ܗܦܟ *hpak/nehpok*; ~ *b-*

go before (verb) ܩܕܡ *qdam/neqdam* ; Pa *qaddem* to precede, go before

go down (verb) ܢܚܬ *nḥet/neḥḥat* ; Aph *aḥḥet* to send/bring down; (+^{c}*l*) to go against

go forth (verb) ܢܦܩ *npaq/neppoz*

go in (verb) ܥܠܠ ^{c}*al/ne*^{cc}*ol*

go on (to say, e.g.) ܝܣܦ Aph *awsep*

go out (light, lamp) (verb) ܕܥܟ *d'ek/ned'ak*

go up (verb) ܣܠܩ *sleq/nessaq*; have (someone) come/go up

go, to go ܐܙܠ *ezal/nêzal*

goat ܓܕܝܐ *gadyā* pl *gdayyā*

God ܐܠܗܐ *alāhā*

gold ܕܗܒܐ *dahb̲ā*

Golgotha ܓܓܘܠܬܐ *gāgultā*

good (thing, deed) ܛܒܬܐ *ṭābtā*

good news (to spread good news) (verb) Pa *sabbar* (see "think," "imagine")

good ܛܒ *ṭāb*

gospel ܟܪܘܙܘܬܐ *kārōzutā*

gout ܦܛܓܪܐ *peṭgārā*

governor ܗܓܡܘܢܐ *hegmōna*

governorship ܗܓܡܘܢܘܬܐ *hegmōnutā*

grace ܫܘܟܢܐ *šukānā*

grandee ܪܘܪܒܢܐ *rawrbānā*

grasp (verb) ܠܒܟ *lbak/nelbok*

gratitude *qubal-ṭaybutā* (see "before")

grave ܩܒܪܐ *qabrā*

great ܪܒ *rabb* pl *rawrbin*;

Greek ܝܘܢܝܐ *yawnāyā*

greetings ܫܠܡܐ *šlāmā*

grievous (to be grievous) (verb) ܩܫܐ Ethpa *etqašši* *ᶜal*

grow strong (verb) ܬܩܦ *tqep/netqap*

grow up (verb) ܪܒܐ *rbā* (*rbi*)/*nerbē*

guard ܢܛܘܪܐ *nāṭōrā*; ܡܛܪܬܐ *maṭṭartā*; *nṭar maṭṭartā* to keep watch; guard (verb) ܢܛܪ *nṭar/neṭṭar* ; Pa *naṭṭar* to keep under watch; Ethpe *etnṭar* to be kept

guardian ܡܕܒܪܢܐ *mdabbrānā*

guilt ܚܘܒܐ *ḥawbā*; to find guilty Pa *ḥayyeb* (see "succumb," "conquered")

habit ܥܝܕܐ *ᶜyādā*

hair ܣܥܪܐ *saᶜrā*; strand of hair ܡܢܐ *mennā*

half ܦܠܓܐ *pelgā*; ܦܠܓܘܬܐ *pelgutā*

hand ܐܝܕܐ *idā* (f, const *id-/yad-*, abs *yad*) pl *idē/idayyā*

hand over (verb) Aph *ašlem* (see "finished," follow")

handmill ܪܚܝܐ *raḥyā*

hang up ܬܠܐ *tlā/netlē*; Ethpe *ettli* to be hung

Hannan ܚܢܢ *ḥannān* (pr n)

happen (verb) ܓܕܫ *gdaš/negdaš* (see "cross," "transgress")

happy ܦܨܝܚ *pṣiḥ*

hard ܥܛܠ *ᶜṭel/ᶜaṭlā*; ܥܣܩ *ᶜseq/ᶜasqā*

harm ܣܘܪܚܢܐ *surḥānā*; to do harm to ܣܪܚ *sraḥ/nesroḥ b-*; ܢܟܐ Aph *akki*; Ettaph ܐܬܬܟܝ *ettakki* to be harmed

harp ܩܝܬܪܐ *qitārā*

haste ܣܘܪܗܒܐ *surhābā*

hasten (verb) ܣܪܗܒ *sarheb/nsarheb*

hastily *msarhbā'it* (see "hasten," "timorous")

hate (verb) ܣܢܐ *snā/nesnē*

hateful *snē/sanyā* (see "hate")

having (see "seize")

hawk ܒܙ *bāz*

he is ܗܘܝܘ *huyu* (for *hu-hu*)

he ܗܘ *hu, haw* (m sing) that

head ܪܫܐ *rêšā*

heading ܪܫܐ *rêšā*

heal (verb) Pa *dakki* to heal; Ethpa *etdakki* to be healed (see "pure"); ܐܣܐ Pa *assi/nassē,* Ethpa *etassi* to be healed; healer ܐܣܝܐ *āsyā*; healing ܐܣܝܘܬܐ *āsyutā* (pl)

health ܚܘܠܡܢܐ *ḥulmānā*

hear (verb) ܫܡܥ *šmaᶜ/nešmaᶜ*; Aph *ašmaᶜ* to make hear; Ethpe *eštmaᶜ* to be heard

heart ܠܒܐ *lebbā*

heat ܚܘܡܐ *ḥummā*

heaven ܫܡܝܐ *šmayyā* (pl)

heavenly body ܟܘܟܒܐ *kawkbā*

heavy sleep ܛܘܠܥܐ *ṭulā'ā*

heavy ܝܩܝܪ *yaqqir*

heed, pay heed to *ḥāar/nḥur b-* (see "look," "gaze at")

heel ܥܩܒܐ *ᶜeqbā* (f)

height ܪܘܡܐ *rawmā*; ܡܪܘܡܐ *mrawmā*

Heliopolis ܐܠܝܘܦܘܠܝܣ *êliopolis*

hell ܓܗܢܐ *gehhannā*

help ܥܘܕܪܢܐ *ʿudrānā*; to help ܥܕܪ *ʿdar/neʿdar*

hen ܬܪܢܓܘܠܬܐ *tarnāgultā*

hence ܡܟܐ *mekkā*

henceforth ܡܟܝܠ *mekkêl*

here ܗܪܟܐ *hārkā*; ܬܢܢ *tnan*

Herod ܗܪܘܕܣ *hêrōdes*

hesitate Eshtaph, *eštawḥar* (see "delay")

hidden from (to be hidden from) ܚܦܐ Ethpa *etḥappi ʿal*

hidden things ܡܛܫܝܬܐ *maṭšyātā*

hide (verb) ܛܫܐ Pa *ṭašši* ; Aph *aṭši* to store in a secret place; Ethpa *eṭṭašši* to hide oneself; Pa *kassi* ܟܣܐ *ksā/neksē*

high priest *rēš-kāhnē* (see "head")

high ܪܡ *rām* (for verbs see ܪܘܡ)

hind ܚܪܝ *ḥrāy*

hinder ܥܟܪ Pa *ʿakkar*

hire (to hire) (verb) ܐܓܪ *egar/negor*

hold (verb) ܠܒܟ *lbak/nelbok*

hold out (verb) ܘܫܛ Aph *awšeṭ*

hole in the ground ܚܘܠܢܐ *ḥulānā*

hole ܢܩܥܐ *neqʿā*

holy (to make holy) (verb) ܩܕܫ Pa *qaddeš*; Ethpa *etqaddaš* to be made holy, sacred

Holy Spirit ܩܘܕܫܐ *qudšā*, as in *ruḥā d-qudšā*

holy ܩܕܝܫ *qaddiš*

honor (verb) ܝܩܪ Pa *yaqqar*

honor ܐܝܩܪܐ *iqārā*; ܡܝܬܪܐ *myattrā*

honored ܝܩܝܪ *yaqqir*

hoof ܦܪܣܬܐ *parstā*

hope ܣܒܪܐ *sabrā*

horn ܩܪܢܐ *qarnā* pl *–ātā*

horoscope ܡܠܘܫܐ *malwāšā*

horse ܪܟܫܐ *rakšā* pl *rakšā*; ܣܘܣܝܐ *susāyā*

host ܚܝܠܘܬܐ *ḥaylutā* pl – *lawwātā*

hot ܫܚܝܢ *šaḥḥin*

hour ܫܥܬܐ *šāʿtā* pl *šāʿē* (abs *šāʿā* pl *šāʿin*)

house ܒܝܬܐ *baytā* pl *bāttē* (const sing *bēt-*)

household (adj) ܒܝܬܝܐ *baytāyā*

how many ܟܡܐ *kmā* (+ abs pl)

how much ܟܡܐ *kmā* (+ abs pl)

how ܟܡܐ *kmā* (+ abs pl); ܐܝܟܢܐ *aykannā; aykannā d-* those who; ܐܝܟܢ *aykan*

however ܓܝܪ *gēr* (postpositive); ܒܪܡ *bram*; ܕܝܢ *dēn* (postpositive)

howl ܝܠܠ Aph *aylel*

Hülägü ܗܘܠܐܟܘ *hulāku* Ilkhan, r. 1256-65

human ܒܪܢܫܐ *bar-nāšā*

humble ܡܟܝܟ *makkik*; to humble ܡܟܟ Pa *makkek*; Ethpa *etmakkak* to be humbled

Humiah (pr n) ܚܘܢܝܐ *ḥunyā*

humiliate (verb) ܡܟܟ Pa *makkek*; Ethpa *etmakkak* to be humbled

humility ܐܢܫܘܬܐ *nāšutā*

hunger (verb) *kpen/kapnā* hungry ܟܦܢ *kpen/nekpan*

hungry (see "hunger")

hurt (to hurt) (verb) ܣܪܚ *sraḥ/nesroḥ b-*

husband ܒܥܠܐ *ba'lā*; ܓܒܪܐ *gabrā*

hymn ܬܫܒܘܚܬܐ *tešboḥtā*

hypocritical (to be hypocritical) ܢܣܒ *nsab b-appē*

I ܐܢܐ *enā*

Iberian ܐܝܒܪܝܐ *iberāyā*

Ibn al-'Al-qami ܒܪ ܥܠܩܡܝ *bar'alqami* d. 1258, vizier to Musta'sim

Ibr Kurar (pr n) ܒܪ ܟܘܪܪ *bar kurār*

id est ܟܐܡܬ *kemat*

idle ܒܛܠ *baṭṭāl*; ܒܛܝܠ *bṭil*; *baṭṭitl* in vain, of no effect

idol ܦܬܟܪܐ *ptakrā*

if (contrafactual) ܐܠܘ *ellu*

if (possible condition) ܐܢ *en*

ill (to do ill to); treat ill ܥܘܠ Aph *a^c^wel b-*

ill ܚܘܒܐ *ḥawbā*; ܟܪܝܗ *krih*

illuminated ܢܗܝܪ *nahhir*

image ܨܠܡܐ *ṣalmā* (abs *ṣlem*); ܕܡܘܬܐ *dmutā*

imagination ܦܢܛܣܝܐ *panṭāsiā* φαντασία

imagine (verb) ܗܓܓ Ethpa *ethaggag*; ܣܒܪ *sbar/nesbar*

immediately ܡܚܕܐ *meḥdā*; *bāh b-šā^c^tā*, *bar šā^c^teh* (see "hour"); ܥܓܠ *^c^gal, ba-*

impious ܪܫܝܥ *rašši^c^*

impost ܬܒܥܬܐ *tba^c^tā*

imprinted (to be imprinted) (verb) Ethpe *eṭṭba'* (see "seal," "sink")

imprison (verb) ܚܒܫ *ḥbaš/neḥboš*

imprisonment ܚܒܘܫܝܐ *ḥbušyā*

in (place) ܒ *b(a)-*

in front of (+ pron encl I) ܩܘܒܠ *qubal*, *l-qubal*; ܩܕܡ *qdām* (+ pron encl II)

in mourning ܐܒܝܠ *abil*

in proportion to ܠܦܘܬ *lput*

in short ܦܣܝܩܬܐ *pāsiqātā, b-*

in the presence of (+ pron encl I) ܠܘܬ *lwāt*

inasmuch as *^c^al d-* (see "over"); *kmā d-* ܟܡܐ *kmā* (+ abs pl)

incense ܒܣܡܐ *besmā*

incline (verb) Ethpe *eṣtli* (see "pray")

increase (to increase) (verb) Ettaph *ettawsap* (see "add"); ܝܬܪ Pa *yattar*

indeed ܓܝܪ *gēr* (postpositive)

inflict pain (verb) ܫܢܩ Pa *šanneq*

inform (verb) Aph *awda‘* to inform (see "know")

inherit ܝܪܬ *iret/nêrat*; Aph *awret* to bequeathe to

inheritance ܝܪܬܘܬܐ *yārtutā*

injury ܣܘܪܚܢܐ *surḥānā*

inner room ܬܘܢܐ *tawwānā*

inside ܓܘ *gaww* (also *gaww men, b-gaww, l-gaww*)

insignificant ܩܠܝܠ *qallil*; ܙܥܘܪ *z‘ōr*

insolent ܡܪܚ *marrāḥ*

instead of ܚܠܦ *ḥlāp* (+ pron enc II)

instruct (verb) Pa *darreš* to instruct (see "dispute with")

instructed (to be instructed) (verb) ܡܗܪ Ethpa *etmahhar*

intelligence ܣܘܟܠܐ *sukālā*

intense ܬܩܝܦ *taqqip*

intermediary ܡܨܥܝܘܬܐ *meṣ^{c}āyutā*

invite (verb) ܙܡܢ Pa *zammen*; ܩܪܐ *qrā/neqrē*; (see "call")

Ionian ܝܘܢܝܐ *yawnāyā*

iron ܦܪܙܠܐ *parzlā*

it is necessary for ܘܠܐ *wālē l-*

Italy ܐܝܛܠܝܐ *iṭālyā*

Jacob ܝܥܩܘܒ *ya‘qob*

jail *bēt-ḥbušyā* (see "imprisonment")

jasper ܐܝܣܦܘܢ *iyāspōn*

Jerusalem ܐܘܪܫܠܡ *orêšlem*

Jesus ܝܫܘܥ *išō‘*

Jew ܝܗܘܕܝܐ *yudāyā (-yhudāyā)*

job ܥܒܕܐ *^{c}bādā*

John ܝܘܚܢܢ *yōḥannān*

join (verb) ܢܩܦ *npeq/neqqap*

Jordan ܝܘܪܕܢܢ *yordnān*

Joseph ܝܘܣܦ *yōsep*

journey ܡܪܕܝܬܐ *marditā*; to journey ܚܙܩ *ḥzaq/neḥzoq*

Judaea ܝܗܘܕ *ihud (-yhud)*

Judah ܝܗܘܕܐ *ihudā/yudā*

Judas ܝܗܘܕܐ *ihudā/yudā*

judge (verb) ܕܘܢ *dān/ndun*

judgment seat ܒܝܡ *bêm*

jurisdiction ܐܘܚܕܢܐ *uḥdānā*

just as *kmā d-* ܟܡܐ *kmā* (+ abs pl)

just ܟܐܢܐ *kênā*; justly *kênā'it*

justice ܟܐܢܘܬܐ *kênutā*

keep (a promise) (verb) Aph *aššar* (see "fix firmly")

keep (flocks) (verb) ܪܥܐ *r^{c}ā/ner^{c}ē*

keep (verb) ܢܛܪ *nṭar/neṭṭar*; Pa *naṭṭar* to keep under watch; Ethpe *etnṭar* to be kept

keep possession of (verb) ܩܕܐ Pa *qaddi*

kick ܪܦܣܐ *repsā*

kill (verb) ܩܛܠ *qṭal/neqṭol* ; Pa *qaṭṭel* to slaughter; Ethpe *etqṭel* to be killed

kind ܙܢܐ *znā* pl *znayyā* (abs *zan* pl *znin*); *ba-znā* in a (like) manner

kindle (verb) ܢܒܪܫ *nabreš/nnabreš*

kindness ܛܝܒܘܬܐ *ṭaybutā*

king ܡܠܟܐ *malkā* (abs *mlek*)

kingdom ܡܠܟܘܬܐ *malkutā*; pl *-kwātā*

kiss (verb) ܢܫܩ *nšaq/neššoq*

kneel (verb) ܒܪܸܟ *brek/nebrak*

knock (verb) ܢܩܫ *nqaš/neqqoš*

know (verb) ܝܕܥ *ida'/nedda'*; Aph *awda'* to make known; Ethpe *etida'* to be known

knowledge ܝܕܥܬܐ *ida'tā*

known ܝܕܝܥܐ *idi'*

Kurd ܟܘܪܕܝܐ *kurdāyā*

labor (verb) ܥܡܠ *ᶜmal/neᶜmal*

labor ܥܡܠܐ *ᶜalmā*; ܠܐܘܬܐ *leutā*; ܥܒܕܐ *ᶜbādā*

laborer ܦܥܠܐ *pāᶜlā*

lacking ܚܣܝܪ *ḥassir*

lad ܥܠܝܡܐ *ᶜlaymā*

lamb ܥܠܓܐ *ᶜelgā*; ܐܡܪܐ *emrā*

lame (to be lame) (verb) ܚܓܪ *ḥgar/neḥgar*

lame ܚܓܝܪ *ḥgir*; ܚܓܝܣ *ḥgis*

lamp ܠܡܦܝܕܐ *lampêdā*; ܠܡܦܐܕܐ *lampêdā*

land ܐܪܥܐ *arᶜā* (abs *araᶜ*) pl *arᶜē/arᶜawwātā*

language ܠܫܢܐ *leššānā*

lap ܚܢܐ *ḥannā*

large amount ܣܘܓܐܐ *sogā*

last ܐܚܪܝ *ḥrāy*

law ܢܡܘܣܐ *nāmōsā*

lawless *dlānāmōs* (see "law")

lay before (verb) Aph *armi* (see "cast down," "fallen," "prostrate")

lay down (verb) Aph *armi* (see "cast down," "fallen," "prostrate")

lay waste (verb) ܚܪܒ *ḥrab/neḥrob*

lead (verb) ܕܒܪ *dbar/nedbar*

lead back (verb) Aph *apni* (see "return," "come back")

leader ܦܩܘܕܐ *pāqodā*; ܡܕܒܪܢܐ *mdabbrānā*

lean (verb) ܚܢܐ Ethpa *etḥanni*

leap (verb) ܫܘܪ *šwar/nešwar*

learn (verb) ܝܠܦ *ilep/nêlap* (impt *ilap*)

learning ܝܘܠܦܢܐ *yulpānā*

leave (cause to leave) (verb) Aph *appez* (see "go forth"); ܫܒܩ *šbaq/nešboq*; Ethpe *eštbeq* to be abandoned, forsaken; to be forgiven

leaven ܚܡܝܪܐ *ḥmirā*

left (hand) ܣܡܠܐ *semmālā*;

leg ܪܓܠܐ *reglā* (f)

lend (verb) Aph *ašel* (see "ask," "demand")

lengthy (to be lengthy), go on for a long time (verb) ܓܪ Aph *agar*

leprous ܓܪܒ *greb/garbā*

lest ܠܡܐ *l-mā*

letter ܐܓܪܬܐ *eggartā*

life (collective) (see "animal); ܢܦܫܐ *napšā* (f, abs *npeš*) pl *–ātā*; ܚܝܐ *ḥayyē* (pl)

lift up (verb) Aph *asseq* (see "go up"); ܪܘܡ Aph *arim*; Ettaph *ettrim* to be lifted up; ܬܠܐ *tlā/netlē* light (to be light) (verb) ܢܗܪ *nhar/nenhar*; Aph *anhar* to shine, make light

light (to light) (verb) Aph *adleq* (see "lit")

light ܢܘܗܪܐ *nuhrā*; ܢܗܝܪ *nahhir*

lightning ܒܪܩܐ *barqā*

like (prep) ܐܟܘܬ *akwāt*

like (to be like) (verb) ܕܡܐ *dmā/nedmē l-*; Ethpa *etdammi l-* to resemble

like (to make like) (verb) ܣܒܗ Pa *sabbah*

like ܐܝܟ *ak* ; *ak d-* as

likeness ܨܠܡܐ *ṣalmā* (abs *ṣlem*); ܛܘܦܣܐ *ṭupsā*

likewise ܐܟܢܐ *aknā*; ܐܟܚܕ *akḥad*; ܗܟܘܬ *hākwāt*

limb ܗܕܡܐ *haddāmā*

limit (without limit) *dlāḥušbān* (see "reckoning")

line ܥܩܪܐ ^{c}*eqqārā*

lion ܐܪܝܐ *aryā* pl *–yawwātā*

liquor ܫܟܪܐ *šakrā*

lit (to be lit) (verb) ܕܠܩ *dleq/nedlaq*

little bit ܩܠܝܠ *qallil*

little ܩܠܝܠ *qallil*; ܙܥܘܪ *z'ōr*

liturgy ܛܟܣܐ *ṭaksā, ṭeksā*

liturgy, to perform a liturgy (see oblations)

live (verb) ܚܝܐ *ḥyā/neḥḥē* and *nêḥē*; Aph *aḥḥi* to give life; ܥܡܪ ^{c}*mar/ne*^{c}*mar*

living things (see "animal)

living ܚܝ *ḥayy*

lo ܗܐ *hā*

load ܡܘܒܠܐ *mawblā* (abs/const *mawbal*, f)

loaf (of bread) ܓܪܝܨܬܐ *griṣtā*

lodging ܐܘܢܐ *awwānā*

long (time) ܢܓܪ *nagger*

look (verb) ܚܘܪ *ḥāar/nḥur l-*

look for (verb) ܒܥܐ *b'ā/neb'ē*

look out (of a window, e.g.) (verb) ܕܘܩ Aph *adiq*

loosen (verb) ܫܪܐ *šrā/nešrē*

Lord God Sabaoth *māryā ḥayltānā* (see "strong," "mighty")

lord of all ܡܪܟܠ *mārē-kol*

lord ܡܪܐ *mārā* (const *mārē*) pl *mārayyā/mārawwātā*

Lord, the ܡܪܝܐ *māryā*

loss ܚܘܣܪܢܐ *ḥusrānā*

lost ܐܒܝܕ *abid*

loud ܪܡ *rām* (for verbs see ܪܘܡ)

love (verb) Aph *aḥḥeb* (see "burn"); ܪܚܡ *rḥem/nerḥam*

love ܪܚܡܬܐ *reḥmtā*

lower (verb) ܪܟܢ Aph *arken* ; Ethpe *etrken* to bow down; ܪܟܢ Aph *arken* ; Ethpe *etrken* to bow down

low-lying ܡܡܟܟ *mmakkak*

luck ܓܕܐ *gaddā*

Ma'nu (pr n) ܡܥܢܘ *ma*^{c}*nu*

Macedonia ܡܩܕܘܢܝܐ *māqedōniyā*; *māqedōnāyā* Macedonian

made ready ܓܡܝܪ *gmir*

Magdalene ܡܓܕܠܝ *magdlāy*

maiden ܥܠܝܡܬܐ *^{c}laymtā*

maidservant ܐܡܬܐ *amtā* pl *amhātā*

maimed ܦܫܝܓ *pšig*

make (verb) ܥܒܕ *^{c}bad/ne^{c}bed*

make king (verb) Aph *amlek* (see "advise")

make whole (verb) ܚܠܡ Aph *aḥlem*

maker ܥܒܘܕܐ *^{c}ābōdā*

Makkika (pr n) ܡܟܝܟܐ *makkikā*

malice ܒܝܫܘܬܐ *bišutā*

man ܒܪܢܫܐ *bar-nāšā*; ܓܒܪܐ *gabrā*

manage (verb) Pa *dabbar* (see "lead")

management ܦܘܪܣܢܐ *pursānā*

manger ܐܘܪܝܐ *oryā*

manner; ܙܢܐ *znā* pl *znayyā* (abs *zan* pl *znin*); *ba-znā* in a (like) manner

many ܣܘܓܐܐ *sogā*; ܣܓܝ *saggi*

marble ܫܝܫܐ *šišā*

March ܐܕܪ *ādār*

Marcianus ܡܪܩܝܢܘܣ *marqiānos*

Mark ܡܪܩܘܣ *marqos*

market ܫܘܩܐ *šuqā*

marriage ܚܠܘܠܐ *ḥlōlā*

martyr ܣܗܕܐ *sāhdā*

martyrdom ܣܗܕܘܬܐ *sāhdutā*

marvel ܬܕܡܘܪܬܐ *tedmurtā* pl *tedmrātā*

marvelous ܬܗܝܪ *thir*

Mary ܡܪܝܡ *maryam*

Maryab (pr n) ܡܪܝܗܒ *māryab*

master builder ܐܪܕܟܠܐ *ardeklā*

master ܪܒܐ *rabbā*; ܒܥܠܐ *ba'lā*; ܡܪܐ *mārā* (const *mārē*) pl *mārayyā/mārawwātā*

matter ܫܪܒܐ *šarbā*

matter, affair ܨܒܘܬܐ *ṣbutā* pl *ṣebwātā*

Matthew ܡܬܝ *mattay*

Maximian ܡܟܣܡܝܢܘܣ *maksemyānos*

May ܐܝܪ *êyār*

mean ܫܝܛ *šiṭ*

measure (verb) Pa *maššaḥ* (pass part *mmaššaḥ* measured, moderate) (see "anoint")

measure of weight ܡܢܝܐ *manyā*

measurement ܡܫܘܚܬܐ *mšuḥtā* pl *mušḥātā*

medicinal herb ܥܩܪܐ *^{c}eqqārā*

medicine *sammā* pl *sammānē* (see "blind")

meditate (verb) Ethpa *etḥaššab* (see "count," "reckon"); ܗܓܐ Ethpa *ethaggi*; ܪܢܐ *rnā/nernē*

meet (verb) ܐܪܥ *era^{c}/nero^{c}*; ܙܕܩ *zādeq*

meeting house ܒܝܬ ܨܘܒܐ *bēt-ṣawbā*

meeting place ܨܘܒܐ *ṣawbā*

meeting ܐܘܪܥܐ *ur^{c}ā* (abs *ura^{c}*)

melt (verb) ܦܫܪ *pšar/nepšar*

member ܗܕܡܐ *haddāmā*

memorial ܥܘܗܕܢܐ *ʿuhdānā*; ܕܘܟܪܢܐ *dukrānā*

memory ܥܘܗܕܢܐ *ʿuhdānā*

mental ܡܠܝܠ *mlil*

merchant ܬܓܪܐ *tāgrā*

mercy (have mercy on) (verb) Pa *raḥḥem ʿal* (see "love")

mercy ܪܚܡܐ *raḥmā*; ܡܪܚܡܢܘܬܐ *mraḥḥmānutā*

Mesopotamia ܒܝܬ ܢܗܪܝܢ *bēt-nahrinc*

message ܐܝܙܓܕܘܬܐ *izgaddutā* ; ܫܠܝܚܘܬܐ *šliḥutā*

messenger ܫܠܝܚܐ *šliḥā*

messiah ܡܫܝܚ *mšiḥ*; *mšiḥā* the Christ

middle ܦܠܓܐ *pelgā*; ܡܨܥܬܐ *mṣaʿtā* (const *meṣʿat*); ܦܠܓܘܬܐ *pelgutā*

midnight *pelgut-lêlyā* (see "middle")

midst ܡܨܥܬܐ *mṣaʿtā* (const *meṣʿat*)

might ܚܝܠܐ *ḥaylā*; ܥܘܫܢܐ *ʿušnā*

mighty ܥܫܝܢ *ʿaššin*

mighty ܓܢܒܪ *gabbār*; ܚܝܠܬܢ *ḥayltān*; ܓܢܒܪ *gabbār*

mild ܪܟܝܟ *rakkik*

mile ܡܝܠܐ *milā*

mill ܪܚܝܐ *raḥyā*

millstone *rayḥyā da-ḥmārā* (of a gristmill turned by a donkey) (see "mill")

mina ܡܢܝܐ *manyā*

mind ܪܥܝܢܐ *reʿyānā*; ܬܪܥܝܬܐ *tarʿitā*

ministration ܬܫܡܫܬܐ *tešmeštā*

mirror ܡܚܙܝܬܐ *meḥzitā*

missing ܚܣܝܪ *ḥassir*

mistress ܡܪܬܐ *mārtā*

mock Aph *ahhel b-* (see "praise")

moderate ܡܡܫܚ *mmaššaḥ*

moist ܪܛܝܒ *raṭṭib*

moisture ܪܛܝܒܘܬܐ *raṭṭibutā*

mollify (verb) ܪܘܚ Pa *rayyaḥ*

moment ܥܕܢܐ *ʿeddānā*

money ܟܣܦܐ *kespā*

Mongol ܡܘܓܠܝܐ *moglāyā*

month ܝܪܚܐ *yarḥā* (abs *iraḥ*)

more than ܝܬܝܪ *yattir men* ; ܐܘ *aw*

more *yattirā'it* (see "more than")

morning ܨܦܪܐ *ṣaprā* pl *ṣaprwātā*

Moses ܡܘܫܐ *mušē*

mother ܐܡܐ *emmā* pl *emmhātā*

motion (pertaining to motion) ܡܙܝܥܢܝ *mziʿānāy*

mount (verb) ܪܟܒ *rkab/nerkab*

mountain peak ܫܢܐ *šennā* (f)

mountain ܛܘܪܐ *ṭurā*

mounted soldier ܦܪܫܐ *parrāšā*

mourning ܐܒܠܐ *eblā*

mouse ܥܘܩܒܪܐ *ʿuqbrā*

mouth ܦܘܡܐ *pumā*

move far away (verb) ܪܚܩ Aph *arḥeq*

much ܣܓܝ *saggi*

multitude ܟܢܫܐ *kenšā*

murder ܩܛܠܐ *qeṭlā*

murderer ܩܛܘܠܐ *qāṭōlā*

murmur (verb) ܪܛܢ *rṭan/nerṭan*

Muslim (to become Muslim) (verb) ܗܓܪ Aph *aphgar*

Muslim ܡܫܠܡܢܐ *mašlmānā*

Musta'ṣim, last Abbasid caliph, r. 1242-58 ܡܘܣܬܥܨܡ *musta^c^ṣem*

mute *ḥreš/ḥaršā* (see "silent"); ܫܬܝܩ *šattiq*

mutter (verb) ܪܛܢ *rṭan/nerṭan*

myriad ܪܒܘ *rebbō* (abs)

Najm al-Din (pr n) ܢܓܡ ܐܠܕܝܢ *najm aldin*

naked ܥܪܛܠ *^c^arṭel(lāy)*

name (verb) ܩܪܐ *qrā/neqrē*; (see "call")

name ܫܡܐ *šmā* (abs *šem*) pl *šmāhē*; to be named ܫܡܗ Ethpa *eštammah*

narrate (verb) ܬܢܐ *tnā/netnē*

natal star ܡܠܘܫܐ *malwāšā*

nation ܐܘܡܬܐ *ummtā*

nature ܟܝܢܐ *kyānā*; pertaining to nature ܟܝܢܝ *kyānāy*

Nazarene ܢܨܪܝܐ *nāṣrāyā*

Nazareth ܢܨܪܬ *nāṣrat*

near *^c^al-yad* (see "over"); ܩܪܝܒ *qarrib*; ܥܠܝܕ *^c^alyad*

nearly ܩܪܝܒܘܬܐ *qarributā d-*

Nebo ܢܒܘ *nebō*

necessary (to be necessary) (verb) Ethpe *etb'i* (see "seek," "look for")

necessary ܡܬܒܥܝܐ *metb^c^ē/metba^c^yā*

necessity ܣܢܝܩܘܬܐ *sniqutā*; ܣܘܢܩܢܐ *sunqānā*

neck ܨܘܪܐ *ṣawrā*

need (in need of) ܣܢܝܩ *sniq ^c^al*; ܣܢܩ Ethpe *estneq ^c^al*

need (verb) ܣܢܝܩܘܬܐ *sniqutā*

need ܣܘܢܩܢܐ *sunqānā*

needed (verb) Ethpe *etb'i* (see "seek," "look for")

needle ܡܚܛܐ *mḥaṭṭā*

neglect (verb) ܗܡܐ Aph *ahmi men*

negligence ܒܣܝܢܐ *besyānā*

negligible (to be negligible) (verb) Ethpe *eṭṭ'i* (see "wander," "astray")

negligible ܡܬܛܥܐ *meṭṭ^c^ē*

neighbor ܫܒܒܐ *šbābā*

neighborhood ܫܒܒܘܬܐ *šbābutā*

nerve ܓܝܕܐ *gyādā*

new ܚܕܬ *ḥdat/ḥadtā* (emph *ḥadtā – ē/ḥdattā ḥadtātā*)

next to ܨܐܕ *ṣêd* (+ pron encl II; also spelled ܨܝܕ); ܨܝܕ *ṣêd* (with pron encl II usually spelled ܨܐܕ)

next ܒܬܪܟܢ *bātarken*

night ܠܠܝܐ *lêlyā* pl *laylē/laylawwātā*

nine ܬܫܥ *tša^c^* (f)/*teš^c^ā* (m)

noble ܪܫܢܐ *rêšānā*; ܡܝܩܪܐ *myaqqrā*; ܝܩܝܪ *yaqqir*

nobleman ܚܐܪܐ *ḥêrā*

nonetheless ܒܪܡ *bram*

north, the north ܓܪܒܝܐ *garbyā; (gabbā) garbyāyā* north side

not (is not) ܠܘ *law = lā-(h)u*; also as negative prefix as in *law saggi* not much; not very

not much *law saggi* (see "not")

not very *law saggi* (see "not")

notable ܡܝܩܪܐ *myaqqrā*

nourish (verb) ܬܪܣܝ *tarsi/ntarsē*

nourishing ܡܬܪܣܝܢ *mtarsyān*

nourishment ܣܝܒܪܬܐ *saybartā*

November ܬܫܪܝܢ / ܬܫܪܝ *tešri(n) ḥrāy*

now ܟܝ *kay* (particle of emphasis); ܗܫܐ *hāšā*

Noyan (Mongolian princely title) ܢܘܝܢ *noyān*

number ܡܢܝܢܐ *menyānā*

nutritious ܡܬܪܣܝܢ *mtarsyān*

O (vocative) ܐܘ *aw*

oath ܡܘܡܬܐ *mawmtā*

oblation ܩܘܪܒܢܐ *qurbānā*

oblations, to make oblations, to perform the liturgy ܩܪܒ Pa *qarreb*

October *tešrin qdēm* (see "November")

odious *snē/sanyā* (see "hate")

of (prep) ܕ *d(a)-*

offend (verb) ܟܫܠ Aph *akšel*

offense ܡܟܫܘܠܐ *makšulā*

offer (verb) Aph *armi* (see "cast down," "fallen," "prostrate"); ܝܫܛ Aph *awšeṭ*

oil ܡܫܚܐ *mešḥā*

old (to grow old) (verb) ܣܐܒ *seb/nesab*

old man ܣܒܐ *sābā*

old ܥܬܝܩ *ᶜattiq*; ܩܫܝܫ *qaššiš*; ܩܕܝܡ *qaddim* ; *men qdim* of old, long ago, from eternity

on account of ܡܛܠ *meṭṭul* ; *meṭṭul d-* for, because; ܡܛܘܠ variant spelling of *meṭṭul*; ܡܛܠܬ *meṭṭlāt* – form of *meṭṭul* when followed by enclitic pronouns II; ܚܠܦ *ḥlāp* (+ pron enc II)

on the one hand… on the other hand ܡܢ *man* usually followed by *dēn*

on ܒ *b(a)-*

on ܥܠ *ᶜal* (with pron encl II, *ᶜl-*)

one another ܚܕܕܐ *ḥdādā*; *ḥad 'am ḥad* with one another

one ܚܕ *ḥad/ḥdā* ; *ḥad 'am ḥad* with one another

only ܝܚܝܕܝ *iḥidāy*

open (verb) ܦܬܚ *ptaḥ/neptaḥ*; Pa *pattaḥ* to cause to be opened; Ethpe *etptaḥ* to be open, opened

opening ܟܘܬܐ *kawwtā* pl *kawwē* (abs *kawwā* pl *kawwin*) (f)

openly ܓܠܝܐ *gelyā, b-*

opinion ܬܪܥܝܬܐ *tarᶜitā*

or ܐܘ *aw*

order (verb) ܦܩܕ *pqad/nepqod*

order ܛܟܣܐ *ṭaksā, ṭeksā*; ܦܘܩܕܢܐ *puqdānā*

organ ܐܘܪܓܢܘܢ *orgānon*

orient ܡܕܢܚܐ *madnḥā* (abs/constr *madnaḥ*)

ornament ܨܒܬܐ *ṣebtā* pl *–tē*

other ܐܚܪܢܐ *ḥrêtā/ḥrētā* pl *ḥrānē/ḥranyātā*

outcry ܩܥܬܐ *qᶜātā*

outside of ܒܪ *bar (l-bar men)*

over *lᶜel men* (see "above"); ܥܠ *ᶜal* (with pron encl II, *ᶜl-*)

overcome (verb) ܙܟܐ *zkā/nezkē*

overflow (verb) ܫܦܥ *špaᶜ/nešpaᶜ*

overlay (verb) ܩܪܡ *qram/neqrom*

overlayed ܩܪܝܡ *qrim*

overtake (verb) ܕܪܟ Aph *adrek*

overthrow (verb) ܙܟܐ *zkā/nezkē*

overwhelm (verb) ܛܘܦ Aph *aṭip*

pagan ܚܢܦܐ *ḥanpā*

paganism ܚܢܦܘܬܐ *ḥanputā*

page *yāteb-waᶜdā* (see "sit," "stay," "dwell")

pain ܟܐܒܐ *kêbā*; ܢܟܝܢܐ *nekyānā*

painter ܨܝܪܐ *ṣayyārā*

palace *traᶜ –malkutā* (see "gate," "doorway"); ܐܦܕܢܐ *āpadnā*

Palestine ܦܠܣܛܝܢܐ *palesṭinē*

Pallut (pr n) ܦܠܘܛ *palluṭ*

parable ܡܬܠܐ *matlā*

paradise ܦܪܕܝܣܐ *pardisā, pardaysā*

paralyzed ܡܫܪܝ *mšarray*

parent ܝܠܘܕܐ *yālōdā*

parrot ܛܝܛܝܩܘܣ *ṭiṭikos/ṭayṭikos*

partake ܠܥܣ *lᶜes/nelᶜas*

pass the night (verb) ܒܘܬ *bāt/nbut*

passion ܚܫܐ *ḥaššā*; ܪܚܡܬܐ *reḥmtā*

path ܫܒܝܠܐ *šbilā*

paw ܦܪܣܬܐ *parstā*

peace treaty ܩܝܡܐ *qyāmā d-šaynā* (see "contract")

peace ܫܠܡܐ *šlāmā*; ܫܝܢܐ *šaynā*; ܫܠܝܐ *šelyā*

pearl ܡܪܓܢܝܬܐ *margānitā* pl *–nyātā*

pebble ܩܘܦܣܐ *qupsā*

penetrate (verb) ܒܙܚ *bzaḥ/nebzoḥ*

people ܐܢܫܐ *nāšā;* anybody, somebody *nāš,* nobody *lānāš*; ܥܡܐ *ᶜammā* pl ܥܡ̈ܡܐ *ᶜammē*

perceive (verb) Eshtaph *eštawdaᶜ* (see "know"); ܪܓܫ Aph *argeš*; ܣܟܠ Ethpa *estakkal*

perceptive ܪܓܝܫ *rgiš*

perchance ܟܒܪ *kbar*

perfected ܓܡܝܪ *gmir*

perhaps ܛܟ *ṭāk* τάχα

perish ܐܒܕ *ebad/nêbad* to perish; Aph *awbed* to cause to perish

permit ܦܣܣ Aph *appes*

permitted ܫܠܝܛ *šliṭ*

persecute ܪܕܦ *rdap/nerdop* (+ *bātar*)

persecution of ܪܕܘܦܝܐ *rdupyā ᶜal*

persevere in (verb) ܐܡܢ Ethpe *etemen b-*

Persia ܦܪܣ *pāres*

Persian ܥܓܡܝܐ *ᶜajāmāyā*; ܦܪܣܝܐ *pārsāyā*

person ܒܪܢܫܐ *bar-nāšā*; ܩܢܘܡܐ *qnomā*

persona ܦܪܨܘܦܐ *parṣōpā*

personally *qnomā'it* (see "person")

persuade (verb) ܦܝܣ Aph *apis* (with nonspirantized *p*, derives from πεισαι); *mpis leh* he was persuaded; Ettaph *ettpis*, usually *eṭṭpis* to be persuaded, instructed

pertaining to the soul ܢܦܫܢܝ *napšānāy*

Peter (m) ܟܐܦܐ *kêpā*

petition (verb) ܒܥܘܬܐ *bā'utā*

Pharisee ܦܪܝܫܐ *prišā*

phial ܦܝܠܐ *pyālā* pl *pyālās*

Philip (pr n) ܦܝܠܝܦܘܣ *pilippaws*

philosopher ܦܝܠܘܣܘܦܐ *pilosopā*

Phoenicia ܦܘܢܝܩܐ *puniqē*

pigment *sammā* pl *sammānē* (see "blind")

piled up (to be piled up) (verb) ܟܫܐ Ethpe *etkši*

pine ܐܪܙܐ *arzā*

pit ܓܘܡܨܐ *gumāṣā*

pity (to have pity) (verb) ܚܘܣ *ḥās/nḥus*; ܚܘܣܢܐ *ḥawsānā*; pitiness – *dlā-ḥawsān*

placate (verb) Pa *raᶜᶜi* (see "tend," "keep," "rule")

place (verb) Aph *aqim* (see "rise up," "arise"); ܣܘܡ *sām/nsim*; Ettaph *ettsim* to be put, be located

place ܐܬܪܐ *atrā* pl *–rē/-rawwātā*; ܕܘܟܬܐ *dukktā*

plan (verb) Ethpa *etḥaššab* (see "count," "reckon")

plan ܦܘܪܣܐ *pursā*

plant (verb) ܢܨܒ *nṣab/neṣṣob* ; Ethpe *etnṣeb* to be planted

plant firmly (verb) ܣܬܬ Pa *sattet*

plaster (verb) ܟܠܫ Pa *kalleš*

plate (verb) ܩܪܡ *qram/neqrom*

pleasant ܪܓܝܓ *rgig*; ܒܣܝܡ *bassim*

pledge ܘܥܕܐ *wa'dā*

plot (verb) Ethpa *etḥaššab* (see "count," "reckon"); Ethpa *etparras* (see "spread")

plot ܦܘܪܣܐ *pursā*

plow (verb) ܦܠܚ *plaḥ/neploḥ*

point the finger (verb) *pšaṭ ṣebᶜā* (see "spread," "stretch out")

policeman ܓܙܝܪܝܐ *gzirāyā*

pool ܡܥܡܘܕܝܬܐ *maᶜmōditā*

poor ܡܣܟܢܐ *meskênā*

porch ܐܣܛܘܐ *eṣtwā*, στοά

portico ܐܣܛܘܐ *eṣtwā*, στοά

possessing (see "seize")

possible, it is ܐܢܢܩܐ *ananqê* (ἀνάγκη) *ananqê*

pound ܡܢܝܐ *manyā*

pour out (verb) ܐܫܕ *ešad/nešod;* Ethpe *etešed* to be spilled, shed pour over oneself (verb) ܢܨܠ Ethpe *etnṣel*

power ܚܝܠܐ *ḥaylā*

powerful (see "seize")

praise (verb) ܗܠܠ Pa *hallel* ; ܫܒܚ Pa *šabbaḥ*; Ethpa *eštabbaḥ* to be praised

praise ܬܫܒܘܚܬܐ *tešboḥtā*

pray (verb) ܨܠܐ Pa *ṣalli* (*ʿal* for); Ethpe *eṣtli* to incline

prayer ܨܠܘܬܐ *ṣlōtā* pl *ṣlawwātā*

pre- ܡܩܕܡܘܬ *mqaddmut*

preach (verb) ܟܪܙ Aph *akrez*

preaching ܟܪܘܙܘܬܐ *kārōzutā*

precede (verb) Pa *qaddem* (see "go before," "do first")

pre-dawn ܫܦܪܐ *šaprā*

prefiguration *mqaddam-ṣā'ar* (see "representation")

pregnant (to become pregnant) (verb) *qabbel baṭnā* (see "receive," "get")

prepare (verb) ܬܩܢ Pa *taqqen*; ܛܝܒ Pa *ṭayyeb*

prepared ܥܬܝܕ *ʿtid* (*d-* + impf, to do something)

present (to be present) Ethpa *eṭṭayyab* (see "prepare")

prevail (verb) ܬܩܦ *tqep/netqap*

previously ܠܘܩܕܡ *luqdam*

price ܛܝܡܐ *ṭimā* (usually pl)

priest (verb): to serve as a priest, perform priestly functions ܟܗܢ Pa *kahhen*

priest ܟܗܢܐ *kāhnā*; ܟܘܡܪܐ *kumrā*

priesthood ܟܗܢܘܬܐ *kāhnutā*

priestly ܟܗܢܝ *kāhnāy*

prince ܪܫܢܐ *rêšānā*

prison *bēt-ḥbušyā* (see "imprisonment"); ܒܝܬܐܣܝܪܐ *bēt-asirē*

prisoner ܐܣܝܪܐ *asirā*

proceed (verb) Aph *ašqel* (see "remove," "take away"); ܪܕܐ *rdā/nerdē*

proclaim (verb) ܟܪܙ Aph *akrez*

proclaimer ܟܪܘܙܐ *kārōzā*

procurator ܐܦܝܛܪܦܐ *epiṭrāpā* ἐπίτροπος

profession ܬܘܕܝܬܐ *tawditā*

property of ܕܝܠ *dil* (+ pron encl I)

prophet ܢܒܝܐ *nbiyā*

prosperity ܫܝܢܐ *šaynā*

prostrate (verb) ܪܡܐ *rmē/ramyā*

protection ܓܢܐ *gennā*

Protonice (pr n) ܦܪܘܛܘܢܝܩܐ *proṭoniqê*

prove ܢܣܐ Pa *nassi*

psalm ܙܡܘܪܐ *zāmōrā*; ܙܡܝܪܬܐ *zmirtā*

psychological ܢܦܫܢܝ *napšānāy*

publicly ܓܠܝܐ *gelyā, b-*

purchase (verb) ܩܢܐ *qnā/neqnē*

pure (to be pure) (verb) ܕܟܐ *dkā/nedkē*

pure ܣܢܝܢ *snin*

purify (verb) ܫܘܓ Aph *ašig*

pursue (verb) ܪܕܦ *rdap/nerdop*

Pusaq (pr n) ܦܘܣܩ *pusāq*

put (verb) Aph *aqim* (see "rise up," "arise"); ܣܘܡ *sām/nsim*; Ettaph *ettsim* to be put, be located put away (verb) ܪܚܩ Aph *arḥeq*

put in authority (verb) ܫܠܛ Pa *šalleṭ*

put on (verb) ܠܒܫ *lbeš/nelbaš*

quantity ܟܡܝܘܬܐ *kmāyutā*

queen ܡܠܟܬܐ *malktā*

quickly ܥܓܠ *ᶜgal, ba-*

radiant (to be radiant) (verb) ܦܪܓ Aph *apreg*

rage ܚܡܬܐ *ḥemmtā*; ܪܘܓܙܐ *rugzā*

rain ܡܛܪܐ *meṭrā*

raise (verb) Aph *asseq* (see "go up"); ܥܠܐ Pa *ᶜalli*

raise up (verb) ܪܘܡ Aph *arim*; ܙܩܦ *zqap/nezqop* ; Ethpe *ezdqep* to be crucified

rank ܛܟܣܐ *ṭaksā, ṭeksā*

ray ܙܠܝܩܐ *zalliqā*

read (verb) ܩܪܐ *qrā/neqrē*; Ethpe *etqri* to be read out, called

ready (to be ready) Ethpa *eṭṭayyab* (see "prepare")

ready ܥܬܝܕ *ᶜtid* (*d-* + impf, to do something)

rear (verb) ܬܪܣܝ *tarsi/ntarsē*

rear ܚܨܐ *ḥaṣṣā*

reason ܥܠܬܐ *ᶜelltā* pl ܥܠܠܬܐ *ᶜellātā*

rebel (verb) ܡܪܕ *mrad/nemrad*

receive (verb) ܢܣܒ *nsab/nessab* ; ܩܒܠ Pa *qabbel*

reckon (verb) ܚܫܒ *ḥšab/neḥšob*

reckoning ܚܘܫܒܢܐ *ḥušbānā*; *dlāḥušbān* without limit

recline (verb) Ethpe *estmek* (see "rest against"); recline at table (verb) ܓܣܣ Aph *agess*

recognize (verb) Eshtaph *eštawdaᶜ* (see "know")

recovery ܚܘܠܡܢܐ *ḥulmānā*

redeem (verb) ܩܢܐ *qnā/neqnē*

reflect (verb) ܪܢܐ *rnā/nernē*

regal ܡܠܟܝ *malkāy*

regard (verb) ܒܝܢ Ethpa *etbayyan*

region ܦܢܝܬܐ *pnitā*

registrar of tribute ܛܒܘܠܪܐ *ṭabbulārā*

reign (*ᶜal* over) (verb) Aph *amlek* (see "advise")

rejoice (verb) ܦܪܓ Aph *apreg*; ܪܘܙ *rwaz/nerwaz*; ܚܕܐ *ḥdi/neḥdē*

rejoicing ܪܘܙܐ *rwāzā*

relate (verb) ܫܥܐ Ethpa *eštaᶜᶜi*

released (to be released) (verb) ܫܡܪ Ethpa *eštammar*

rely (verb) ܚܢܐ Ethpa *etḥanni*

remain ܦܫ *pāš/npuš*; ܩܘܐ Pa *qawwi*

remaining ܩܝܡ *qayyām*

remember (verb) ܥܗܕ Ethpa *etᶜahhad*; ܕܟܪ *dkar/nedkar* (pass part *dkir* has act & pass senses); Ethpe *etdkar* to remember; Ethpa *etdakkar* to be mindful of

remembrance ܕܘܟܪܢܐ *dukrānā*

remote ܡܒܥܕ *mabᶜad*

remove (verb) ܪܚܩ Aph *arḥeq*; ܫܩܠ *šqal/nešqol*; Ethpe *eštqel* to be removed rend (verb) ܬܠܚ *tlaḥ/netloḥ*

renounce (verb) ܟܦܪ *kpar/nekpor b-*

repeat (verb) ܬܢܐ *tnā/netnē*

repent (verb) ܬܘܒ *tāb/ntub*

repentance ܬܝܒܘܬܐ *tyābutā*

reply *punāy-pet-gāmā* (see "return"); Pa *panni* (see "return," "come back"); ܥܢܐ ^{c}*nā/ne*^{c}*nē*

report ܛܒܐ *ṭebbā*

represent (verb) ܨܘܪ *ṣār/nṣur* (pass part ܨܝܪ *ṣir*)

representation ܨܐܪ *ṣā'ar* (see ܨܘܪ)

reproach ܚܣܕܐ *ḥesdā*; ܡܟܣܢܘܬܐ *maksānutā*

request (verb) ܒܥܘܬܐ *bā'utā*

require (verb) ܬܒܥ *tba*^{c}*/netba*^{c}

resemble (verb) Ethpa *etdammi l-* to resemble (see "seem," "like")

rest (the rest; remainder) ܫܪܟܐ *šarkā*

rest against (verb) ܣܡܟ *smak/nesmok*

rest ܢܝܚܬܐ *nyāḥtā*; ܢܝܚܐ *nyāḥtā*

rest, to be at rest ܢܘܚ *nāḥ/nnuḥ* ; Aph *aniḥ* to give rest to; Ettaph *ettniḥ* to rest

retain (verb) ܩܕܝ Pa *qaddi*

return (int) (verb) ܗܦܟ *hpak/nehpok*; Pa *happek*

return (trs) (verb) ܗܦܟ Pa *happek*

return (verb) ܦܘܢܝܐ *punāyā*; ܦܢܐ *pnā/nepnē*; Aph *apni* cause to return; Ethpe *etpni*; ܥܛܦ ^{c}*ṭap/ne*^{c}*ṭop*; Pa ^{c}*aṭṭep* to clothe; to give back

reveal (verb) ܓܠܐ *glā/neglē* ; Pa *galli* to reveal; Ethpe *etgli* to be revealed; *glē/galyā* open, revealed; *galyā'it* openly, in public

revelation ܓܠܝܢܐ *gelyānā*

revert (verb) Aph *apni* (see "return," "come back")

revile (verb) ܓܕܦ Pa *gaddep b-/l-/ 'al* ; Ethpa *etgaddap* to be reviled

reward (verb) ܦܪܥ *pra*^{c}*/nepro*^{c}

rib ܐܠܥܐ *el*^{c}*ā* (f)

rich (to grow rich) (verb) ܥܬܪ ^{c}*tar/ne*^{c}*tar*

rich ܥܬܝܪ ^{c}*attir*

riches ܥܘܬܪܐ ^{c}*utrā*

ride (verb) ܪܟܒ *rkab/nerkab*

right (hand, side) ܝܡܝܢܐ *yamminā*

right (to make right) (verb) ܬܩܢ Pa *taqqen*; Aph *atqen* to set in order

right ܬܪܝܨ *triṣ*; ܙܕܩ *zādeq*

righteous ܙܕܝܩ *zaddiq*

rip out (verb) ܥܩܪ ^{c}*qar/ne*^{c}*qor*

rip up (verb) ܥܩܪ ^{c}*qar/ne*^{c}*qor*

rise (sun) (verb) ܕܢܚ *dnaḥ/nednaḥ* ; Aph *adnaḥ* to make (the sun) rise

rise (verb) ܩܡ *qām*

rise up (verb) ܩܘܡ *qām/nqum*

rite ܛܟܣܐ *ṭaksā, ṭeksā*

river ܢܗܪܐ *nahrā* pl *–rawwātā*

road (f) ܐܘܪܚܐ *urḥā*

robber ܓܝܣܐ *gayyāsā*

rock ܟܐܦܐ *kêpā* (f); ܫܘܥܐ *šō*^{c}*ā*

roll (verb) ܟܪܟ *krak/nekrok*

roll away (verb) ܥܓܠ Pa *ᶜaggel*

Roman ܪܗܘܡܝܐ *rōmāyā*

Rome ܪܗܘܡܐ *rōmê*

rooftop ܐܓܪܐ *eggārā*

root ܥܩܪܐ *ᶜeqqārā*

round about ܚܘܕܪܐ *l-ḥudrā*

royal ܡܠܟܝ *malkāy*

rubbed off (verb) ܩܦܠ Ethpe *etqpel*

rubbed out (verb) ܩܦܠ Ethpe *etqpel*

rule (verb) Aph *amlek* (see "advise"); Pa *dabbar* (see "lead"); ܪܥܐ *rᶜā/nerᶜē*

rule ܡܠܟܘܬܐ *malkutā*; pl *-kwātā*

run (verb) ܪܗܛ *rheṭ/nerhaṭ* (impt *harṭ*)

sabbath ܫܒܬܐ *šabbtā*

sack ܣܩܐ *saqqā*

sacred ܩܕܝܫ *qaddiš*

sacrifice ܕܒܚܐ *debḥā*

sacrifice(verb) ܕܒܚ Pa *dabbaḥ*

sad (to be sad) (verb) ܟܡܪ Ethpe *etkmar*; ܚܫܫ *ḥaš/neḥḥaš*

sad ܟܡܝܪ *kmir*

sadly, mournfully ܚܫܫܝܬ *ḥaššišā'it*

sainted ܩܕܝܫ *qaddiš*

Salome (pr n) ܫܠܘܡ *šālōm*

salt ܡܠܚܐ *melḥā* (f)

salvation ܦܘܪܩܢܐ *purqānā*

Samaritan ܫܡܪܝܐ *šāmrāyā*

sanctify (verb) ܩܕܫ Pa *qaddeš*; Ethpa *etqaddaš* to be made holy, sacred

sand ܚܠܐ *ḥālā*

sandal ܡܣܢܐ *msānā*

Satan ܣܛܢܐ *sāṭānā*

Saturday ܫܒܬܐ *šabbtā*

save (verb) ܦܨܐ Pa *paṣṣi*; ܫܘܙܒ *šawzeb/nšawzeb*; Eshtaph *eštawzab* to be delivered

savior ܦܪܘܩܐ *pārōqā*

say (verb) ܐܡܪ *emar/nêmar* (*l-* someone, *ᶜal* about); Ethpe *etemar* to be said

say gently (verb) ܪܬܡ Pa *rattem*

scabbard ܬܝܩܐ *tiqā*

schoolmaster ܣܦܪܐ *sāprā*

scourge (verb) ܢܓܕ Pa *negdā*

scrape off (verb) ܓܪܪ *gar/neggor*

scratch (verb) ܚܪܛ *ḥraṭ/neḥroṭ*

scribe ܣܦܪܐ *sāprā*

scripture ܟܬܒܐ *ktābā*

scrutinize(verb) ܒܩܐ Ethpa *etbaqqi*

sea ܝܡܐ *yammā* pl ܝܡ̈ܡܐ *yammē*

seal (verb) ܛܒܥ *ṭbaʻ/neṭbaʻ* ; ܚܬܡ *ḥātmā*

seal ܛܒܥܐ *ṭabʻā*

search into (verb) ܒܨܐ *baṣṣi* Pa

season ܥܕܢܐ *ᶜeddānā*

seat ܟܘܪܣܝܐ *kursyā* pl *–sawwātā*

second ܬܪܝܢܐ *trayyānā/trayyānitā*

secretly ܒܟܣܝܐ *kesyā, b-*

securely *zhirā'it* (see "wary")

see (verb) ܚܙܐ *ḥzā/neḥzē*; Ethpe *etḥzi* to be seen, appear

seek (verb) ܒܥܐ *b'ā/neb'ē* ; ܬܒܥ *tba^c/netba^c*

seem (verb) ܕܡܐ *dmā/nedmē l-*; Ethpa *etdammi l-* to resemble

seem good to (verb) ܫܦܪ *špar/nešpar l-*

seize (verb) ܐܚܕ *eḥad/neḥod* past part (*aḥid*) has both act & pass senses, also means possessing, having, powerful;

self (reflexive pron) ܢܦܫܐ *napšā* (f, abs *npeš*) pl *–ātā*; ܩܢܘܡܐ *qnomā*

sell (verb) Pa *zabben* (see "buy")

send (verb) ܫܕܪ Pa *šaddar*; Ethpa *eštaddar* to be sent, dispatched; ܫܠܚ *šlaḥ/nešlaḥ* Ethpe *eštlaḥ* to be sent

sense ܪܓܫܐ *regšā*

senselessness ܡܬܢܫܝܢܘܬܐ *metnaššyānutā*

sensory ܡܪܓܫܢ *margšān*

sepulchre ܒܝܬܩܒܘܪܐ *bēt-qburā*

sermon ܡܐܡܪܐ *mêmrā*

servant ܥܒܕܐ *^cabdā*

serve (verb) ܫܡܫ Pa *šammeš*; ܦܠܚ *plaḥ/neploḥ*

service ܬܫܡܫܬܐ *tešmeštā*

servitude (to be reduced to servitude) (verb) (see "work")

set forth (verb) Aph *ašqel* (see "remove," "take away")

set free (verb) ܦܨܐ Pa *paṣṣi*

set in order (verb) Aph *atqen* (see "right," "get ready," "prepare"); ܨܒܬ Pa *ṣabbet*

set on fire (verb) ܚܒܒ *ḥab/neḥḥob*

set up (verb) ܩܒܥ *qba^c/neqbo^c* ; Ethpe *etqba^c* to be set up (cross, e.g.)

settle (trs) (verb) Aph *ašri* (see "stop," "camp")

seven ܫܒܥ *šba^c* (f), *šab^cā* (m)

severe ܩܫܐ *qšē/qašyā*; ܚܪܝܦ *ḥarrib*

Severus ܣܘܝܪܘܣ *seweros*

sew (verb) ܚܘܛ *ḥāṭ/nḥuṭ*

shame ܚܣܕܐ *ḥesdā*

shamed by (to be shamed by) (verb) ܢܟܦ Ethpa *etnakkap b-*

shape ܕܡܘܬܐ *dmutā*

share (verb) ܫܘܬܦ Ethpau *eštawtap*

sharp ܚܪܝܦ *ḥarrib*

she ܗܝ *hi*

shed (verb) ܐܫܕ *ešad/nešod;* Ethpe *etešed* to be spilled, shed

sheep ܥܪܒܐ *^cerbā*; ܥܢܐ *^cānā*

shepherd ܪܥܝܐ *rā^cyā* pl *rā^cayyā/rā^cawwātā*

shine (to shine) (verb) ܢܗܪ *nhar/nenhar*; Aph *anhar* to shine, make light; ܦܪܓ Aph *apreg*; ܢܨܚ *nṣaḥ/nenṣaḥ*

shining ܢܨܝܚ *naṣṣiḥ*

ship ܣܦܝܢܬܐ *spittā* pl *–ē/spinātā*

Shmeshgram (pr n) ܫܡܫܓܪܡ *šmešgram*

shoe ܡܣܢܐ *msānā*

shop ܚܢܘܬܐ *ḥānutā* pl *–nwātā*

shoulder ܟܬܦܐ *katpā* pl *–ē/-ātā* (f)

shout ܐܠܠܬܐ *illtā* pl *yallātā*

show (verb) ܚܘܐ Pa *ḥawwi*

shut (verb) Ethpe *etthed* to shut (see "seize")

Shwida (pr n) ܫܘܝܕܐ *šwidā*

sick (get sick) (verb) ܟܪܗ Ethpe *etkrah*

sick ܟܪܝܗ *krih*

sickness ܚܫܐ *ḥaššā*; ܟܐܒܐ *kêbā*

side ܓܒܐ *gabbā* (abs *gebb*)

sight ܚܙܬܐ *ḥzātā*

sign ܐܬܐ *ātā*; pl. ܐܬܘܬܐ; ܪܡܙܐ *remzā*

signet ܥܙܩܬܐ *ᶜezqtā*

signs (by signs) ܡܪܡܙ *mermaz*

silence ܫܬܩܐ *šetqā*; keep silence (verb) ܫܬܩ *šteq/neštoq*

silent (to be silent) (verb) ܚܪܫ *ḥreš/neḥraš*; *ḥreš/ḥaršā* dumb, deaf, mute

silk ܫܐܪܐ *šērā*; ܪܟܝܟ *rakkik*

silken ܫܐܪܝ *šērāy*

Siloam ܫܝܠܘܚܐ *šilōḥā*

silver ܣܐܡܐ *sêmā*; ܟܣܦܐ *kespā*

Simeon ܫܡܥܘܢ *šemᶜōn*

Simon ܫܡܥܘܢ *šemᶜōn*

Sindban (pr n) ܣܢܒܢ *sinbān*

sing psalms (verb) ܙܡܪ Pa *zammar*

sink (int) (verb) ܛܒܥ *ṭbaʻ/neṭbaʻ* ; Pa *ṭabbaʻ* to sink (trs);

sinner ܚܛܝܐ *ḥaṭṭāyā*

sister ܚܬܐ *ḥātā* pl *aḥwātā*

sit (verb) ܝܬܒ *iteb/netteb*; *yāteb-waʻdā* page

six ܫܬ *šet* (f), *(e)štā* (m)

skilled (to be skilled) (verb) ܡܗܪ Ethpa *etmahhar*

skilled ܡܗܝܪ *mhir*

slander (verb) ܩܪܨܐ *qarṣā*

slaughter (verb) ܢܟܣ *nkas/nekkos*; Ethpe *etnkes* to be slaughtered

slaughter ܩܛܠܐ *qeṭlā*

slave ܥܒܕܐ *ᶜabdā*

sleep (verb) ܕܡܟ *dmek/nedmak*

sleep ܫܢܬܐ *šentā*

sleep, slumber ܢܘܡ *nām/nnum*

small cattle ܥܢܐ *ᶜānā*

small ܕܩܕܩ *daqdaq* ; ܙܥܘܪ *zʻōr*

smite (verb) ܡܚܐ *mḥā/nemḥē ᶜal*

smother (verb) ܚܢܩ *ḥnaq/neḥnoq*

snatch (verb) ܚܛܦ *ḥṭap/neḥṭop*

soaked, to get soaked (verb) ܬܪܐ *trā (tri)/netrē*

society ܥܢܝܢܐ *ᶜenyānā*

soften (verb) ܪܘܚ Pa *rayyaḥ*

sojourning (verb) *šrē/šaryā* (pass part) (see "stop," "camp")

sole ܝܚܝܕܝ *iḥidāy*

solemnize (verb) ܙܘܚ Pa *zayyaḥ*

something ܡܕܡ *meddem*

son ܒܪܐ *brā* (constr *bar-*) pl *bnayyā* (abs *bnin*) son; ܒܪܝ *ber* my son

sons ܒܢ̈ܝܐ *bnayyā*

sorrow ܚܫܐ *ḥaššā*

sorrow (verb) ܚܫ *ḥaš/neḥḥaš*

sort ܙܢܐ *znā* pl *znayyā* (abs *zan* pl *znin*); *ba-znā* in a (like) manner

soul ܢܦܫܐ *napšā* (f, abs *npeš*) pl *–ātā*

sound ܚܠܝܡ *ḥlim*

source ܡܒܘܥܐ *mabbuᶜā*

south ܬܝܡܢ *tayman* ; *taymnāy* southern; (*gabbā*) *taymnāyā* south side

sow (verb) ܙܪܥ *zra'/nezro'*

spacious ܪܘܝܚ *rawwiḥ*

Spain ܐܣܦܢܝܐ *espānyā*

span ܙܪܬܐ *zartā* pl *–ē*

speak (verb) ܡܠܠ Pa *mallel*; Ethpa *etmallal* to be spoken, told

species ܓܢܣܐ *gensā*

spend (money) (verb) Aph *appez* (see "go forth")

spend the night (verb) ܒܬ *bāt/nbut*

spice ܒܣܡܐ *besmā*

spirit ܪܘܚܐ *ruḥā* pl *–ē/-ātā* (f)

spit (verb) ܪܩ *raq/nerroz*

spread (verb) ܦܫܛ *pšaṭ/nepšoṭ*; ܦܪܣ *pras/nepros*(trs & int)

spring up (verb) ܫܘܚ *šwaḥ/nešwaḥ*

spring ܡܒܘܥܐ *mabbuᶜā* ; ܡܥܝܢܐ *mᶜinā* (f)

sprinkle (verb) ܪܣܣ *ras/nerros*

spur (verb) ܒܥܛ *b'aṭ/neb'aṭ*

stall ܚܢܘܬܐ *ḥānutā* pl *–nwātā*

stamp ܪܦܣܐ *repsā*

stand up (verb) ܩܡ *qām*

standing ܩܝܡ *qayyām*

star ܟܘܟܒܐ *kawkbā*

stay (verb) ܝܬܒ *iteb/netteb*; *yāteb-wa'dā* page; ܦܫ *pāš/npuš*; ܩܘܐ Pa *qawwi*

staying (verb) *šrē/šaryā* (pass part) (see "stop," "camp")

steal (verb) ܓܢܒ *gnab/negnob* to steal

stick ܩܝܣܐ *qaysā*

stitch (verb) ܚܛ *ḥāṭ/nḥuṭ*

stone (f) ܟܐܦܐ *kêpā*

stone (verb) ܪܓܡ *rgam/nergom*

stop (verb) ܫܪܐ *šrā/nešrē* (ᶜ*al* at, near); ܩܡ *qām*

story ܫܪܒܐ *šarbā*; ܬܫܥܝܬܐ *tašᶜitā* pl *tašᶜyātā*

straightforward ܬܪܝܨ *triṣ*

strange ܢܘܟܪܝ *nukrāy*

stranger ܐܟܣܢܝܐ *aksnāyā*

stream ܢܗܪܐ *nahrā* pl *–rawwātā*

strength ܚܘܝܠܐ *ḥuyālā*; ܥܘܫܢܐ ᶜ*ušnā*

strengthen (to gain strength) ܥܫܢ *ʿšen/neʿšan*; ܚܝܠ Pa *ḥayyel*

stretch out (verb) ܦܫܛ *pšaṭ/nepšoṭ*

strip bare (verb) ܫܠܚ *šlaḥ/nešlaḥ*

strong (to be strong) (verb) Ethpa *etḥayyal* (see "strengthen")

strong drink ܫܟܪܐ *šakrā*

strong ܚܝܠܬܢ *ḥayltān* ; ܥܙܝܙ *ʿazziz*

stumble (verb) Aph *aḥgar*, ~ *ʿal qupsā* to stumble on a pebble (see "lame")

stupor ܛܘܠܥܐ *ṭulāʿā*

succumb (verb) ܚܘܒ *ḥāb/nḥub*

suffer (verb) ܚܫܫ *ḥaš/neḥḥaš*

suffice, be sufficient (verb) ܣܦܩ *spaq/nespaq*

Sulayman Shah (pr n) ܫܐܗ ܣܘܠܝܡܢ *sulaymān šāh*

sum ܟܢܝܫܘܬܐ *knišutā*

summer ܩܝܛܐ *qayṭā*

summon (verb) ܩܪܐ *qrā/neqrē*; (see "call")

sun ܫܡܫܐ *šemšā* (m & f)

Sunday ܚܕܒܫܒܐ *ḥadbšabbā*

supply (verb) ܬܪܣܝ *tarsi/ntarsē*

supreme ܥܠܝ *ʿellāy*

surround (verb) ܚܕܪ *ḥdar/neḥdor* and *neḥdar* to surround *(b-, l-)*; *ḥdār* around (+ pron encl II)

surround (with a wall) (verb) ܟܠܠ Pa *kallel*

surveyor ܡܫܘܚܐ *māšoḥā*

swaddling clothes ܥܙܪܘܪܐ *ʿazrurē* (pl)

swear (verb) ܝܡܐ *imā/nêmē* ; Aph *awmi* to make (someone) swear, bind with an oath

swift ܩܠܝܠ *qallil*

swiftly *qallilāʾit* (see "swift")

sword ܣܝܦܐ *saypā*

symbol ܛܘܦܣܐ *ṭupsā*

synagogue ܟܢܘܫܬܐ

Syria ܣܘܪܝܐ *suryā*

Syrian ܣܘܪܝܝܐ *suryāyā*

table land ܬܩܢܐ *taqnā d-ṭurā*

tabularius ܛܒܘܠܪܐ *ṭabbulārā*

take (verb) ܢܣܒ *nsab/nessab* ; ܝܒܠ Aph *awbel*

take away (verb) ܫܩܠ *šqal/nešqol*; (see "remove"); ܪܘܡ Aph *arim*; Ettaph *ettrim* to be taken away; ܚܛܦ *ḥṭap/neḥṭop*

take heart (verb) ܠܒܒ Ethpa

take in (verb) Pa *kanneš* (see "gather")

take off (clothes) (verb) ܫܠܚ *šlaḥ/nešlaḥ*

take out (verb) Aph *appez* (see "go forth")

tale ܬܫܥܝܬܐ *tašʿitā* pl *tašʿyātā*

taper ܩܪܝܘܢܐ *qeryōnā*

tarry (verb) ܟܬܪ Pa *kattar*; ܐܘܚܪ Aph *awḥar*

task ܥܠܡܐ *ʿalmā*; ܣܘܥܪܢܐ *suʿrānā*

Tatar ܬܬܪܝܐ *tātārāyā*

tax ܬܒܥܬܐ *tbaʿtā*

teach (verb) ܐܠܦ *allep* (Pa)

teacher ܡܠܦܢܐ *mallpānā*

teaching ܝܘܠܦܢܐ *yulpānā*;
ܡܠܦܢܘܬܐ *mallpānutā*

tear ܕܡܥܐ *dem'ā* (f)

tear to pieces (verb) ܒܣܒܣ *basbes/nbasbes*

tell (verb) ܫܥܐ Ethpa *ešta^{cc}i*; ܐܡܪ *emar/nêmar* (*l-* someone, ^{c}*al* about)

tell abroad (verb) Pa *sabbar* (see "think," "imagine")

temple ܗܝܟܠܐ *hayklā*

temptation ܢܣܝܘܢܐ *nesyōnā*

ten thousand *rebbō-rebbwān*

ten ܥܣܪ ^{c}*sar* (f), ^{c}*esrā* (m)

tend (verb) ܪܥܐ *r^{c}ā/ner^{c}ē*

tent ܝܪܝܥܬܐ *yāri'tā*

term ܦܪܘܬܣܡܝܐ *protesmiā* προθεσμία

terrified (to be terrified) (verb) ܪܗܒ Ethpa *etrahhab*

terrified (to be terrified) (verb) ܣܪܕ Ethpa *estarrad*; Ettaph *ettziḥ* (see "tremble")

test ܢܣܐ Pa *nassi*

testament ܕܝܬܩܐ *daitêqê* διαθήκη

testify (verb) ܣܗܕ *shed/neshad* (*b-*, ^{c}*al* to); Pa *sahhed* to testify

thanks *qubal-ṭaybutā* (see "before")

that (conj) ܕ *d(a)-*

that (f sing) ܗܝ *hay*

that (rel conj) ܕ *d(a)-*

that is to say ܟܐܡܬ *kemat*

that is ܟܐܡܬ *kemat*

them (f) ܐܢܝܢ *ennēn*

them (m) ܐܢܘܢ *ennon*

then ܟܝ *kay* (particle of emphasis);
ܒܬܪܟܝܢ *bātarken*; ܕܝܢ *dēn* (postpositive); ܡܕܝܢ *mādēn*;
ܗܝܕܝܢ *haydēn*

there are not ܠܝܬ *layt*

there is not ܠܝܬ *layt*

there is/are ܐܝܬ

there ܬܡܢ *tammān*

therefore ܗܟܝܠ *hākêl*; ܒܓܕܘܢ *bagdon*; ܡܕܝܢ *mādēn*

these (pl) ܗܠܝܢ *hālēn*

they (f) ܐܢܝܢ *ennēn*

they (m pl) ܗܢܘܢ *hennon*

they (m) ܐܢܘܢ *ennon*

thing (see "word"); ܦܬܓܡܐ *petgāmā*; ܥܠܬܐ ^{c}*elltā* pl ܥܠܠܬܐ ^{c}*ellātā*; ܡܕܡ *meddem*

think (verb) Ethpa *etḥaššab* (see "count," "reckon"); ܣܒܪ *sbar/nesbar*

third ܬܠܝܬܝ *tlitāy*

thirst (verb) ܨܗܐ *ṣhā* (*ṣhi*)/*neṣhē* ; pass part (*ṣhē/ṣahyā*) thirsty

thirsty (see "thirst")

this (f sing) ܗܕܐ *hādē* (f sing)

this (m sing) ܗܢܐ *hānā*

Thomas ܬܐܘܡܐ *tōmā*

thoroughly (to do thoroughly) (verb) Shaph *šamli* (see "full")

those (m pl) ܗܢܘܢ *hānon*

thousand ܐܠܦܐ *alpā* (abs *ālep*)

threat ܠܘܚܡܐ *luḥāmā*

three ܬܠܬ *tlāt* (f)/*tlātā* (m)

throne ܟܘܪܣܝܐ *kursyā* pl – *sawwātā*; ܬܪܘܢܘܣ *trōnos*

throng together (verb) ܚܒܨ *ḥbaṣ/neḥboṣ*

through ܝܕ *yad*, *b-yad*

throw (verb) ܫܕܐ *šdā/nešdē*

thunder ܪܥܡܐ *ra*ᶜ*mā*

Thursday *ḥammšābšabbā* (see "five")

thus ܗܟܢܐ *hākannā*; ܗܟܝܠ *hākêl*; ܗܟܢ *hākan*

Tiara ܚܘܕܐ *ḥawdā*

Tiberius ܛܝܒܪܝܣ *ṭiberis*

tidings ܣܒܪܬܐ *sbartā*

Tigris ܕܩܠܬ *deqlat*

till (verb) ܦܠܚ *plaḥ/neploḥ*

time (a long time) ܢܘܓܪܐ *nugrā*

time limit ܦܪܘܬܣܡܝܐ *protesmiā* προθεσμία

time ܙܒܢܐ *zabnā* (abs *zban*); *zban-zban* from time to time; *ba-zban* once upon a time; ܥܕܢܐ ᶜ*eddānā*

timorous ܪܗܝܒ *rhib*;

timorously *rhibā'it* (see "timorous")

to ܠ *l(a)*

today ܝܘܡܢܐ *yawmānā*

together ܐܟܚܕܐ *akḥdā*

toil (verb) ܠܐܐ *lā/nêlē* ; ܥܡܠ ᶜ*mal/ne*ᶜ*mal*

token ܐܬܐ *ātā*; pl. ܐܬܘ̈ܬܐ

tomb ܩܒܪܐ *qabrā*

tomorrow ܡܚܪ *mḥār*

tongue ܠܫܢܐ *leššānā*

tooth ܫܢܐ *šennā* (f)

torch ܕܠܩܐ *dalqā* (abs *dleq/dlaq*)

torture ܫܢܕܐ *šendā*

total ܟܢܝܫܘܬܐ *knišutā*

totality ܟܠܝܘܬܐ *kollāyutā*

totter (verb) ܙܥܙܥ Ethpal *ezda'za'*

touch (verb) ܡܘܫ *māš/nmuš*

tower ܒܘܪܓܐ *burgā*; ܡܓܕܠܐ *magdlā*; ܦܘܪܟܣܐ *purkāsā* πύργος

trace ܫܒܝܠܐ *šbilā*

track ܫܒܝܠܐ *šbilā*

trade ܬܓܘܪܬܐ *tgurtā*; ܐܘܡܢܘܬܐ *umānutā*

trained ܡܗܝܪ *mhir*

trample (verb) Pa *dayyeš* (see "tread")

tranquility ܫܠܝܐ *šelyā*

transgress(ᶜ*al*) ܥܒܪ ᶜ*bar/ne*ᶜ*bar*

travel ܚܙܩ *ḥzaq/neḥzoq*

tread (verb) ܕܘܫ *dāš/nduš*

treasure (verb) ܓܙܐ *gazzā*

treasure ܣܝܡܬܐ *simtā*

treat with contempt (verb) ܫܘܛ *šāṭ/nšuṭ*

tree ܐܝܠܢܐ *ilānā*

tremble (verb) ܙܘܥ *zāʻ/nzuʻ*; to make tremble ܪܥܠ Aph *arᶜel*; trembling ܪܬܝܬܐ *rtêtā*

trespass ܚܘܒܐ *ḥawbā*

trespasser ܚܝܒܐ *ḥayyābā*

trial ܢܣܝܘܢܐ *nesyōnā*

tribe ܫܪܒܬܐ *šarbtā*

tribute ܡܕܐܬܐ *madatā*

triumph ܢܨܚܢܐ *neṣḥānā*

triumphant (to be triumphant) (verb) Ethpa *etnaṣṣaḥ* (see "shine")

trouble ܠܐܘܬܐ *leutā*

troubled (verb) ܫܚܩ Ethpa *eštaḥḥaq*; ܫܓܫ Ethpe *eštgeš*

true ܫܪܝܪ *šarrir*

truly *šarrirā'it* (see "true"); ܟܝ *kay* (particle of emphasis)

trumpet ܫܝܦܘܪܐ *šipōrā*

trust (verb) ܬܟܠ Ethpe *ettkel ᶜal*

trust ܣܒܪܐ *sabrā*

trusting in ܬܟܝܠ *tkil ᶜal*

trusty ܫܪܝܪ *šarrir*

truth ܫܪܪܐ *šrārā*

try ܢܣܐ Pa *nassi*

tryst ܘܥܕܐ *wa'dā*

turn (verb) Aph *apni* (see "return," "come back")

turn over (verb) Aph *ašlem* (see "finished," follow")

turned (to be turned) Ethpa *etkarrak* (see "wrap," "roll")

turned around (to be turned around) (verb) Ethpa *ethappak* (see "return," "convert," "go back on")

turret ܒܘܪܓܐ *burgā*

twist (verb) Pa *karrek* (see "roll," "wrap"); Ethpa *etkarrak* twisted

two ܬܪܝܢ *trēn/tartēn* (+ pron encl, *tray-*, as *trayhon* the two of them, both of them)

type of armor ܒܪܙܢܩܐ *barzanqā*

type ܛܘܦܣܐ *ṭupsā*

tyrant ܛܪܘܢܐ *ṭrunā*

under ܬܚܘܬ *tḥut* (+ pron encl II); ܬܚܬ *taḥt, l-taḥt*; under ܬܚܝܬ *tḥēt*

understand (verb) Eshtaph *eštawdaʻ* (see "know"); ܣܟܠ Ethpa *estakkal*

understanding ܣܘܟܠܐ *sukālā*

unexpectedly ܫܠܝܐ *šelyā, men šelyā, men-šel(y)*

unfortunate ܡܣܟܢܐ *meskênā*

unheard of ܢܘܟܪܝ *nukrāy*

uninhabited ܚܪܒ *ḥreb/ḥarbā*

unjust ܥܘܠܐ *ᶜawwālā;*

unless ܐܠܐ ܐܢ *ellā en*

unsheathe (verb) ܫܡܛ *šmaṭ/nešmoṭ*

until ܥܕܡܐ ܕ *ᶜdammā d-* (conj); ~ *l-* until (prep)

up to ܥܕ *ᶜad*

upright ܬܪܝܨ *triṣ*

urge on (verb) ܒܥܛ *bʻaṭ/nebʻaṭ*

utterly ܓܡܪ *gmār, la-*

vain (in vain) *baṭṭitl* of no effect (see "idle"); ܣܪܝܩ *sriq* value ܛܝܡܐ *ṭimā* (usually pl)

vanish (verb) ܛܠܩ Ethpa *eṭṭallaqu*

vehement ܥܙܝܙ *ᶜazziz*

veil ܬܚܦܝܬܐ *taḥpitā*

verily *šarrirā'it* (see "true"); ܐܡܝܢ *āmên*

very ܛܒ *ṭāb*; ܣܓܝ *saggi*

vessel ܡܐܢܐ *mānā*

vexed (to be vexed) (verb) ܥܣܩ Ethpa *etᶜassaq*; ܫܚܩ Ethpa *eštaḥḥaq*

vial ܦܝܠܐ *pyālā* pl *pyālās*

victim ܕܒܚܐ *debḥā*

victorious (to be victorious) (verb) Ethpa *etnaṣṣaḥ* (see "shine")

victory ܢܨܚܢܐ *neṣḥānā*; ܙܟܘܬܐ *zākutā*

vigilance ܥܝܪܘܬܐ *ᶜirutā*

village ܩܪܝܬܐ *qritā* pl *qeryātā/quryā*

vineyard ܟܪܡܐ *karmā*

violent (to make violent) Aph *aᶜšen* to make violent (see "strengthen")

violent ܥܫܝܢ *ᶜaššin*; ܬܩܝܦ *taqqip*

virgin ܒܬܘܠܬܐ *btultā*

vision ܚܙܘܐ *ḥezwā*

visit (verb) ܣܥܪ *sᶜar/nesᶜar*

vizier ܘܙܝܪܐ *wazirā*

voice ܩܠܐ *qālā*

vow (verb), to make a vow ܢܕܪ *ndar/neddor*

vow ܢܕܪܐ *nedrā*

wage ܐܓܪܐ *agrā*

wail ܝܠܠܬܐ *illtā* pl *yallātā*

wait for (verb) ܣܟܐ Pa *sakki*; ܩܘܐ Pa *qawwi*

waiver (verb) Aph *aḥgar* (see "lame")

wake (verb) ܥܘܪ *ᶜār/nᶜur*; Ettaph *ettᶜir* to wake up

wakefulness ܥܝܪܘܬܐ *ᶜirutā*

walk; to make (someone) walk (verb) ܗܠܟ Pa *hallek*

wall ܐܣܐ *essā*; ܐܣܬܐ *estā*

walled city ܟܪܟܐ *karkā*

wander (verb) ܛܥܐ *ṭ'ā/neṭ'ē*; *ṭ'ē/ṭa'yā* astray

wander about (verb) Ethpa *etkarrak* (see "wrap," "roll")

want (verb) ܨܒܐ *ṣbā/neṣbē* ; Ethpe *eṣṭbi* to want

warn against (verb) ܙܗܪ Pa *zahhar 'al*; Ethpa *ezdahhar b-* to beware of, watch over

wary ܙܗܝܪ *zhir*

wash (verb) ܣܚܐ *sḥā/nesḥē*; ܫܘܓ Aph *ašig*

wash away (verb) ܫܘܓ Aph *ašig*

washing ܡܣܚܘܬܐ *masḥutā*

waste away (verb) ܦܫܫ Ethpau *etpawšaš*

watch (verb) ܥܘܪ *ᶜār/nᶜur*; ܡܛܪܬܐ *maṭṭartā*; *nṭar maṭṭartā* to keep watch

watch over (verb) Ethpa *ezdahhar b-* to beware of, watch over (see "warn against")

watchman ܢܛܘܪܐ *nāṭōrā*

water ܡܝܐ *mayyā* (pl)

way ܐܘܪܚܐ *urḥā*

way of life ܗܘܦܟܐ *hupākā*

we ܚܢܢ *ḥnan*

weak (to become weak) (verb) ܪܦܐ Ethpa *etrappi*

wealth (usually pl) ܢܟܣܐ *neksā*; ܥܘܬܪܐ *ʿutrā*

wealthy ܥܬܝܪ *ʿattir*

wear (verb) ܠܒܫ *lbeš/nelbaš*

wearing ܠܒܝܫ *lbiš*

weary *lē* pl *leyn* (emph ܠܐܝܐ *layā* pl ܠܐܝ̈ܐ *layyā*) (see "toil"); ܥܡܝܠ *ʿmil*

Wednesday *arbʿābšabbā*

weep (verb) ܒܟܐ *bkā/nebkē*

weeping ܒܟܬܐ *bkātā*

weighty ܬܩܝܦ *taqqip*

welter (in blood) (verb) ܦܠܦܠ Ethpal *etpalpal*

western ܡܥܪܒܝ *maʿrbāy*

what for? ܠܡܢܐ *l-mānā*

what? ܡܐ *mā*; *l-mā* lest; ܡܢܐ *mānā*; *mān* (see "from")

whatever ܡܐ ܕ *mā d-*; ܡܕܡ *meddem*

when ܡܐ ܕ *mā d-*; ܟܕ *kad*; ܐܡܬܝ *emat*

whenever ܟܠܡܐ ܕ *kollmā d-*

where? ܐܝܟܐ *aykā*

whether ܕܡ *dam(en)*

which ܕ *d(a)-*

which? (f) ܐܝܕܐ; *aydā d-* she who; ܐܝܢܐ *aynā; aynā d-* he who

while ܥܕ *ʿad*

whisper (verb) ܠܚܫ Pa *laḥḥeš*

white ܚܘܪ *ḥewwār*

whiten (verb) ܚܘܪ Pa *ḥwwar*

whitewash (verb) ܟܠܫ Pa *kalleš*

who ܕ *d(a)-*

who? *man* (see "from")

why? ܠܡܢܐ *l-mānā*; ܠܡܢܐ *l-mānā*

wicked ܒܝܫ *biš*; ܥܢܢܬ *ʿannāt*

wife ܐܢܬܬܐ *atttā,* pl *neššē*

wilderness ܕܒܪܐ *dabrā*; ܡܕܒܪܐ *madbrā*

will ܨܒܝܢܐ *ṣebyānā*

wind ܪܘܚܐ *ruḥā* pl *–ē/-ātā* (f)

wine ܚܡܪܐ *ḥamrā*

wing ܓܦܐ *geppā*

winter ܣܬܘܐ *satwā*

wipe out (verb) ܓܪ *gar/neggor*

wisdom ܚܟܡܬܐ *ḥekmtā*

wise ܚܟܝܡ *ḥakkim*

with (instrumental) ܒ *b(a)-*

with ܠܘܬ *lwāt* ; ܥܡ *ʿam* (+ pron encl I, *ʿamm-*)

withdraw from (verb) ܩܦܣ Ethpe *etqpes men*

withdraw ܦܪܙ *praq/neproz*

withhold (verb) Ethpe *etkli* to be withheld; *etkalyat tba^c^tā mennhon* they were exepted from taxes ܟܠܐ *klā/neklē*

witness (verb) ܣܗܕ *shed/neshad* (*b-*, *^c^al* to); Pa *sahhed* to call to witness; Aph *ashed* to bear witness

woe ܘܝ *wāy*

woman ܐܢܬܬܐ *atttā,* pl *neššē*

womb ܟܪܣܐ *karsā* (abs/const *kres*)

women ܢܫ̈ܐ *neššē* (pl)

wonder ܬܕܡܘܪܬܐ *tedmurtā* pl *tedmrātā*

wood (piece of) ܩܝܣܐ *qaysā*

word ܦܬܓܡܐ *petgāmā*; ܡܐܡܪܐ *mêmrā*; ܡܠܬܐ *melltā* pl *mellē* (f); thing, event; (m) λόγος

work (verb) Aph *a^c^bed* make work; Ettaph *etta^c^bad* to be put to work; Shaph *ša^c^bed* to reduce to servitude (see "make," "do"); ܥܡܠ *^c^mal/ne^c^mal*; ܥܒܕܐ *^c^bādā*

working (of the land, e.g.) ܬܘܩܢܐ *tuqānā*

world ܥܠܡܐ *^c^ālmā* (abs *^c^ālam*)

wormwood ܡܪܪܐ *mrārā*; *ekal* ~ to be galled

worship (verb) ܣܓܕ *sged/nesgod*; ܦܠܚ *plaḥ/neploḥ*

worshipper ܣܓܘܕܐ *sāgōdā*

worthy ܫܘܐ *šāwē* (m), *šāwyā* (f)

wound ܡܚܘܬܐ *mḥutā* pl *maḥwātā*

wrap (verb) ܟܪܟ *krak/nekrok*

wretched (to be wretched) (verb) ܕܘܐ *dwā/nedwē*

write (verb) ܟܬܒ *ktab/nektob* Ethpe *etkteb* to be written, inscribed, enrolled

writer ܡܟܬܒܢܐ *maktbānā*

year ܫܢܬܐ *šattā* pl *šnayyā* (abs *šnā* pl *šnin,* const *šnat-*)

yes ܐܝܢ *ên*

yoke ܢܝܪܐ *nirā*

you (f pl) ܐܢܬܝܢ *attēn*

you (f sing) ܐܢܬܝ *att*

you (m pl) ܐܢܬܘܢ *atton*

you (m sing) ܐܢܬ *att*

young man ܥܠܝܡܐ *^c^laymā*

young woman ܥܠܝܡܬܐ *^c^laymtā*

Zacharias ܙܟܪܝܐ *zkaryā*

Select idioms or grammatical features:

introduces a new section or thought ܬܘܒ *tub*

it would be better for *paqqāḥ-wā l-* (see "expedient")

for a long time ܛܘܪܐ *tawrā (saggi'ā)*

gain strength (verb) ܥܫܢ *^c^šen/ne^c^šan*; Aph *a^c^šen* to make violent

quotation: to dinciate that the phrase in which it occurs is a quotation ܠܡ *lam*

a long time ܢܘܓܪܐ *nugrā*

if it is/was (a fact, true) that ܐܢܗܘ ܕ *enhu d-*

introduces the topic of a sentence, usually followed by *dēn*; ܡܢ *man* μεν; *man… dēn* μεν… δε , on the one hand… on the other hand

without limit *dlāḥušbān* (see "reckoning")

in the twinkling of an eye ܬܡܪܐ *temrā d-*^{c}*aynā, ak meṭrap*

Corrigenda to the Readings in the Grammar: p. 164, line 5: for ܐܚܝ̇ܐ read ܐܚ̈ܝܐ; p. 169, line 90: for ܬܕ̈ܡ read ܡܕ̈ܡ; p. 173, line 20, end, add ܠܦܘܪ̇ܗ; p. 189, line 20: for ܐܚܠܝܪ̈ܐ, read ܐܚ̈ܠܝܪ̈ܐ.

Addenda to Syriac-English Vocabulary in the Grammar: p. 199: ܕܡܐ *dmā* (abs *dem*) blood; p. 203: ܚܫܝܫܐܝܬ *ḥaššišā'it* sadly, mournfully; p. 203: ܛܝܒ Pa *ṭayyeb* to appoint; p. 216: ܨܒܘܬܐ *ṣbutā* pl *ṣebwātā* matter, affair; p. 217: ܩܪ̇ܒ Pa *qarreb* to make oblations, to perform the liturgy; p. 220: ܫܡܠܝ *šamli* see ܫܠܡ; p. 222 ܬܡܝܗ *tammih* astonishing.

www.ingramcontent.com/pod-product-compliance
Lightning Source LLC
Chambersburg PA
CBHW031155160426
43193CB00008B/376
* 9 7 8 1 5 8 8 1 4 0 4 5 6 *